W9-CDC-818

The Psychology of Hope

An Integration of Experimental, Clinical, and Social Approaches

Ezra Stotland

BF323
E8
S75

THE PSYCHOLOGY OF HOPE

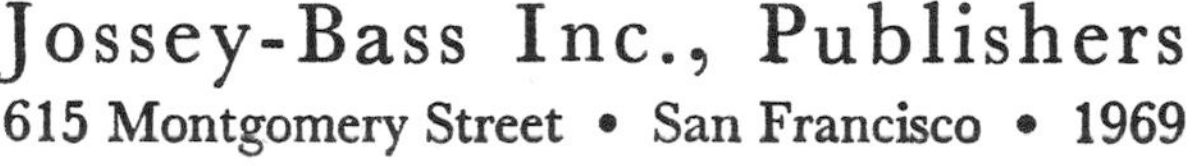

Jossey-Bass Inc., Publishers
615 Montgomery Street • San Francisco • 1969

JUN 7 1972
169017

THE PSYCHOLOGY OF HOPE

by Ezra Stotland

Copyright © 1969 by Jossey-Bass, Inc., Publishers

Copyright under Pan American and
Universal Copyright Conventions

All rights reserved. No part of this book may be reproduced in any form—except for brief quotation in a review—without written permission from the publishers. All inquiries should be addressed to:

Jossey-Bass, Inc., Publishers
615 Montgomery Street
San Francisco, California 94111

Library of Congress Catalog Card Number 76-75934

Standard Book Number SBN 87589-031-8

Manufactured in the United States of America
Composed and printed by York Composition Company, Inc.
Bound by Chas. H. Bohn & Co., Inc., New York
Jacket design by Willi Baum, San Francisco

FIRST EDITION
First printing: January 1969
Second printing: September 1969

6901

THE JOSSEY-BASS BEHAVIORAL SCIENCE SERIES

General Editors

WILLIAM E. HENRY, *University of Chicago*

NEVITT SANFORD, *Stanford University and Wright Institute, Berkeley*

Preface

The Psychology of Hope is the last volume of a trilogy. It began with *The End of Hope: A Social-Clinical Study of Suicide* by Arthur L. Kobler and myself, and now ends with what might be the beginning of hope—as a respectable construct in scientific psychology and as an even more useful one in clinical psychology. In between the two "ends" of the trilogy was another volume, *Life and Death of a Mental Hospital,* which Kobler and I also wrote.

The first volume was the study of an epidemic of suicide among patients in a small mental hospital. The significance of hope and its loss in the psychodynamics of suicide became abundantly clear to Kobler and myself and became the core of our theorizing about suicide. The second volume was an effort to examine the social context of the suicides to learn how it influenced the levels of hope among the patients. At the time we wrote this volume, it was very clear to us that hope was significant for many other events in the lives of mental patients, in addition to suicide. In fact, we not only reviewed much of the social-psychologically oriented research on mental patients available at that time; we wrote a chapter integrating much of that literature around the theme of hope. For reasons of editorial policy and consistency, this chapter was not included in the published version of the book. However, there were pressures, we felt, to develop that chapter. In the course of the work on the manuscript, William E. Henry, the general editor of Jossey-Bass, happened to read this unpublished chapter and was favorably impressed. Furthermore, after the *Life and Death* book came out, this chapter gave us a sense of incompleteness, of useful work left undone.

By the time I finally found enough time in my schedule to work on an expansion of the chapter, Kobler's interests had shifted to other problems. I went on to complete the work myself. Nevertheless, the core of the thinking was developed with Kobler; and parts of Chapters Ten through Thirteen were written originally at the time we were working together. Furthermore, he read the entire manuscript of this book and provided some very useful critical comments, which are greatly appreciated.

During the preparation of *The Psychology of Hope* I received much encouragement and valuable criticism from the members of staff seminars run by Michael Adams at the Veterans Administration Mental Hygiene Clinic which was then in the Smith Tower in Seattle. The freewheeling intellectual, scientific, and humane quality of these seminars provided a source of strength. To the members of the seminar—Michael Adams, Patricia Crowder Goodin, Henry Fischer, Roy Fowler, Lewis Garmize, Lillian Gideon, Patricia Lunneborg, Patricia Simester, Allen Wieson, and especially Arnold Katz—I am immeasurably thankful. Arnold Katz was especially helpful because of his acutely probing questioning and warm and constant encouragement, both during the seminars and in hours of discussion outside of it.

Preparation of this book was partially financed by a grant from the Graduate Research Fund ("171" Funds) of the University of Washington. Kathleen Packard, Sandra Knight, and Catherine Gosho did yeoman work on some of the typing. Barbara Hilyer assisted greatly with the chore of proofreading. To all of these, my appreciation.

Most importantly, Shirley Buckingham clarified the language and ideas by questioning and probing every word in the manuscript, and then retyping it.

My deepest gratitude and love to my wife, Patricia, for sharing my anxieties and hopes while I worked on the book.

EZRA STOTLAND

Seattle
January 1969

Contents

The Psychology of Hope

Prologue

A Necessary Condition

The importance of hope for man has long been known to layman and professional. It is widely accepted that with hope, man acts, moves, achieves. Without hope, he is often dull, listless, moribund. Faced with a situation that threatens a loss of hope, he may desperately try to cling to it, to restore it, to protect it. Yet despite a common awareness of the role hopefulness plays in determining behavior, rarely has it been introduced into the mainstream of psychology and psychiatry.

Psychologists are generally averse to the use of so subjective a term as *hope,* but in psychiatry, the sense of hopefulness has been mentioned, primarily in terms of its therapeutic importance (French, 1952; Menninger, 1963; Frank, 1961); only French has developed it as part of an overall theory. Among psychologists, *hope* has been used by Lewin (1951) in a cognitive approach and by Mowrer (1960) in a behavioristic one.

The American College Dictionary (1960) defines *hope* as follows:

> noun 1. Expectation of something desired; desire accompanied by expectation. 2. A particular instance of such expectation or desire: *a hope of success.* 3. Confidence in a future event; ground for expecting something; *there is no hope of his recovery.* 4. A person or thing that expectations are centered in; the hope of the family. transitive verb 5. To look forward to with desire and more or less confidence. 6. To trust in the truth of a matter (with a clause): *I hope that you are satisfied.* intransitive verb 7. To have an expectation of something desired; *We hope to see you, to hope for his pardon.*

The definition used in this book is based on meanings one, two, five and seven; such use facilitates, we believe, its integration into the terminology of some approaches to experimental psychology. The essence of these meanings of hope is an expectation greater than zero of achieving a goal. The degree of hopefulness is the level of this expectation or the person's perceived probability of achieving a goal. It is therefore possible to integrate the definition of hope with approaches that use a concept of "expectation," such as Tolman's (1948), Rotter's (1954), and Atkinson's (1964). *Hope* can therefore be regarded as a shorthand term for an expectation about goal attainment.

In these experimental approaches (and the present one as well), the *expectation* of attaining a goal is not the same thing, conceptually, as its *desirability.* Of course, it is possible and, in fact, rather likely, that persons will believe success is more probable for a desirable event than for an aversive one. On the other hand, for most people and animals there are limits to the degree of distortion in favor of the probability of desired outcomes. If such distortion were so strong that there could be no meaningful distinction between expectation and desirability, the human race, and lower species as well, would have died out long ago owing to lack of preparation for future states of hunger, cold, and thirst. Another factor limiting the distortion level is the clarity of the available data—distortion would be great in the case of a "partly cloudy–partly sunny" weather forecast, in which case we would expect both the best and the worst.

Despite the translation of hopefulness into the terms of experimental psychology and the emphasis some theorists have given it, its full significance has not been treated systematically; Mowrer's work (1960) is, perhaps, the exception. The present volume is an attempt to develop the outlines of a theory about the level of hopefulness and to apply this theory to data from both experimental and field studies. The questions it attempts to answer concern causes and consequences of different levels of expectation of goal achievements. These questions can be asked about a wide range of organisms, from human to rat, in an equally wide range of situations: experimental neuroses, social influence on mental patient behavior, human behavior in stressful situations, to name a few.

Before going into the theory and data, I should clarify several points. In only a few of the studies are there direct measures of the degree of hopefulness, the level of expectation of goal achievement. Even if all the researchers had been oriented toward the present theory, they often would have had great difficulty obtaining reliable and valid direct measures of hopefulness. Asking someone how hopeful he is usually elicits a blank stare. Asking him to estimate his chances of attaining a goal is feasible only sometimes, and his answer may be subject to all sorts of response biases, such as the tendency to give socially desirable responses. Accordingly, hopefulness is treated here mainly, but not exclusively, as a construct used to tie together antecedent and consequent events, a mediating process. In order to explain why a given antecedent event led to a given behavioral outcome, it is often possible, plausible, and even necessary to assume that a given level of hopefulness was in fact involved.

At this point we must consider whether it is not dangerous to use such subjective language. For an answer, let us begin with the assumption that the existence of consciousness in the universe is undeniable. I assume that the reader is conscious and the reader assumes that I am conscious, at least while I write. *If* scientific laws apply to all phenomena in the universe—a proposition scientists could hardly reject—then these laws must apply also to consciousness. One way of treating consciousness scientifically is to regard it as an epiphenomenon—an effect having no causal power of its own. This treatment implies that consciousness "exists" in some disembodied state. "But," an epiphenomenalist may object, "I make no such assumption." If he in fact makes no such assumption then he must join the author in the thesis that consciousness is one aspect of an event that also has a physical aspect. Therefore consciousness, as an aspect of an event, can have a causal effect. Only taste and usefulness determine whether one refers to this event in its physical or its conscious aspect. Since we have limited knowledge of the physical, we have little choice at present but to use the subjective label.

The existence of consciousness is only one answer to the question of the use of the subjective term *hope*. Others are: (1) The reader is at liberty to translate hope into its more hard-nosed version—expectations of the attainment of goals. If the theory still makes sense to the reader and if the data are still consistent with the theory, no crucial harm has been done. (2) The theory will be applied to the widest possible range of data (this is basic to the whole point of this volume). The precepts of science favor a theory that covers a wide range of data over one with narrow parameters, all other factors being equal. Accordingly, if a theory about hopefulness serves easily and plausibly as an explanation of these wide-ranging data, then these precepts of science would argue for acceptance of the theory. In other words, if a single theory can be used to integrate data of widely differing sorts, it is a highly useful scientific theory. In large part, the burden of the present volume is that the theory of hope does have wide generality and, therefore, scientific merit. The fact that its central term is subjective should not then be crucial. (3) It is futile to argue that because we cannot now always measure hope directly, we should not use it as a scientific concept. There is no certainty that there will never be a way to measure consciousness (Feigl, 1958). The failure up to this point is, after all, ours. Furthermore, indirect indices, such as asking the subject to report his estimated probability of success, are sometimes available. As mentioned previously, there are important difficulties in using these measures, but in many situations the difficulties may not be so serious as to preclude their use. Improvements in techniques of measurement, rather than rejection of the concept, should be the answer.

The next major point the reader should bear in mind is that this theory is not a total theory of behavior. Its parameters are simply some aspects of the motivation of organisms. It does not purport to explain the choice of goals, the process of learning a given habit, the etiology of mental illness. This theory is directed not at explaining the causes of "sick" behavior but rather at the events that result from such behavior. It is directed not at the process of therapy but at pointing out a necessary condition (albeit not a sufficient one) for therapy to be effective; that condition is hopefulness.

I make no claim to originality with regard to the major points. Wherever possible I will cite others who have said the same things. The primary intent and value of the present volume is to document the generality of the ideas, ideas that have often been stated with a disregard for their catholicity, as well as to test the ideas systematically. Finally, the theory's applicability to many types of data will be demonstrated. The purpose, then, is integrative.

The theory has been formulated in a set of general propositions, which are stated in the next chapter. These propositions are used to derive hypotheses by joining a given proposition with some simple, plausible assumption, by joining two or more propositions, or by doing both. Nevertheless, the theory has not been formulated into an elegant axiomatic system, complete with full complement of axioms, implicit definitions, allowable processes of deduction, and operational definitions. I feel strongly that too great a concern for the formally logical often distracts from a concern for the psychological significance of the concepts used. Lewin (1951) warned us long ago against premature formalization; the author heeds his warning.

Basic to the rejection of elegant formalizations is the feeling that psychology has not yet secured a firm grasp of the important factors in the behavior and experience of people. Even today, there is plenty of room for the addition of new concepts and for the reaffirmation of old but neglected ones. This is an attempt to perform the latter service. Thus, the theory is presented in broad strokes; not all the questions it raises can be answered empirically at the moment. Yet a more elegant theory will not emerge until a less elegant one is at least broached.

CHAPTER 1

The Theory

In this chapter, we will present an overview of the theory, indicating briefly its propositions and explicating them sufficiently to give some general idea as to the nature of the theory. Detailed explications of the propositions, derivation of hypotheses, and the citing of data in detail will be presented in subsequent chapters.

The first proposition of the theory is a formal statement of an ancient truism: hopefulness is a necessary condition for action. People who are hopeless have been described as inactive, apathetic, dull. They feel, most simply, that there is no point in expending energy for no gain at all. Conversely, people who are hopeful are usually described as active, vigorous, energetic.

> Proposition I: *An organism's motivation to achieve a goal is, in part, a positive function of its perceived probability of attaining the goal and of the perceived importance of the goal.*

In this proposition, the term *goal* is to be interpreted broadly, subsuming anything from life goals to laboratory mash, modified only by the precept that it must be perceived or symbolized by the organism itself. If it is not so perceived or symbolized, then it can not be deemed a goal.

Motivation, as used in the proposition, refers primarily to action, to doing something rather than doing nothing, simply vegetating. That something can be overt or covert; it can entail skeletal, perceptual, or cognitive behavior (*cf.* Lewin, 1951). Secondly, motivation refers to the directed quality of the action taken; the organism will choose acts that seem more likely to lead to goal attainment over acts that seem less likely to do so, and it will attend to those aspects of the environment that are relevant either in an instrumental or in a consummatory way. Attention to perceived relevancies can occur on both the symbolic and overt levels; what is perceived as irrelevant will be avoided, ignored, left unattended, not thought about. Needless to say, changes in the relevant aspects of the environment will cause a greater reaction in the organism than changes in nonrelevant aspects.

This line of reasoning leads to the following two hypotheses: (1) the organism will selectively attend to those aspects of the environment that are relevant to its goal attainment; (2) the greater the perceived probability or expectation of goal attainment, the more likely the organism is to act to attain the goal. The second hypothesis receives direct support from such diverse sources as studies of instrumental learning, of the effects of experimental and "natural" manipulation of expected probabilities, of reactions of animals to stressful situations in the laboratory, of normal people in the face of difficulty. Arguments supporting the first hypothesis will be presented in the next chapter.

In addition to influencing motivation, hope of attaining a goal and the importance of that goal also influence the organism's affective states.

> Proposition II: *The higher an organism's perceived probability of attaining a goal and the greater the importance of that goal, the greater will be the positive affect experienced by the organism.*

Positive affect can be described as joy, euphoria, pleasure, satisfaction. Little research, if any, has been done in the field of positive affect, especially in its physiological aspects. Furthermore, most research that has been conducted on positive affect has treated it as synonymous with sensory pleasure—sweetness, for example. This sensory emphasis is analogous to treating anxiety as if it were a residual of the reaction to pain. In both cases, the sensory emphasis is far too limiting, since there are many instances in life in which a person feels joy without any particular physical pleasure, such as the joy of hearing good news. One of the rare instances of pertinent research comes from Murphy (1962), who observed a small group of children in a wide variety of settings. She writes, "Increasing mastery [of new situations] is accompanied by increasing zest, and gratifying repetition (p. 192)." Later she writes, "Children who enjoyed new situations also tended to show more capacity to struggle, or determination and drive to mastery (p. 201)."

Surely the reader can recall instances in his own life that are consistent with Proposition II.

Because of the lack of research on positive affect, because of the greater social significance of problems of anxiety, most of the concern of the present volume is with negative affect or anxiety. This emphasis, however, should not be construed to mean that joy is theoretically less important than anxiety.

> Proposition III: *The lower an organism's perceived probability of attaining a goal and the greater the importance of that goal, the more will the organism experience anxiety.*

Anxiety is a state in which there is physiological arousal and subjectively negative affect. This definition does not lend itself to easy measurement. Sometimes subjective reactions are difficult to obtain because of problems of communication, such as inaccurate word usage and reluctance to admit to negative feelings. Sometimes subjective reactions are completely beyond present measurement techniques because the subjects under study are animals. Sometimes various measures of physiological reactions are unobtainable or, if they are obtainable, they may be unrelated to one another. Nevertheless, the term *anxiety* has to be retained and used, despite its ambiguity, because of its obvious central importance to psychology. Furthermore, we feel certain that any observer of certain forms of behavior in animals, such as excessive defecation and urination, would not be averse to referring to them as indicators of anxiety.

Some of the supporting data for the propositon come from studies showing that animals "break down" in the face of inescapable pain. But the present approach does not view anxiety as a function of pain so much as the inability to avoid it. This approach thereby differs from those that define anxiety as the residual of pain reaction.

The next proposition concerns the organism's reactions to being anxious. It also has the quality of reflecting a truism (that anxiety is noxious) and thus needs little explication here.

> Proposition IV: *Organisms are motivated to escape and avoid anxiety; the greater the anxiety experienced or expected, the greater the motivation.*

The core variable in the first four propositions has been the level of expected probability of achieving goals. Therefore, it is necessary to examine the determinants of the level of expected probability. In other words, the propositions thus far have concerned the organism cognizing its relationship to goals, that is, its perceived probability of attaining them. The next propositions, then, will concern cognitive processes, so that the cognizing of relationships to goals can be treated as merely a specific instance of cognizing in general, however important an instance it is.

The key concept in these cognitive propositions is that of *schema.* Each individual is assumed to have many schemas pertaining to himself and to aspects of the world around him. Schemas are the more complex aspects of an individual's cognitive structure. Being more complex, they often take on a propositional form, such as describing a relationship between a class of objects and some attribute. Examples of schemas would be "I can drive a car"; "All tall men are heavy"; "If Joe likes her, he should take her out."

Schemas themselves are built up out of concepts. In the examples above, the ingredient concepts are *I, can drive, a car, all, tallness, men,* and so on. Thus, schemas can be defined as cognitive structures consisting of associations between concepts. An association between concepts means that the existence of one of the concepts implies the existence of the other. The existence of *I* implies *can drive a car.* The concepts included in a schema are called the *constituent concepts* of that schema.

Before we proceed with the discussion on schemas, we should note that the term *concept* is used here to refer not only to classes of objects but also to classes of events such as a sale or an election, as well as to relationships between other concepts—such as owning, causing, being able, or being greater than. Thus, a schema can consist of an association among three concepts, one of which is a concept of relationship; for example, "aggressive salesmen can sell houses." Two of the concepts (*salesmen, houses*) refer to classes of objects while the third (*can sell*) is a concept of relationship and implies a class of events, sales.

Schemas can be abstract or concrete in varying degrees. Some may be as broad as mathematical and philosophical systems; others may concern only a given situation. More importantly, schemas can be hierarchical. A more abstract schema may incorporate a more specific one, much as a concept subsumes a specific case or example.

The first cognitive proposition refers to the acquisition of schemas:

> Proposition V: *The organism acquires schemas as a result either (1) of his perception of a number of events in which examples of the same concepts are associated; or (2) of communication from other people.*

This proposition indicates that the acquisition of schemas is not necessarily a function of the organism's having been rewarded for acquiring it. It is obvious that undesirable schemas may be acquired; for example, that so-and-so is a malicious person; that I fail at such and such. Furthermore, this proposition indicates that the learning process is assumed to be purely perceptual.

Schemas may be in a latent or solely dispositional state in the organism, present within him, but not influencing action. Conversely, schemas may also be in state of arousal in which they have a directive influence in any given situation. In this state, they direct the person's perception of the situation; they influence his interpretation of what is occurring; they are reflected in his "mental set." When a schema is shifted from a dormant or latent state to an aroused state, we will call this event the *invocation of the schema.* The next proposition concerns the conditions under which a schema is invoked:

> Proposition VI: *A schema is invoked by the organism's perceiving an event similar to a constituent concept of the schema or by the individual's receiving a communication from another directing him to invoke the schema; the greater the similarity between the event and the constituent concept, or the greater the importance of the person directing him, the more likely is the schema to be aroused.*

It is patent that schemas are not likely to be invoked in equal degree nor are they equally likely to remain in a state of arousal when events inconsistent with them are perceived. This variance is partially a result of the differential occurrence of the invoking events and partly the result of the differences among the schemas themselves.

> Proposition VII: *The probability that a schema will be invoked and remain aroused is, in part, a positive function of the number of times that it has been invoked previously; of the number of events previously perceived as consistent with the schema; of the importance to the organism of the person, if any, from whom one acquired the schema.*

In the present discussion, the degree of invocability of a schema refers to both the invocability and the tendency to remain aroused. Sometimes, for purpose of euphemism, invocability in both senses will be referred to as strength.

The seven propositions presented throughout this chapter

are the heart of the theory. As indicated in the beginning, the theory does the work of generating hypotheses by having the propositions either combined with one another, or by joining simple assumptions to each of the propositions. Thus, hypotheses can be generated about the schemas that an organism develops about its own behavior, about its attainment of goals, about the effects other people have on goal attainment, about the relationships between schemas and anxiety, and so forth. How this is accomplished will be seen in the following chapters.

CHAPTER 2

Hope and Action

Proposition I indicated that motivation was a positive function of the perceived probability of goal attainment and of the importance of the goal. Motivation is indicated by the organism's acting, either overtly or cognitively, toward the attainment of goals. These actions include attending to and thinking about those aspects of the environment that are perceived as relevant to goal attainment.

In contrast to other definitions of motivation, this one does not focus on the so-called energizing feature. Although energy expenditures may be greater when the organism acts than when it does not act, this expenditure of energy in and of itself is not the crucial factor. Furthermore, the symbolic expression of motivation—thinking about ways to solve a problem—may not involve high levels of energy expenditure. A person in a state of motivational conflict may think very intensively about the conflicting goals without moving a single muscle.

This "non-energizing" conception of motivation is not contradictory to the notions that a person may tense muscles used in an act he is thinking about; but muscle tensions are not always concomitants of thought. It is hard to imagine what muscles an astrophysicist would tense when he thinks about outer space. Furthermore, someone who argues that energizing is a critical function of motivation would have to argue that the amount of energy expended is an index of motivation. But this can lead to ridiculous conclusions: the astrophysicist who paces is more motivated than the one who sits.

In Proposition I, the importance of the goal is one of the determinants of motivation. Thus, an individual might be highly motivated to achieve a goal with low expectations of attainment but of great importance to him; or he might be highly motivated for a goal of minor importance but of high probable attainment. Notice that in the present formulation, motivation refers to action, not to affective states. The person who strives for highly probable goals of low importance may do it without much enthusiasm. In quite the same way a person may be rather unhappy while striving mightily for an almost unobtainable goal of great importance to him. He may spend a whole lifetime in this unhappy state; but such a life is not evidence against the present formulation. Action, not affect, is the key.

The importance of hope, of expectation of success in attaining goals, has been underlined by a number of theorists. In a psychoanalytic vein, French has written (1952):

> We summarize the process of activation of goal-directed behavior: First, the motivating pressure of a need seeks discharge in diffuse motor activity. Next, hope of satisfaction, based on present opportunity and memories of previous success, stimulates the integrative mechanisms to form a plan, a plan for realizing this hope. Finally, hope of satisfaction activates this plan so that it exerts a guiding influence, concentrating motor discharge on efforts to put the plan into execution.

> . . . Integrative capacity should vary as a positive function of one's confidence of attaining a goal (p. 53).

Sullivan (1953) believed that motivation to attain security was one of the basic determinants of human behavior. Security may be defined as high perceived probability of future goal attainment. Lewin (1951) had similar ideas:

> Even more than suffering, persistency depends on the time perspective of the individual. As long as there is hope that the difficulty may be overcome for that price in effort or pain which the individual is ready to pay, he goes on trying. . . .
>
> Persisting depends on two factors: the value of the goal and the outlook for the future (p. 107).

Tolman's (1948) position was also consistent with this viewpoint. He assumed that the organism would act if there was some expectancy that it would and could achieve its goals. If there was no expectancy that any response could lead to the achievement of a goal, then the organism would not "behave."

More recently, Rotter (1954) and Atkinson (1964) have made expectations of goal achievement, as well as importance of the goal, central to their theories. After reviewing the whole field of motivation, Cofer and Appley (1964) argue that behavior can be understood in terms of anticipations, rather than in terms of drive. Tolman, Rotter, Atkinson, and Cofer and Appley generally consider the individual's expectation of goal attainment to be a function only of his perception of the efficacy of his own behavior. Tolman and Rotter specifically tie expectancy drives to the notion that, "if I do such-and-such, I will attain this goal (reward or reinforcement)." We do not limit goal attainment in this way. An individual may perceive that his goal attainment is dependent on the behavior of other people or on acts of nature or God. Thus the present formulation allows for a far greater variety of factors, primarily social in nature, to influence the level of expectation and to influence it in a variety of ways. These influences will be spelled out in subsequent chapters.

Hope and Action

We may hypothesize that each of the two proposed determinants of motivation, importance of the goal and the expectation of achieving it, can lead to the occurrence of the following indicators of motivation: (1) overt action toward the goal; (2) covert symbolic action toward the goal; and (3) selective attention to aspects of the environment relevant to attaining the goal. Combining each of the two determinants with each of the three indicators generates six hypotheses. They are:

1. The greater the expectation of attaining a goal, the more likely the individual will act to attain it.
2. The more important a goal is, the more likely is the individual to attend selectively to aspects of the environment relevant to attaining it.
3. Increased importance of the goal leads to more overt action to attain it.
4. Increased importance of the goal leads to more thought about *how* to attain it.
5. Increased expectation of goal attainment leads to more thought about how to attain the goal.
6. Increased expectation of goal attainment leads to more selective attention to aspects of the environment relevant to attaining the goal.

Hypotheses one and two will be discussed below as the hypotheses for which there are known supportive data. Hypotheses three and four are self-evident. The last two (numbers five and six) are not self-evident, but I am unaware of any corroborative research. They are presented here as evidence of the heuristic value of the present theory.

The first hypothesis for which evidence will be cited is "the more important a goal is, the more likely is the individual to attend selectively to aspects of the environment relevant to attaining it."

Easterbrook (1959) has thoroughly reviewed the research

pertinent to the problem of the influence on perception of an individual's being oriented toward some goal. His conclusion is that "high drive"—an organism's having an important goal—is associated with a limitation in the range of cues to which it will attend. Easterbrook also implies that the research indicates that the individual will concentrate on cues relevant to his goal. As the range of cues becomes more limited because of increasing importance of goals, the more likely are irrelevant cues to be ignored. This is exactly what is maintained here.

More recently, Jones and Gerard (1967) have reviewed data pertaining to the problem of the conditions determining whether or not a person will attend to stimuli that have been associated with pain. Their conclusion: if attention to these stimuli mediates a person's goal attainment, including the avoidance of the pain itself, he will attend to these stimuli; if attention to these stimuli does not help him to attain his goals, he will not attend to them.

Our argument does not imply that the individual will necessarily be better able to attain more important goals than less important ones. Studies have repeatedly shown that when a goal is extremely important to an organism, its problem solving ability tends to go down. However, this drop in performance probably occurs mainly in those cases in which the problem actually is such that the organism cannot solve it unless the organism attends to aspects or events which it does not perceive as relevant. On the other hand, if the problem is such that the perceived and the actual relevancies overlap, then the organism may be more likely to achieve his goals. If the aspects of the environment on which the organism centers are completely relevant to and sufficient for goal attainment, high importance would lead to greater goal attainment. However, such tasks or situations may be quite unusual. In many cases, in a changing world, the individual may be mistaken about relevance. Therefore, in such situations, the more important the goals, the less likely he is to attend to the truly relevant ones and the less likely he is to be successful. Easterbrook cites data consistent with the present argument.

Hope and Action

The second hypothesis for which data will be presented is "the greater the expectation of attaining a goal, the more likely the individual will act in order to attain it." In the most rudimentary sense, the data in the area of operant or instrumental learning can be considered to support this hypothesis. A particular habit dies when hope of achieving a reinforcement or reward ceases. If there is some hope, the organism will continue to act. This interpretation of instrumental learning has not only been formulated by Tolman, a cognitive theorist, but has also been developed at length by Mowrer (1960), who is far more "behavioristic." Mowrer described the process of learning in terms of the organism's learning to hope —learning that a given event signals an oncoming reinforcement. In fact, he argues that hope is a prerequisite for action, paralleling the present thesis.

In direct confirmation of the proposition, Zipf (1963) gave human subjects a task of tapping three holes in each of one hundred circles. After the baseline rate of performance was established for subjects, they were informed of the probability of working fast enough to gain a two-dollar reward. The probability was experimentally varied in steps from 0 to 1.00. The subjects' increases in speed were directly proportional to the perceived probability. Diggory (1966) reports a study by Rosen that shows that subjects speeded up as they were made to discover that the probability of their attaining the goal of performing a card-sorting task at a certain high speed, was increasing. Diggory, Klein, and Cohen (1964) gave subjects a task of tapping out with their arms the numbers that had been associated with cards presented to them. They were given a goal of tapping out a certain number in a given period of time. On each of the subjects' trials they were given bogus information about their level of performance on that task. Subjects who were told they were doing better had a higher level of muscular action potential in their working arms during the rest periods between tasks. Birch (1964) found that subjects reached more rapidly for puzzles with which they were successful than for those with which they had failed.

Battle (1965) first had junior high school students indicate the grade they expected to receive in their mathematics course. Later, an experimenter, who did not know the students, gave them an extremely difficult mathematics problem and told them they could quit working on the problem any time they wanted and could then work on a "second task," which had nothing to do with mathematics. The students who expected higher grades in mathematics persisted longer on the task. Presumably these students also had higher expectations of completing the task.

The importance of hope as a prerequisite for action, even action to avoid death, is illustrated in a remarkable study by Richter (1957). He removed from animals a part of their bodies upon which they normally rely for adaptation. Without this part of their bodies, they had little basis for hope when faced with an extreme threat to their survival and, accordingly, gave up. Richter had a group of thirty-four wild rats whose most important contact with the world of other alert, aggressive rats was, according to him, their whiskers. After he had clipped their whiskers, he placed the rats in containers of water with jets of water playing on the top to prevent their floating. Normally, rats placed in such containers swim for a very long time, but all the de-whiskered wild rats gave up quickly and died. Richter gives the following description:

> The first rat swam around excitedly on the surface for a very short time, then dove to the bottom, where it began to swim around, moving its way along the glass wall. Without coming to the surface a single time it died two minutes after entering the tank (p. 194).

Richter found that the rats' heart and respiratory rates slowed down before death, as if they were giving up. He writes:

> The situation of these rats scarcely seems one demanding fight or flight—it is rather one of hopelessness. . . . The rats are in a situation against which they have no defense (p. 196).

On the other hand, Richter found that if he briefly immersed de-whiskered rats a few times, pulling them out very rapidly after their immersion, they soon regained their capacity to swim around like normal rats. The immersion in the water was no longer a hopeless situation for them.

Furthermore, he found that of twelve laboratory-raised rats, only three died as a result of de-whiskered immersion. These rats had not learned to depend so heavily on their whiskers for survival. Clearly, hope of survival is essential for action for survival.

Richter's water jar is analogous to cases in which people are confronted with a potential disaster, such as being in a building on fire. Quarantelli (1954) has surveyed the reports of human behavior in such situations and concludes that "the flight of panic arises only when being entrapped is sensed or thought of as a possibility rather than an actuality (p. 273)." That is, people will attempt to flee the danger only if they expect they can attain the goal of being in a safe place. Quarantelli states "Persons in panic feel powerless to bring the threat itself under control but they do not despair of getting out of danger by fleeing (p. 274)." He reports that if the person feels that he cannot possibly escape, he does not panic, does not flee, but sits down, so to speak, to await death.

Hope is important even for the persons who escaped from fires but were burned. Hamberg, Hamberg, and de Goza (1953) studied behavior of severely burned patients. They described the process of moving toward recovery with a minimum of psychological problems as follows: "The recovery mechanisms in these cases may be broadly defined as *mobilization of hope of recovery, followed by* the restoration of interpersonal relationships, and self-esteem, including transaction from enforced passivity to constructive activity ([p. 11] italics supplied)."

Bettelheim (1960) reviews his experience as a concentration camp inmate in Nazi Germany and describes some prisoners who came to be described as "Moslems" because of their fatalism:

> Prisoners who came to believe the repeated statements of the guards—that there was no hope for them, that they would never leave the camp except as a corpse—who came to feel that their

> environment was one over which they could exercise no influence whatever, these prisoners were, in a literal sense, walking corpses. . . . They were people who were so deprived of affect, of self-esteem, and every form of stimulation, so totally exhausted, both physically and mentally, that they had given the environment total power over them (p. 151).

Bettelheim reports that these prisoners soon died, not even trying to get food for themselves.

Nardini (1952) reports that among American prisoners of war in Japanese camps the conditions were so bad and efforts at survival so difficult that after an extended period of suffering some of the prisoners lay down to die; they suffered so-called "apathy deaths," which had no obvious physical basis.

We see then that data from controlled laboratory experiments, on both humans and on animals, from schools, from peacetime disaster, from hospitals, from concentration and prisoner-of-war camps, all point to the importance of hope for action, even action to prevent the greatest of all disasters, death. Lazarus (1966), who reviewed the literature on psychological stress, also concludes:

> In short, real hopelessness is here proposed as a condition of inaction in the face of threat. This is not to say that there aren't other factors that may be involved, such as the suddenness of the condition or the social structure of the situation, but that a crucial antecedent of inaction and apathy is that there is no hope that an active response can be viable (p. 263).

Also consistent with our general theoretical position is Lewin's (1951) interpretation of the phenomenon of the positive goal gradient, the increase in motivation that occurs as the organism gets psychologically closer to its goal. According to Lewin, the degree of closeness can be interpreted as the number of different activities the individual perceives he has to perform in order to achieve his goal. If it is assumed that the organism's perceived probability of completing each of the activities is less than perfect, then the perceived probability of attaining the ultimate goal increases as the organism approaches it. That is, the subjective product of the probabilities of completing the various activities increases as the number of remaining activities declines. This increase in perceived probability then leads to an increase in motivation (the goal gradient). Diggory (1966) found a positive relationship between closeness to a goal and subjective probabilities of success.

This interpretation of the positive goal gradient can be tested by a number of hypotheses. One is that the number of different activities in which an organism expects to have to engage in, that is, the number of obstacles it expects to have to overcome, determines the slope of the goal gradient—the more activities, the more gradual the slope. This prediction simply reflects the fact that generally the greater the number of activities en route to a goal, the less will be the increment in perceived probability of success resulting from the completion of each activity.

Another hypothesis is that if the organism repeats the series of activities and successfully attains the goal several times, the goal gradient will become more gradual as the number of repeated successes increases. The rationale for this hypothesis is that, after each repetition, the organism will be more hopeful the next time it completes the first activity in the series. Still another hypothesis is that the slope of the goal gradient is a function of the perceived difficulty of each of the tasks en route. In fact, if the task perceived to be most difficult is presented first in the series, the slope of the positive goal gradient might flatten.

All of this analysis is based on the goal gradient in a situation in which there are a series of activities. However, the goal gradient has been determined in situations in which the only activity was running down a runway. We do not intend to argue that each step constitutes another activity or task for the subject unless the steps are exceedingly difficult, as in the case of a crippled person or animal. Instead, the present analysis can be applied to the straight running situation by assuming that, in the organism's experience, increased distance from a goal had been associated with lower probability of attainment. It is not unlikely that in some previous experience, the organism has been blocked before attaining goals. The potential of being blocked obviously increases with distance from the goal. The organism then generalizes to the runway this association between physical distance and blocking. Clearly, this interpretation could also be tested by appropriate experimental variations in the organism's prior experiences.

Since not all situations are positive, any valid theory must concern itself with the negative. It has been found that the decrease in motivation to move *away* from a negative goal is greater than the increase in motivation to move *toward* a positive goal as one gets closer to it. Examined in the light of the present theory, a negative goal gradient can be interpreted as a situation in which the organism's goal is that of being in any one of the many places or situations other than the negative one it is in. Thus, a negative goal gradient really entails a positive goal that encompasses a much broader class of places and situations than does a positive goal. Since the class of such goals is more extensive, the organism is more likely to attain them rather rapidly. Once it attains the goals, the organism no longer needs to act. This speed of attaining the positive goal of moving away from the negative would explain the sharper drop-off of negative goal gradients than of positive ones.

Why negative goal gradients at all? Doesn't the present theory suggest that the organism is more motivated to escape the closer it is to escaping? This suggestion implies a negative goal gradient with a slope that is the reverse of those usually found. If the behavior of individual subjects in experimental studies were examined, it might be discovered that they are motivated with increasing strength as they move through the negative region and arrive closer to the boundary through which they anticipate escape. However, this increase in motivation may often be hidden by the fact that, in most studies, the subjects can very quickly attain the goal of getting out of the negative zone. The animal simply jumps over a wall, for example. If the animal had to engage in a series of activities, it could be expected to be more motivated in those activities that are closer to the point of escape.

One test of the present interpretation could be made by experimentally controlling the degree to which each step away from the negative goal entails a lower probability of being forcibly returned to the negative region. If, after an organism has left the negative region, each step further away reduces the probability of being returned to it, then a goal gradient with a slope opposite to those found presently would be predicted. This goal gradient, however, would drop to "no motivation" as soon as the organism was in the region of no probability of return to the negative region. This drop should not be so surprising since there is an equivalent phenomenon when the organism enters a "goal box." Once he is inside the box, the goal has been attained and the organism's running speed reduces. In short, then, the hypothesis indicates that these gradients are not fixed aspects of nature but can be flattened out and reversed directionally.

At this point, the apparent conflict between the present formulation and Atkinson's (1964) theory of achievement motivation needs airing. He argues that the incentive value of a goal (its motivating qualities) is negatively related to its probability of attainment. Easy tasks are not highly motivating. Clearly, his position has the smell of intuitive validity—we are not generally motivated to achieve trivial goals. On closer examination, however, we find that in his system the value of performing a task is a matter not only of the incentive value of the task, but also of the incentive value of success. Atkinson himself raises the question, "What is it about success that makes it valuable to some people?" He concludes that success has value to them because of their pride. He writes "Let us turn now to the matter of the value of the incentive. In sizing up the task, how much pride of accomplishment does the individual anticipate if he achieves his goal? Certainly there is much less of a sense of accomplishment in completion of certain tasks than others (p. 24)."

It then becomes important whether one defines the goal of the individual's motivation as the completion of the task or as the enhancement of pride. It is evident that Atkinson regards the "real" goal as the enhancement of pride; the achievement of success is only ancillary. If success can be obtained only in ways that do not enhance pride, for example, by cheating, then motivation to attain success would be low for those who "pride themselves" for not cheating. The point here is that the attainment of difficult goals is more instrumental to increasing pride than the attainment of easy goals. In our formulation, the expected probability of attaining the goal of an increase in pride by performing a very simple task is quite low and, therefore, people do not choose it. On the other hand, the expected probability of attaining the goal of an increase in pride by means of a difficult task is generally quite high; therefore, people do choose it, provided it is not so difficult that it cannot be completed. Moreover, if some action were both easy as well as greatly enhancing to his pride, a person would be most likely to take it. For example, a person who takes great pride in collecting certain art objects accidentally finds one which is both rare and cheaply priced. Regardless of Atkinson's formulation, he would plausibly buy it.

Atkinson cannot easily reject the last example as irrelevant to his theory because pride in success was not involved. If he did so, he would then reason somewhat circularly: in some situations, pride is enhanced by difficult tasks; these are the situations to which the theory of achievement motivation applies. In other situations, pride is not correlated with difficulty; the theory does not apply to these. Nevertheless, Atkinson does share the idea that expectation of goal attainment greatly influences motivation.

Data from studies of partial reinforcement are rather confusing with respect to the hypothesis under consideration. In partial reinforcement, the organism receives a reward (attains a goal) on only some of the occasions in which it makes a particular response or acts in a particular way. Since the perceived probability of goal attainment must be lower here than in a situation of consistent reinforcement, the organism would be expected to respond less. In general, data supporting this expectation are found in those studies where there are a limited number of opportunities to respond. Antithetically, at least two studies (Weinstock, 1958; Goodrich, 1959) have shown that if the organism is given many opportunities to respond, a reversal occurs on the later trials. On these trials, the organisms who are partially reinforced run sooner and faster than those who are consistently reinforced. Although this reversal is not of great magnitude, it has been found to be reliable. Admittedly, this reversal is difficult to explain in the present formulation. Nevertheless, this exception does not loom large in the considerable evidence that is consistent with the hypothesis relating action to perceived probability—or hope.

CHAPTER 3

Hope and Anxiety

In the previous chapter, we examined the relationship between hope and action. We now turn to the problems of the effect of hope on anxiety. As presented in Chapter Two, Proposition III maintains that an individual's hopelessness about important goals results in anxiety. Anxiety was defined as a negative subjective state as well as a state of physiological arousal.

Two issues related to the definition of anxiety should be mentioned. The first is that the problem of the existence or nonexistence of unconscious anxiety is not central to the present theory and therefore can be bypassed without generating excessive difficulty. Secondly, the distinction between anxiety and fear can be treated with greater depth after the notion of schema is introduced.

Anxiety as described here should be distinguished from states of the organism sometimes referred to as *tension* or *arousal*. States of tension or arousal are usually described as motivationally significant. The organism is described as having a given level of tension, which demands expression in action, or as being aroused to act. Anxiety, on the other hand, is an affective state, involving a subjectively negative state. Whether or not tension and anxiety are distinguishable physiologically remains unclear, although Mandler, Mandler, Kremen, and Sholiton (1961) found some indications that at the autonomic level, a different system may be involved in tension (arousal) and anxiety.

The idea put forth here, that anxiety is the result of perceived low probability of attaining important goals, has been stated by a number of theorists, especially those who have observed anxiety in natural settings.

Freud (1936) wrote "Anxiety arose as a response to a situation of *danger*. It will be regularly reproduced thenceforward whenever such a situation recurs ([p. 72] italics supplied)." "The situation which the infant appraises as 'danger,' and against which it desires reassurance, is therefore one of not being gratified, of an increase in tension arising from non-gratification of its needs—a situation against which it is powerless (p. 76)." "In both respects, alike as an automatic phenomenon and as a safety signal, anxiety proves to be a product of the psychic helplessness of the infant which is the obvious counterpart of its biological helplessness (p. 77)."

Goldstein (1940) refers to the "catastrophic situation," a situation with which the organism cannot cope. He postulates that the organism experiences great anxiety in these situations. This situation also refers in part to what Maslow (1941, 1943) defined as a threat to the organism's integrity. To the extent that this threat involves the organism's inability to function effectively to satisfy its needs, the catastrophic and threat situations overlap. Maslow also implies that great anxiety is a consequence of this experience. Horney (1937) also has referred to basic anxiety as a consequence of being helpless in a threatening environment. In their study of the emotional reactions of soldiers in World War II, Grinker and Speigel (1945b) wrote ". . . the problem of anxiety in this context centers about the position of the ego in regard to mastery, independence and freedom of activity (p. 129)." In a paper entitled "Anticipated frustration as a determinant of anxiety," Whiteman (1957) presented the same idea.

Our proposition receives empirical support from a more systematic study showing that a person whose chances of attaining his goals are lowered by a loss of status and income experiences anxiety—if it is assumed that anxiety will manifest itself in an increase of physical ailments or concern with physical ailments. Kasl and French (1962) report that in a factory, the fifty-three men who moved up to higher status jobs decreased their visits to the infirmary while the thirty men who went down in occupational status increased their visits.

Another case of hopelessness with respect to important goals is pessimism about escape from pain. Unavoidable electric shock has been used sometimes in classical conditioning studies in which a stimulus is presented just prior to the infliction of pain. In their reviews of the experimental literature about such situations, Solomon and Brush (1956) and Mowrer (1960) both conclude that emotional upset and anxiety result. Furthermore, if animals are confined in a situation of constant, loud, painful noise, they would be expected to experience anxiety, since they cannot shut their ears. Some rodents even have psychotic-like (audio-genetic) seizures under such conditions. "Susceptible rats appeared 'scared to death.' Such rats appeared to be vainly trying to escape from a highly undesirable and frightening stimulus in the form of the ringing bell. The shaking, running, teeth chattering . . . seemed to indicate a general fear reaction (Griffiths, 1942, p. 18)."

It would be interesting to determine whether only intermittent painful noise or painful noise with intermittent intervals of silence would have the same effect as constant noise. The "breaks" would give the organism at least some hope of relief. By the same token, it may be possible to generate seizures in animals by constant shock instead of intermittent shock as used in most of the existing studies of animal reactions to shock. These intermittent shocks do not usually generate anxiety great enough to lead to seizures.

Furthermore, Proposition III would also lead to the prediction that, if an individual's goal in a situation is to avoid pain and if he has learned an action that will avoid pain, he will not be anxious. Bersh, Matterman, and Schoenfeld (1956) gave subjects an electric shock after the subjects heard a certain tone, while they measured the subjects' cardiac responses. The subjects were told that they could avoid the shock if they lifted their fingers. All of the subjects did so and the cardiac reaction to the tone dropped out. Solomon and Wynne (1953) reported that rats showed less upset after they had learned to avoid shock. Solomon and Wynne (1954) also report fewer overt signs of anxiety as a rat learns to make the correct response to avoid pain. More recently, Solomon (1964) has written:

> Anyone who has tried to train a rat in a T maze using food reward for a correct response, and shock to the feet for an incorrect response, knows that there is a period of emotionality during early training, but that, thereafter, the rat, when the percentage of correct responses is high, looks like a hungry, well-motivated, happy rat, eager to get from his cage to the experimenter's hand, and thence to the start box (p. 250).

Parallels to these laboratory situations occur in real life. Miller (1959) has written:

> Many additional practical points can come out of the naturalistic study of fear; for example, the importance of knowing exactly what to expect or planning and knowing what to do to minimize the danger, of concentrating on the task at hand, of breaking seemingly impossible tasks into manageable steps and concentrating on the performance of each step (p. 268).

Haggard (1949), in his report on emotional stress on submarine sailors in World War II, writes:

> For maximal protection against emotional stress, the individual

> should have experienced all possible contingencies that might arise, and should have learned how to handle them. . . . A sense of helplessness results, on the other hand, when an individual is caught off guard or untrained to act effectively in a situation. Panic frequently follows (p. 449).

One advantage of the present theoretical approach to anxiety is that it is applicable to a wider range of anxiety-arousing situations than other approaches. For instance, the proposition that anxiety is a function of hopeless expectations about goal attainment implies that any perceived event that reduces the expectations of goal attainment will tend to increase anxiety. As will be shown, there are a great variety of such events, ranging from blocking of the person's own activities to his perception of some other person, even one with whom he might not communicate. The advantage of describing the cause of anxiety as a function of reduced expectations is that it provides a common theoretical way of explaining why a variety of events or factors influence anxiety. Thus, anxiety as a result of frustration or the blockage of an individual's sequence of responses becomes just one of the many types of anxiety-causing events. The theories of Mandler and Watson (1966), Berkowitz (1962), Dollard, Miller, Doob, Mowrer and Sears (1939), in which anxiety, rage, and aggression are assumed to be outcomes of frustration, are at least partially subsumable under the present approach, since a frustration is an event that often increases hopelessness. In addition, there can be special cases of anxiety that involve a sequence of responses that is complete, that is not frustrated, but the goal is not attained. A person who walks to a beach for a sun bath, covers himself with ointment, lies down to enjoy the sun and then finds that suddenly a dark cloud has blocked the sun, and will do so for a long while, might feel quite upset. His sequence of responses was completed. Nevertheless, he did not attain his goal. In short, any event perceived by the organism to reduce his expectations will increase anxiety, regardless of whether this event involves his own actions.

The present approach also has a wider range of applicability than those that treat anxiety as a residual of a pain reaction, this residual having been attached to some stimulus that was regularly antecedent to pain. This more behavioristic definition is deficient for present purposes because it is not possible in many cases to show that physical pain was experienced by an organism in the acquisition of anxiety. In some cases of experimental neurosis, no physical pain whatever was inflicted and yet it is clear that the organism became anxious.

Moreover, the present formulation fits data from studies of the persistence of actions acquired because they led to the avoidance of pain, while theories based on anxiety as a residual of pain reaction are not consistent with these data. Such theories typically explain the marked persistence of avoidance reactions by citing the rewarding quality of reducing the anxiety aroused by the recurrence of cues that had in the past preceded pain. The data cited above from studies by Bersh, Matterman, and Schoenfeld (1956), Solomon and Wynne (1953, 1954), and Solomon (1964) all indicate that, after the pain-avoidance reaction has been acquired, anxiety no longer occurs when the organism is in the potentially dangerous situation. Anxiety is not found to occur even before the avoidance response is made. Thus, there is no anxiety to reduce by means of the avoidance reaction. On the other hand, the present approach argues simply that the organism persists in the avoidance response because the occurrence of events signaling danger leads the organism to act to attain the goal of avoiding the pain.

The discussion so far has been focused on the effects on anxiety of different levels of expected goal attainment when the goals have been of high importance. The other hypothesis stemming from Proposition III is that anxiety will increase with the rising importance of a goal with low probability of attainment. This hypothesis does not demand data for its support. Unless they have symbolic meaning to a person, the inability to attain small goals causes little anxiety.

The next proposition of the theory, Proposition IV, states that the organism is motivated to avoid and escape anxiety. If an individual is in a state of anxiety, he might do one or both of two things: he might try to raise the expectations of attaining the goal; or he might lower the importance of the unattainable goals. Doing either of these things, however, may entail great difficulties. In trying to raise the expectation of goal attainment he will probably run into the same difficulties that prevented him from having high expectations in the first place. Furthermore, harking back to Proposition I, one would predict that he would be less likely to act to attain the goal than someone with higher expectations of success. (There are, however, other means by which the organism might raise the expectations other than a direct attack upon the problem. We will examine these ways in Chapters Five and Six.)

If the individual lowers the importance of the goal, he then tends to become depressed, apathetic, withdrawn; goals do not matter to him. At the overt level, he does not act; covertly, he may disavow interest in the goal. However, such reduction in importance of goals is not always easy; some goals, such as having water and air, may be so important and undeniable that they cannot be simply ignored. Nonetheless, under extreme conditions, even the goal of survival may be devalued, as in the cases of Bettelheim's (1960) moribund Moslems and of apathy deaths in prisoner of war camps. Of course, such deaths may be the result both of the low expectations of survival and of the lowered importance of surviving. Only careful study under more controlled conditions could distinguish the reasons for lack of action.

Sometimes a person may shift from a state of apathy and depression into a state of anxiety as a consequence of a small but significant rise in hopefulness effected by the occurrence of certain events. The increased hopefulness makes it less necessary to devalue the goal, but hope is not so high as to preclude anxiety. Grinker and Speigel (1945b) describe such a process among some airmen in World War II:

> They accept the likelihood of death at any moment, but not with the inner harmony of those who are intensely attached to their group, but with fatalistic and bitter resignation. Being certain

> of imminent death, neither the past nor the future has any meaning to them; only the present moment is real (p. 131). . . . The "I don't give a damn" reaction is actually closer to a marked depression than to a successful adaptation, but it does not protect the individual against anxiety. The protection, however, is unstable and often breaks down when the individual comes close to the end of his combat tour. . . . During the last few missions, hope of survival again becomes realistic, and at that point concern for his own fate again returns to the individual. Once he begins to hope and to care, he may suddenly develop intense anxiety (p. 132).

The proposition also maintains that organisms will avoid as well as escape anxiety. This avoidance motivation has a number of consequences. It may in part lead to efforts to keep the level of expectations of goal attainment high and thus to be oriented toward security. He may hoard, practice skills, stay in safe situations, and so on.

The tendency of organisms, as delineated by Lewin (1951), to work toward subgoals rather than ultimate goals can also be explained by the motivation to avoid anxiety. As was pointed out in the discussion of goal gradients, the expected probability of achieving a goal can be treated as the product of the probabilities of completing each of the steps toward this goal. In most cases, the perceived probability of completing at least some of the steps is less than 100 per cent. Therefore, on the whole, the perceived probability of attaining goals requiring fewer steps is greater than that of attaining those requiring more steps; the number of probabilities to be multiplied is less. Since subgoals are, by definition, goals that entail fewer steps en route, the individual will tend to make them more important than ultimate goals in order to avoid anxiety.

A poignant example of people shifting to more and more immediate goals in order to avoid the anxiety created by the orientation to a completely hopeless long-range goal comes from a study of the parents of children with leukemia (Freidman, Chodoff, Mason, and Hamberg, 1963). In lieu of centering on the hopeless goal of their children's survival, these parents dedicated themselves to short-range goals, such as getting their children to a movie *that* evening. The parents reported that it was the hope of attaining such short-range goals that kept them going throughout the last days of their children's lives. The researchers also remark, "Unlike massive denial, hope did not appear to interfere with effective behavior and was entirely compatible with an intellectual acceptance of reality (p. 660)."

If the organism cannot avoid anxiety by raising expectation or by reducing the importance of certain goals, he may direct his attention only toward those goals he expects to attain. This withdrawal from involvement with many important goals often characterizes long-suffering people, such as peasants or, until recently, Negro Americans. In a sense, such people may be afraid of hope itself. The ancient Greeks were ambivalent toward hope and some non-Western peoples may regard hoping as a very dangerous activity.

The notion that organisms tend to avoid anxiety should not be misconstrued to mean that there are no other motivational tendencies. Furthermore, the attainment of these other types of goals may sometimes even involve anxiety. For example, in the work of Atkinson (1964), the person's goal in achievement motivation is enhancement of his pride or avoidance of a loss of pride. The attainment of such goals may, in fact, involve risky behavior, as Atkinson points out. Thus, it may appear that the individual seeks out anxiety when, in fact, his engaging in anxiety-producing tasks may simply be a necessary step to the attainment of some other goal.

CHAPTER 4

Schemas

Now that we have completed the examination of the four propositions dealing with motivation and affect, we can turn to those dealing with cognition. In Chapter One, schemas were defined as associations between the concepts in the individual's cognitive structure. The constituent concepts of schemas were described as being either classes of objects, classes of events, or classes of relationships between and among objects and events. This formulation is analogous to the one made by Haygood and Bourne (1965) between attribute and rule. Attributes are exemplified by size, color, shape, movement, and so on. Rules refer to combinations, simple or complex, of the attributes. The rule is comparable to the schema in the present system.

As Scheerer pointed out (1954), a schema does not have to be conscious, conscious in the sense of the person's being able to verbalize it. Often, the schema consists of an assumption made without ever questioning it enough to have to verbalize it—if something is red, anyone can see that it is red. If the assumption is violated, the individual may then become aware of his schema and may even express it verbally. This level of awareness corresponds to Freud's notion of the preconscious, which comprises the ideas and impulses that can readily be brought into consciousness by appropriate situations. But such potential expression is not a necessary part of a schema; it may remain unconscious.

In the discussion below, examples of schemas are sometimes given in terms of something a person might say. These examples are used here only for purposes of communication; the reader is not to draw the conclusion that the present approach is confined to schemas that are readily verbalized.

Another characteristic of schemas, as mentioned in Chapter Two, is that they can vary in degree of abstractness and can bear hierarchical relationships to one another. The more abstract, higher level schemas are analogous to the computer "programs" described by Miller, Galanter, and Pribram (1960), which are part of the person's cognitive structure ready for application to more specific and limited situations. The idea of hierarchy of schemas is also implied in the notion of strategy in concept learning. The individual learns a technique for discovering concepts. The person's knowledge of this technique is a schema of a higher order than any concept he learns in applying it.

There are two ways of determining the relative hierarchical position of schemas that are related to each other. The first way is to examine the constituent concepts to see which set is more abstract. A schema referring to humanity is more abstract than one referring only to Americans. A schema referring to a person's ability to do things is more abstract than one referring to his ability to repair a car.

The second way of determining the hierarchical level of schemas is more complex. A schema may have a constituent concept that refers to a quality, or configuration, of a number of other schemas. For example, a set of schemas may be alike because they all refer to the weights of members of a team and these weights may encompass quite a wide range. The individual may then develop a schema, "The weights of these members of this team are highly variable." This latter schema is of a higher order than those referring to the weights of the particular team members. The constituent concept of variability of weight cannot exist without the set of lower level schemas, yet the concept of *variability* of weight is not part of any *one* of the lower level schemas. Only by considering the collectivity or whole class of schemas does the constituent concept of variability emerge.

Both the definition of schemas and the discussion of the acquisition of schemas in Chapter One imply that people can learn concepts that refer to classes of objects or events as well as those relating to relationships. That the learning of relationships *per se* is possible has been indicated in a number of studies since the Kohler-Spence controversy about transposition. In this controversy, Kohler (1951) maintained that the organism learns to respond to relationships as relationships, while Spence (1937) argued that the organism learns to respond to a specific stimulus and to other stimuli that are similar to it on some given stimulus dimension. Subsequent research has shown that both are possible. Kuenne (1946) found that children could respond to relationships between stimuli, even when the stimuli changed, provided that they had verbalized the relationship as such, indicating that they had learned the concept of the relationship. Lawrence and de Rivera (1954) performed an ingenious experiment in which rats were taught to turn to, say, the right if the darker of two greys was on the top of a stimulus card, and to the left if it was on the bottom. The rats were given trials with several different combinations of various greys, thereby maximizing the possibility of acquiring the concept of the relationship between the cards. The rats were then presented with pairs of shades of grey that had never been presented to them together before. In some cases, both of the greys presented had been associated with a left turn but the particular vertical or relative arrangement had been associated with right turns. In these cases, the rats responded much more frequently to the arrangement or relationship rather than to the absolute shade of grey. The present theory attributes these results to the fact that the rats were given ample opportunity to learn the concept of the vertical arrangement because of the presentation during training of the same arrangement of several different pairs of shades of grey.

This interpretation of the Lawrence and de Rivera study is confirmed by Johnson and Zara (1960). They have shown that transposition is greatly enhanced if the individual is given different exemplars of the relationship so that he can learn the concept of the relationship. Their subjects were three- to five-year-old children who did not verbalize the concept of the relationship on early training trials. Those that did were rejected. The subjects were presented with a series of squares of different sizes, the smallest called *one,* the largest *eight.* One group of children was trained with squares three and four; another group was trained with both three and four and one and two. The researchers found that the second group learned faster than the first. With divers instances of the same relationship, they learned the relationship sooner. The children were then tested for transposition (squares five and six or seven and eight). The second group, those who had been trained on two different examples of the relationship, transposed more than did the other group. Furthermore, they transposed as much to the squares that were proximate to the training squares as to the more distant ones. The other group of subjects transposed primarily to the squares near the training squares.

At a more complex level, Wells (1963) has shown that subjects can be trained to apply in concept learning a type of strategy they otherwise would be unlikely to use. He gave subjects four concept learning problems that could be solved only by using disjunctive concepts, which are, in general, not used "naturally" by subjects. They were then given a concept learning problem that could be solved by either disjunctive or conjunctive concepts. The trained subjects used the disjunctive solutions more than did a control group.

The trained subjects reported that to solve the problem they had applied techniques that they had acquired during training.

The learning of other types of relationships, such as causing, blocking, helping, and so on, has not been experimentally demonstrated as yet but would no doubt prove a profitable area of investigation if these techniques are used.

Since it is maintained that schemas can be hierarchical, the question arises as to how the higher order, the more abstract schemas are acquired. Proposition V indicated that one of the ways in which a person acquires a schema is by perceiving events that are exemplars of the schema. What are the events the organism perceives when it forms higher order schemas? We assume that organisms can perceive or recall their own perceptual processes—the organism can perceive that it has just perceived something. Also, it can perceive that it has just invoked a given schema or that it is in a state of arousal; "I am thinking about such-and-such," or "I thought that such-and-such idea was right," or "I know that such-and-such is the case." By recalling the prior occasions of the arousal or functioning of given schemas, the individual can develop new schemas that subsume the given one. The new schemas are the higher level schemas.

This analysis would suggest that an individual is more likely to develop higher level schemas if he recalls the occasions when the lower level ones functioned. Thus organisms that reminisce or are frequently reminded of the past either by self or by other organisms will most likely develop more complex schemas.

The idea of the importance of recall in the development of higher level schemas is supported by findings that concepts are easier to develop if the person has displayed before him either all or some of the positive and negative exemplars of the concept so that he does not have to rely on his perhaps fallacious memory (Cahill and Hovland, 1960; Bourne, Goldstein, and Link, 1964). Zeiler (1964) showed that transposition or the learning of relationships is facilitated when the two stimuli involved in the relationship are presented simultaneously rather than successively.

That higher level schemas develop out of lower level ones has been stated by a number of theorists. Neisser and Weene (1962) wrote

> In the laboratory or out of it, new ideas are built on old ones. To attain a typical experimental concept, say, "three borders," S must already be able to identify borders, to count, to distinguish between E's positive and negative statements, and so on. Much cognitive activity is hierarchically organized, in that abstractions at one level form the basis of abstractions at the next (p. 640).

Gagné, Mayer, Garstens, and Paradise (1962) have also pointed out that in order for an an individual to learn, he must acquire knowledge in a hierarchical fashion.

> By means of their systematic analysis, it was possible to identify nine separate entities of subordinate knowledge, arranged in a hierarchical fashion. Generally stated, our hypothesis was that (a) no individual could perform the final task without having these subordinate capabilities (*i.e.*, without being able to perform these simpler and more general tasks); and (b) that any task in the hierarchy could be performed by an individual provided suitable instructions were given, and provided relevant subordinate knowledge could be recalled by him (p. 356).

Later they write

> A theory of knowledge acquisition must propose some manner of functioning for the learning sets in a hierarchy. A good possibility seems to be that they are mediators of positive transfer from lower level learning sets to higher level sets. The hypothesis is proposed that specific transfer from one learning set to another standing above it in the hierarchy will be zero if the lower one cannot be recalled, and will range up to 100% if it can (p. 358).

The fact that schemas are cognitive indicates that they may be symbolized or may be implicated in the individual's symbolic processes. Therefore, symbolic processes can have an influence on a person's schemas. Among the most important symbolic processes for humans are those based on communication from others. Therefore, as Proposition V indicates, communication with others does give rise to schemas as well as provide the concepts that are necessary for the development of higher level schemas. For example, the concept of self may be based in part on the person's receiving communications from others that refer to "you," "Joe," and so on. Furthermore, it is important to note that higher level schemas can be acquired directly from communications rather than being built out of lower level schemas.

In Chapter One, it was pointed out that schemas can be in a state of arousal or in a latent state. The event of movement from latency to arousal was termed *invocation of a schema.* The conditions leading to invocation of a schema were stated in Proposition VI as follows: A schema is invoked by the organism's perceiving an event similar to a constituent concept of the schema or by the individual's receiving a communication from another directing him to invoke the schema; the greater the similarity between the event and the constituent concept, or the greater the importance of the person directing him, the more likely the schema is to be aroused.

Once aroused, a schema will guide a person's perceptions and thoughts, will determine his perceptual and mental sets, may influence his overt behavior. In fact, in many cases the presence of a schema in a state of arousal may be the only sign an observer has that the organism possesses that particular schema. An aroused schema functions like a "program" in operation (*cf.* Miller *et al.*), or a learning set in operation, or an instructional set directing the person's attention to certain aspects of the situation.

The reader will recall that Proposition I also concerned influences on perception but in that proposition the source of the influence was the person's own goals. There is nothing contradictory in stating that aroused schemas influence both perception and the person's goals as well. One can either construe the schematic and goal-related influences as functioning jointly or interpret the individual's turning toward a particular goal at a given time as an event that involves a schema—the schema then directly influencing perception. For present purposes, it makes little difference which way the relationship between the two influences on perception is interpreted, although in other contexts it may make a significant difference.

With respect to communication from others as an invoker of schemas, Lawrence (1963) has pointed out that in many, if not all, psychological studies little attention is paid by the researchers to the significance of the instructions given to the subjects. These instructions indicate which aspect of the situation the subject is to respond to and how he is to respond. According to Lawrence, without these instructions, few of the studies would "work." Harlow (1949) instructed his chimpanzees as to which of several possible types of oddity (with respect to size, shape, and so on) they were to attend to on a given trial in order to gain a reward. They had learned to respond to each type of oddity, but were given a signal by the experimenter as to which type applied on a given trial.

With respect to the invocation of schemas through the perception of events similar to a constituent concept, a complication sets in—simply because, during waking hours, there is always some schema of one sort or another in a state of arousal. The individual does not usually exist in a state of quiescence and is not a purely passive recipient of stimuli, mechanistically responsive. The individual tends to perceive events relevant to the aroused schema and consistent with it. This schema would thus tend to be self-perpetuating. Since such a constriction of perception to relevancies does not always continue to the point of being maladaptive for the perceiver, it is obvious that some events may be so clear, unambiguous, and physically prominent that they are perceived regardless of the aroused schema. The physical situation may change to the point that the aroused schema is no longer supported by perception of an event similar to one of its constituent concepts. When the dimensions of the new stimuli do not correspond to any constituent concepts, the new events, the new physical situation may invoke another schema relevant to the new situation. In short, an aroused schema may have a directive influence on perception, but it is not the only influential factor.

If the new situation is one for which the individual does not have a schema, he may then acquire a new one, provided that he has available concepts that can be brought into a new association in the new situation (*cf.* Tighe, 1965). In the very rare situation in which he has no prior applicable concepts, the individual would become, probably, extremely anxious.

The case in which changes in the physical environment invoke new schemas must be distinguished from the case in which a schema remains aroused but in which events are perceived that are inconsistent with it, that is, that are both relevant to it and contradicted by it. If the individual perceives an event similar to one of the constituent concepts of the schema but also perceives that other aspects of the event are contradictory, the person is said to perceive an event inconsistent with the schema. For example, the person may perceive an infant reciting the multiplication table. In such cases, there can be a number of outcomes. The individual may grossly distort his perception of the situation to make it more consistent; or the schema may become less invocable on subsequent occasions. Which alternative will occur in any given situation probably depends on a host of factors, such as the strength of the schema, the degree of inconsistency between percept and schema, the individual's characteristic way of handling such problems, and so on. (In this discussion, the assumption is made that a schema is aroused or not aroused, that arousal is an all-or-none matter. On the other hand, it is possible to talk about degrees of arousal. In the present discussion and in subsequent chapters, it does not appear to make a crucial difference how the notion of arousal is construed. For purposes of convenience of communication, the all-or-none approach will be used here. Nevertheless, the problem still remains as to which interpretation of arousal is the more empirically valid.)

Not all events in the individual's previous experience which are either consistent or inconsistent with the schema will influence its strength or invocability. Only those events that occurred while the schema was aroused determine subsequent invocability. Events perceived in a different frame of reference, as relevant to a different schema, will not have any effect. A southern white may perceive a brilliant Negro diplomat from some foreign country and this may have little or no influence on his schema regarding American Negroes.

In Propositions V and VI it was stated that schemas can be acquired, invoked and, by implication, made more invocable by the perception of other individuals, by direct experience, or by communication from others. One question provoked by this analysis is what happens when two factors, the directly experiential and the communicated, are in opposition? Since the units used to measure the power of each of these factors are not directly comparable, it is not possible to predict in any situation exactly which will predominate. Nevertheless, one can say that the more powerful source, be it social or direct, will most likely be the dominant one. For instance, the more times a schema has been invoked and found consistent with relevant events, the less likely it is to be overridden by communications, and *vice versa.*

Another very important implication of these propositions is the circular process implied by relating them to the discussion concerning the acquisition of schemas, their invocation, and their directive aspect when aroused. Suppose a schema has been invoked by the individual's having perceived an event consistent with it. Once aroused, it will direct the individual to perceive the world consistently with it to the extent that such perception does not grossly distort physical reality. Perceiving the world consistently with the schema then leads the person to perceive other events, beyond the invoking one, that are consistent with the schema. This continued perception of consistent events serves to maintain the schema's arousal. As this state of arousal continues, the schema gains additional strength and is more likely to remain aroused and to be invocable on future occasions. Of course, if the person perceives a grossly and obviously inconsistent event, the schema may lose invocability. However, in many cases, the "actual" situation is so ambiguous, so equivocal, that the schema will direct the person to perceive consistently with it, to interpret every ambiguity and equivocality in its terms. Thus, in ambiguous situations, schemas will have a tendency to be self-maintaining and therefore self-strengthening. Studies of the imperviousness of social stereotypes to change, of the assimilation of new information to preconceptions, of the importance of primacy effects in person perception, and so on, bespeak the self-sustaining quality of schemas.

Communications from others can also be involved. A schema acquired from others might lead the person to perceive consistently with it and therefore make it more likely to be invoked on subsequent occasions. The validity thereby given to the communicator's ideas might enhance his prestige and effectiveness, making it even more likely that this source can subsequently invoke the same and other schemas as well as "teach" the person a new one.

Proposition VI, concerning invocability of schemas, can be expanded to include the possibility of one schema invoking another at a higher level of abstraction. That proposition pointed out that the perception of some event involving the same concepts or dimensions as a schema leads to the invocation of that schema. The event leading to the invocation of a higher order schema is actually another, lower order schema in a state of arousal. This argument is predicated on the idea that more than one schema can be aroused at the same time, provided that they do not contradict one another. Typically, most multiple arousals of schemas occur when the schemas are hierarchically related. In fact, it would be expected that the continuation of the lower order schema in a state of arousal would lead to the continuation of the higher one as well.

This analysis suggests that there is a tendency for a kind of upward chain reaction to occur: the invocation of a schema at any given level leads to invoking a schema at a higher level, and so on. Since this spiraling effect is not likely to occur equally in all people or animals on all occasions, nor to continue to infinitely high levels of abstraction, a problem is posed: what factors determine the extent of the spiraling? The present theory does not purport to provide an answer, but such factors as intellectual ability, cognitive style, and motivation, as well as perceptual and social processes, may all be relevant.

Once a higher order schema has been invoked by a lower order schema or by a communication from another person, the aroused higher order schema can lead to the invoking of other lower order schemas that it subsumes. This ability of the higher order schema is an example of the capability of aroused schemas to serve a directive and selective function with respect to the perception of corresponding situations. In the case of the higher order schemas, the "perceived situations" are other lower order schemas that it subsumes. Of course, there are many different lower order schemas that could possibly be invoked by a given higher order schema. How much these other schemas actually influence a person's perceptions, thinking, and overt behavior is a result of other factors, such as other aroused schemas, the physical environment, and so on.

One example of how an aroused higher order schema can influence a lower order one concerns classical conditioning. Cook and Harris (1957) told subjects they would be shocked after the presentation of a light but did not in fact shock them. Nevertheless, the subjects showed GSR's (galvanic skin responses) after the light. Subsequently, they were given shock but the GSR's did not increase. Next they were told that they would receive no more shock; the GSR's were quickly eliminated. The symbolic processes evidently were in firm control of the emotional. These findings have been more recently replicated by Bridger and Mandel (1965). Lindley and Mayer (1961) shocked human subjects on their fingers after a signal and measured the amount of finger withdrawal. Although the shock was unavoidable, the subjects learned to withdraw their fingers to the signal. Next, they told half the subjects that they would not be shocked anymore and did not shock them on subsequent trials. Other subjects did not receive such instructions before the extinction trials. The first group took fewer trials without shock to stop withdrawing their fingers.

From the area of instrumental behavior comes another example. Turner and Solomon (1962) gave subjects a shock unless they made specific movements of the toes, although the subjects were not told which movements to make. Some subjects were told "when the shock is presented, there is something you can do to terminate the shock"; others were told only, "from time to time, a tone will sound. From time to time shock will be presented." The first group of subjects were much better able to master the situation than were the second. The higher order schema of "there is a solution" governed the first group's reactions.

Although higher order schemas can have a selective and directive influence on lower order schemas, they do not have exclusive control over lower order schemas. As discussed earlier, perceptions of reality relevant to a schema may in some cases be so clear and unequivocal that the lower order schemas may be changed or weakened by a reality that is inconsistent with the schema. Thus, a discrepancy may arise between a higher and lower order schema after the latter has been changed by reality. In such cases, the individual may resolve that discrepancy in a number of ways: he may change his higher order schema; he may come to perceive the higher and lower order schemas as not relevant to one another; he may even change his perception of the situation in order to restore the lower order schema to its original state of consistency. Which one of these courses is taken by the individual depends on a variety of factors: the degree of unequivocality of the perceived situation, the extent of the discrepancy between the higher and lower order schemas, and the relative invocability of the two orders of schemas are among those factors.

The last factor, relative invocability, is of considerable importance for the problems to be examined in the following chapters. Postulating that, in general, the individual experiences more situations consistent with the higher order schema than with the lower, that the higher order schema, by definition, has a wider number of situations relevant to it, and that it draws support from a number of other lower order schemas, we can then assume it has a higher degree of invocability. Furthermore, the lower order schemas subsumed by it can act as a kind of buffering device between perceived discrepancies and the higher order schema. A lower order schema may "absorb" discrepant perceptions without being changed; the perception may be distorted or misinterpreted. Thus, the lower order schema may protect the higher order schema from change and continue to provide support for it. In short, the higher order schema generally retains a relatively higher level of invocability for a variety of reasons. Accordingly, if a particular lower order schema relevant to a higher is being subjected to pressures to change because of some discrepant perceptions, the most common resolution of this discrepancy would be to "change" the perception of the situation rather than change the higher order schema.

Another implication of the possibility of having more than one schema invoked at a time relates to the propositions concerning the acquisition and the relative invocability of schemas. These propositions hold that acquisition and relative invocability are functions, in part, of the number of times the schema has been invoked previously and the amount of support the schema received on these occasions. If it is possible to have more than one schema aroused at a time, this means that more than one schema can be acquired and become increasingly invocable synchronically. Our response to the classic question, "What is learned?" is that the organism may be learning more than one thing at a time. Why is it necessary for the individual to learn only one thing at a time? The dispute about what is learned may have been answered with too much rigid adherence to parsimony, and, while it may be convenient to assume that he does learn only one thing, it may not be accurate.

Lawrence (1963) has demonstrated one way in which the organism can learn more than one thing at the same time. The organism may learn both what physical dimension(s) or aspect(s) of an object or event should be attended to for rewards, as well as what position on that (those) dimension(s) or aspect(s) is rewarded. He pointed out that the response of attending to a given aspect of a situation can be generalized to other situations independently of the generalizations of particular responses to the particular position on the dimensions. Having learned to attend to a given dimension may facilitate learning to make other discriminations in that dimension in other, or even the same, situations. For example, as Kendler and Kendler (1962) theorize, if an intelligent organism has learned both to "symbolize" a given dimension and to respond differentially to stimuli that differ on the dimension, then it is easier for the organism to learn new and opposite responses to positions on that dimension than to learn both a new dimension and a new discrimination.

A special case of the acquisition of more than one schema at a time is the one in which the schemas are in a hierarchical relationship to one another. That is, the person may learn at more than one level of abstraction at the same time. This is precisely what takes place in concept learning. The individual learns that a particular case is or is not an example of a given concept. At the same time, he may be learning what the concept is, its defining characteristics. Furthermore, the acquisition of learning sets, of nonspecific transfer, of learning to learn, also involves learning at several levels of schema simultaneously.

The general tendency in psychology to answer the question "What is learned?" in the singular is not only a reflection of a search for parsimony but also appears to be a result of the technical difficulty of measuring more than one outcome variable. The researcher may be satisfied if he can show that a particular habit has been strengthened or that the subjects have learned to solve a given type of problem. It may be beyond the technical limitations of his laboratory and beyond the practical limitations on his energy and time to test what other things the subject has learned. In some cases he may be interested only in one type of outcome variable and therefore does not investigate the possibility of measuring others. Yet, there is often an implicit recognition of this multileveled learning. "Sophisticated" subjects are not used; maze-wise animals have some "useful" higher order schemas; and so on.

When it comes to applying the findings of laboratory psychology to real life, ignoring the capacity of the individual to learn at several levels of abstraction is a potential danger. Some of the possible "side effects" of a given technique of teaching may not be fully recognized. For example, programmed learning may be effective not only in teaching a language but in teaching that learning occurs generally in an orderly, systematic way. When a person trained on programmed learning has to face a situation in which fate has not been so accommodating as to present the material in an orderly fashion, this person may be severely handicapped.

It is obvious that there can be all sorts of complicated higher order schemas developing on the basis of the lower order schemas. There is no need to spell out all of the possibilities but it is easily seen that the structure of schemas can be many-leveled. This is not to imply that the schemas are logically integrated in a sort of Aristotelian organization of phyla and species. The organization of schemas may be illogical and inconsistent. Their illogicality can emerge simply because ordinary people and animals do not employ the same criteria of consistency as would, say, a logician.

This analysis immediately raises the question of the determinants of the levels of abstraction at which an individual will acquire schemas, both in general and on particular occasions. It is obvious that he cannot acquire schemas at all *possible* levels, and it is equally obvious that even an animal can acquire an abstraction. Unfortunately, the present approach can only lead to suggestions as to what the possible determinants are, leaving the answers to research.

CHAPTER 5

Schemas About Action

To tie in the cognitive propositions with the motivational ones, we must make some simple assumptions to coordinate the two sets of propositions. These assumptions concern an individual's developing schemas about his own actions, since an action is an event perceivable by him. These schemas can then influence his expectations, aspirations, and actual performances, not only with respect to the actions from which he acquired the schemas, but also in some cases with respect to quite different actions—even actions for survival itself. This generalization is an outcome of the abstract nature of schemas. The assumptions about the organism's having schemas about its actions also help to explain persistence in the face of difficulty, since the individual can develop schemas about the outcome of persistence.

The basic assumption is that an organism can perceive his own behavior, his own overt, symbolic, and perceptual behavior. In humans, this is expressed in such verbalizations as "I thought about that," "I looked at that," "I used to believe that," "I did this," or "I won at this game," and so on. This process of self-observation has been pointed out by James (1890) and by Mead (1934). The latter's concept of the "me" is analogous to the perceiver while his concept of the "I" is like the event observed. It would follow then that the person can develop schemas about his own behavior—"Whenever I try to do that, I succeed"; or "Whenever I think about things that sing, I become uneasy." This is implied by Proposition IV. White (1959) has recently written about the infant's developing a sense of competence on the basis of his perceptions of the consequences of his actions. This process can be described in present terms as the acquisition of a schema that consists of "if I move, there are changes in the environment."

Heider (1958) has described some of the conditions that enhance the probability of an individual's perceiving that a given action of his is relevant to a broader schema that concerns his own ability to act on the environment in given ways. The person is more likely to perceive that an action of his is relevant to such a schema if other people are perceived as being unable to perform the same act, or if he did not act under pressure or with guidance and assistance from others, or if he did not attribute his act to luck or good fortune. Thus, not all situations in which a person acts will be subsumed under a schema concerning the effectiveness of his actions, nor will they necessarily increase the invocability of such schemas. As pointed out above, schemas are strengthened by the person's perceiving situations consistent with them when they were aroused. If a schema about the person's being a cause of his own successes is not aroused, his perception at that time will not strengthen such a schema. Most laboratory studies of learning or problem solving meet the conditions established by Heider for making a particular event relevant to the subjects' schemas about the effectiveness of their own actions. The subjects are instructed that they are to learn to master a task. They are the ones on whom the responsibility falls.

Variations in the perceived cause of an individual's actions may help to explain why clinicians often remark that some of their patients do not become more hopeful after a period of apparent success. These people simply may not perceive their success as being the result of their own actions. Similarly, a person who has had a long string of failures may not always become hopeless if he perceives that his failures are the result of "bad luck" or "flukes." In the studies of the effects of success or failure to be cited in subsequent chapters, the subjects usually are pressed to perceive themselves as the cause of their levels of performance, so that perceived "luck" and "fate" are not significant determinants of reaction to levels of performance (*cf.* Lefcourt, 1966).

The phenomenon of learning sets, or learning to learn, can be interpreted within the present system as the acquisition of a schema about one's own behavior and its consequences. It is interesting to note that Mandler (1962), a behavioristic learning theorist, has also presented an analysis of learning that parallels the present one. Consistent with the thesis we have made about learning at several levels at the same time, Mandler begins his interpretation of learning sets by arguing that the S-R associationists' position and the cognitive positions can be integrated. He analyzes the acquisition of learning sets as follows:

> First the organism makes a series of discrete responses, often interrupted by incorrect ones. However, once errors are dropped out and the sequence of behavior becomes relatively stable—as in running a maze, speaking a word, reproducing a visual pattern—the various components of the total behavior required in the situation are "integrated." Integration refers to the fact that previously discrete parts of a sequence come to behave functionally as a unit and behaves as a single component response has in the past; any part of it elicits the whole sequence. . . . Once a re-

> sponse sequence has been integrated and acts as a unit, it develops a structural (cognitive) representation, a "central" analogue of this new response unit which can function independently of the overt response sequence.
>
> The notion of integration deals in part with the problem of defining units of behavior. When complex behavior is built up from previously disparate units, much trial and error behavior may characterize the slow development of the new, larger unit. The fact that the components may themselves have been overlearned—and structurally represented—lends a peculiar "cognitive" flavor to the explicit or implicit hunt and peck search for appropriate components. However, once the units have been selected and the new sequence has been integrated, it tends to be elicited as a whole and has a quasi-automatic appearance in that it is evoked by the appropriate situational cues (p. 417).

This integrated unity of a behavioral sequence that Mandler describes facilitates the individual's conceiving the sequence as a unit. In Gestalt perceptual terms, it is a "good figure," a readily perceivable unit. Accordingly, it can easily be related to the acquisition of schemas. Mandler continues:

> Analogic structures permit covert trial and error behavior, *i.e.*, cognitive manipulation of previously established behavior. In this sense, the analogic representation of a prior behavior sequence is one possible "hypothesis" to be applied to a particular situation. Given many such structures that are relevant to a situational report, the several structures will occur seriatim and covertly until an appropriate one is expressed behaviorally (p. 417).

Mandler then goes on to argue that the acquisition of a cognitive analogue of behavior occurs only with repeated performance (overlearning). His argument is compatible with Proposition VII, which contends that the invocability of schemas is a function of the number of prior experiences consistent with it while it was aroused. Mandler further assumes that the structure of a schema is acquired simultaneously with the learning of responses themselves.

Mandler's thesis concerns stimuli leading to a sequence of responses. However, Tolman (1948) goes one step further. He argues that the consequences of these responses can be included in the schema also. In other words, an individual's expectation of achieving a specific goal, his hopefulness, is interpretable in this context as the result of the invocation of a schema about his achievement of similar goals. This schema may be based on either his own previous experience or on communications from, or perception of, other people. De Soto, Coleman, and Putnam (1960) gave subjects a task of making the "right" associations to given stimuli. The level of "success" was experimentally varied from one-sixth to five-sixths, the subjects being informed after each trial how well each had done. The subjects were urged to make predictions of their performance level after making each response but before they heard whether they had given the right answer. The results showed that the higher the experimentally varied level of success, the higher were their predicted levels of performance.

Since covert behavior can be an event relevant to schemas, the invocation and the state of having an aroused schema can be perceived by the person himself. If the individual perceives certain events as leading to the invocation of a schema on a number of occasions, he can develop a new schema about events causing invocation of the original schema. An individual may have done something which invokes a given schema: he scratches his head and thereby invokes "I am a thoughtful person." He may engage in a superstitious act and invoke the schema, "things work out well for me." In some cases these symbolic or covert acts may occur "naturally," for reasons that are independent of consequences of the arousal of the schema. In other cases, the individual may have developed a high order schema consisting of the relationship between a given act and the arousal of a given schema. For example, the higher order schema may be, "Every time I scratch my head I feel like a thoughtful person." Thereafter, when the individual is motivated to "feel like a thoughtful person," he may scratch his head. This theme will be developed at greater length in the chapters that follow.

One special case of schemas about the consequences of actions is schemas about the degree of success of these actions. The individual will acquire a schema about his level of ability on a given type of task when he perceives that his actions determine his degree of success in completing a task of that type. This has been demonstrated by De Soto *et al.* (1960), as mentioned above. Feather (1962) has shown that an individual's expectations of success on a given task are a direct function of his previous levels of success of other tasks of a similar type. Rychlak and Eacker (1962) gave a series of tests, all of which were ostensibly designed to measure manual ability. Subjects who believed they had failed made lower predictions of performance on a subsequent task also designed to measure this ability than did those who believed they had succeeded. Whiting and Child (1949) asked subjects to describe their own reactions to their successes in life. One of the effects expressed was the increased confidence in their ability to achieve similar goals in the future. Todd, Terrell, and Frank (1962) found that underachievers in college had lower expectations about their performances in future course work. In short, these data are consistent with Proposition VI, which maintains that schemas are invoked by the perception of events similar to a constituent concept of the schema. In the present case, the constituent concepts are tasks of a given type.

Proposition VI also indicates that when a person perceives a new task that is somewhat different from the type in a given schema, he is more likely to invoke that schema the more similar the new task is to the original ones from which the person acquired the schema. Rotter's students (1954) have supported this observation. Jessor (1954) had his subjects succeed or fail on an arithmetic test. He then measured their expected levels of performance on other arithmetic, vocabulary, motor, and social skill tasks. He found that the levels of performance on the original arithmetic directly influenced the subjects' expectations most on the arithmetic test, next on the vocabulary test, next on motor skills, and least on social skills. Crandall, Katkovsky, and Preston (1962) showed a group of highly intelligent boys eight tasks in four areas: intellectual, physical, artistic, and manual skills. The eight tasks in each area had previously been graded for difficulty and the children were informed of the grading. After being told that they would be tested later, the children were asked which tasks they could perform successfully. Even within this group of highly intelligent subjects, a correlation of .62 between IQ and expectation of success was obtained for boys.

The data then tend to support the hypothesis that previous levels of performance determine expected levels on the same or similar tasks. In Jessor's, Feather's, Rychlak and Eacker's, and Crandall *et al.'s* work, the dependent variable was the individual's level of expectation, his prediction of how well he would do on subsequent tasks. On the other hand, Proposition I indicated that the greater a person's expectation of attaining his goals, the more will he be motivated to act. It follows then that the more successful an individual has been in acting to achieve a given goal, the more likely he is to attempt to achieve this goal on subsequent occasions. In their study of level of expected performance, Crandall *et al.* also found that children with higher levels of expectancies were rated by their teachers as striving more intensely in achievement situations. We have already mentioned that Battle (1965) found that high school students who expected higher grades in mathematics persisted longer on an extremely difficult mathematical problem. Although these correlational studies are open to other interpretations, the results are certainly consistent with the present theory.

In addition to influencing expected levels of performance and consequently actual levels of performance, the level of success will also tend to influence the goals the individual sets for himself. His selection of goals is influenced by his tendency to avoid anxiety as indicated by Proposition III. One way of avoiding anxiety is to eschew goals with lower levels of expected achievement. Therefore, as the individual's expectations of success on a given task rise, the less likely he is to avoid it; the less likely he is to avoid setting goals of doing well on the task. Furthermore, Proposition II indicates that people tend to find joy in succeeding. Accordingly, if the individual's level of expectation of performance on a task rises, he is more likely to set higher goals for himself, not only because there is less threat of anxiety but also because there is more likelihood of a positive affective experience.

The level of goal the individual sets for himself has typically been measured by his level of aspiration—by asking what level of performance he expects to fulfill on the next task trial. Lewin, Dembo, Festinger, and Sears (1944) reviewed the literature on level of aspiration and concluded that one of the determining factors is the subjective probability of attaining a given level of performance. Success in attaining a previous goal leads to raising or, at least, maintaining the level; after failure, the level tends to drop or to remain the same. For example, Frank (1935) gave his subjects two similar tasks; half the subjects were made to fail on the first and half were made to succeed. The latter subjects had higher levels of aspiration on the second task. The effect of previous success is evident not only in the laboratory. It is also evident when the previous experience consists of "real" successes and "real" failures. Lewin (1951) quotes a study by Jucknat in which she divided students into three groups according to level of success in schoolwork. All of the subjects were given mazes in ascending levels of difficulty. She found that the more successful the student, the more difficult was the maze he aspired to complete.

In the discussion of the effects of performance on expectations, it was shown that levels of expectation generalize to similar or related tasks. In a parallel fashion, Lewin *et al.* (1944) conclude that the level of performance on one task will determine the level of aspiration on subsequent tasks to the extent that the second task is perceived as being a continuation of the first. Mischel and Staub (1965) led children to believe that they had succeeded or failed on some rather significant tests. The children then made a series of choices among ten valuable rewards that they could have without solving problems and rewards of greater value that they could have only if they solved some problems. In some cases the problems were similar to the original ones on which the subjects had succeeded or failed; in others, they were different. It was found that the children who succeeded were more likely than those who failed to select problems that would bring more valuable goals, provided that these problems were similar to the original tasks. Whiting and Child (1949) asked subjects how they had reacted to the successes they had attained in their lives. In addition to the increased confidence already mentioned, the subjects reported that success was followed by increased desire for the attainment of similar goals and the appearance of new drives directed at the maintenance or improvement of self-esteem.

From Proposition IV, it would be expected that, in general, subjects would tend to avoid work on tasks at which they have failed. In substantiation of this prediction, Gebhard (1948) found that subjects preferred tasks at which they had succeeded to those on which they had failed. Gewirtz (1959) found that children avoided a task at which they had failed. Cartwright (1942) reports that tasks that had been interrupted because the person had "failed" diminished in preference more than tasks that had been interrupted because of an ostensible error on the part of the experimenter. That such preferences are more than just verbalizations is indicated by Nowlis (1941), who had her subjects work on a cog-in-wheel problem but then interrupted them; next, all of the subjects completed a jigsaw puzzle either as a success or a failure or as neither. Subjects who experienced a success on the second task were more likely than the others to resume the first task, given the opportunity. The success on the second task led to higher expectation of success on the first and therefore resumption of it. The similarity that facilitated the generalization of expectancies from the second to the first task was probably based on their both being presented by the same experimenter in the same situation.

Thus far, the reasoning has been that a person's expectations, aspirations, and preferences would be influenced by his history of successes and failures. If his expectations are influenced thus, it could also be predicted that his performance would also be affected, since expectations leaven motivations and motivations often leaven performance. Of course, this would be expected only on those tasks that are so constructed that increased motivation leads to increased performance. Zipf's (1963) study cited in Chapter Two shows a direct relationship between expectations and performance on a single task. Furthermore, the effect of expectations can be studied indirectly by studying the effect of a given performance level on subsequent ones, with the subjects' expected performance levels after each performance as the mediating process between actual performance levels. The influence of one performance level on another can lead to a kind of benign circle of success breeding more success, or to a vicious cycle of failure begetting more failure. In a sense, the old saws of "can't win for losing" and "nothing succeeds like success" have been placed in a larger context. The following studies show that this does take place.

Sears (1937) gave subjects a card-sorting task and led them to believe that they were either succeeding or failing. The "failing" subjects actually performed worse than the "succeeding" ones. McClelland and Apicella (1947) gave subjects a series of trials on a difficult card-sorting task. They then led some subjects to believe that on two-thirds of the trials they had failed to attain the levels of performance to which they had aspired and had just about attained these levels on the remaining trials. Other subjects were led to believe that they had attained their levels of aspiration on two-thirds of the trials and surpassed them on the others. The first or failure group performed more poorly on the task than did the latter group. Osler (1954) gave school children a long division task, some of the children being led to believe that they had failed on a previous long division task, others being told they had succeeded. The performance of subjects who had ostensibly failed was lowered while "successful" children were not affected. Rhine (1957) told subjects that they could expect to solve about one-half the anagrams he gave them, but gave some of them fifteen easily decipherable anagrams, some of them fifteen of moderate decipherability, and some of them fifteen difficult ones. Then, without any break, he gave all of the subjects the same set of twenty anagrams. The subjects who had succeeded on the first fifteen anagrams because they were easy did better than the other subjects on the last twenty. Feather (1966) gave fifteen anagrams to subjects, half of them being made to succeed and half to fail on the first five anagrams. The group that succeeded did better on the last ten than did those who failed.

The basic line of reasoning here implies that a failure to achieve a goal reduces motivation to achieve it when there are subsequent opportunities to do so. The emphasis in the studies so far reported was on the attainment of positive goals, completion of a laboratory task. In addition, this reasoning can be applied to such goals as escaping from noxious situations, like receiving an electric shock. Thus, an animal that has been unable to escape shock will be less prone subsequently to attempt escape. Dinsmoor and Campbell (1956) gave one group of rats shock inescapably for fifteen minutes through the floor grid of a box. Another group of rats was kept in the same box without shock for fifteen minutes. Then both groups received shock through the grid but they could turn it off momentarily by pressing a bar. The previously shocked groups made considerably fewer escape responses than those who had not received any previous shocks. It is, of course, possible to interpret this study as showing adaptation to the shock itself, but the study by Seligman and Maier (1967) reported below provides strong evidence against this interpretation. Carlson and Black (1960) found that dogs who were not permitted to escape shock by jumping out of a box once the shock had been turned on were, thereafter, less able to learn to avoid it by jumping whenever they heard a signal that preceded the shock by five seconds.

Recent research at Solomon's laboratory shows that an organism's failure to attain a goal of escaping shock in one situation can make him hopeless about attaining this goal in another situation. Overmier and Seligman (1967) gave dogs a series of inescapable shocks while they were suspended in a hammock. Twenty-four hours later the dogs were placed in a shuttle box. There they could avoid shock by jumping over the wall to the other side of the box within ten seconds after they had received a signal and they could escape shock by jumping after the shock was turned on. Other dogs who had not previously received any inescapable shock were also placed in the shuttle box and given the same treatment. The group that had suffered inescapable shock showed a much higher rate of failure to escape and a much longer latency in making avoidance responses. A possible explanation of these findings in terms of competing responses was ruled out by a second experiment by Overmier and Seligman. They obtained the same results that they obtained in the first experiment, even when the dogs were completely immobilized by curare while receiving the unavoidable shock. An explanation in terms of adaptation to shock was also negated by the disclosure that strengthening the shocks in the shuttle box did not have any effect on the amount of interference with the learning of avoidance or escape responses. If the increased shock had reduced the interference, it would have been possible to argue that the decrements in escape-avoidance behavior in the previous experiments were due to the dogs' adaptation to the shock during the period of inescapable shock and that the increased shock in avoidance learning had overcome this adaptation.

From the present theory, it could be suggested that dogs who had had previous experience in escaping shock would not show the low level of avoidance-escape behavior characteristic of those who had not been able to escape. This was confirmed in another study in Solomon's laboratory by Seligman and Maier (1967). Some dogs were given shock while in a hammock but the shock could be shut off if they pressed a panel with their noses. A control group was yoked to the first group so that it received the same number and length of shocks as the first group. Both groups were then placed in the escape-avoidance shuttle box. The dogs who had been able to escape shock showed no failure to escape from the shuttle box, while 75 per cent of the "yoked" groups failed to escape in at least nine out of the ten trials. Seligman and Maier interpret their results in terms of a "learned helplessness," as do Overmier and Seligman in the previous study.

Not only is performance on the same type of task or working toward the same goal affected by previous levels of performance, but performance on different types of tasks given to subjects in the same surroundings, by the same researchers, are affected as well. Lantz (1945) gave boys who were placed behind a barrier the job of getting a ball from a box with various tools. Almost all of the boys succeeded on the first two trials. But the third trial was made so difficult that about half failed. Whether a child succeeded or failed was not found to be related to IQ, physical size, age, or grade. The boys had taken an IQ test prior to the game and then one immediately afterwards. The boys who had succeeded increased somewhat in IQ, especially on verbal absurdities, word meanings, and comprehension. Lantz interprets this result in terms of an increment in thinking and reasoning rather than increased recall. Lantz also reports that the succeeding boys developed greater confidence and willingness to work during the second administration. On the other hand, the boys who failed went down markedly in IQ, especially on comprehension, word meanings, verbal absurdities, rhymes, and digit reversal. There was also a decrease in willingness to work and in self-confidence.

Hutt (1947) gave maladjusted children an IQ test with the subtests given either in the standard sequence or in an "adaptive" sequence. In the latter, the subjects started with items easy enough for the child to pass because they involved little concentration, rapid response, and few involved verbal instructions. If a subject failed a subtest, he was given an easier item; if he passed, a harder one. The average IQ in the adaptative sequences was 102.7; in the standard sequence, 91.7.

The same process was found in another study by McClelland and Apicella (1947). They gave subjects a card-sorting task, leading some of them to believe that they had achieved or surpassed their levels of aspiration on all trials, and leading others to believe that they barely attained them or failed on most of the trials. As we already mentioned in the previous citation of this study, the "failing" group actually began to perform more poorly. Next they gave some of the "failure" group a series of successes on a pursuitmeter. The others were given "no rest." Both groups then returned to the original card-sorting task but without receiving any information as to their performances. The subjects who had had the intervening success experience improved their performance on successive trials, while the "no rest" group got worse.

A parallel effect can be shown for the effects of failure on the intervening task. Moshin (1954) gave some subjects a Thematic Apperception Test while others had to tap a series of blocks in the same order as the experimenter. The latter subjects were led to believe that they were doing very poorly. Then both of these groups were given a series of Passalong tests of increasing difficulty. The subjects who had "failed" the block tapping did worse on this task than those who had taken the TAT.

Another implication of the success-begets-success idea is that if an individual gets off to a successful start in life, he will tend to continue to be successful; if he starts off as a failure, he will tend to be one again and again. As the individual succeeds on one task, his expectancy of success with other similar tasks increases. This expectancy will tend to increase not only the probability of his attempting these tasks but also of succeeding, since many tasks are so structured that increased effort leads to success. This new success would then lead to more hopefulness with respect to other tasks that are the same or similar, and so the march is on. Furthermore, the individual may develop a higher order schema based on the variety, as such, of tasks at which he is now successful: "I am good at all sorts of things." In White's terms (1959), he will have developed a sense of competence. He is especially likely to develop this higher order schema if he is reminded from time to time of his various successes. This may occur "naturally" simply by his continuing to reside in the same place or around the same people. Then again, once he does develop this higher order schema of general competence, new tasks that he confronts will invoke this schema, since they are examples of "all sorts of tasks."

Some of Murphy's (1962) observations of three- to five-year-olds are pertinent here. She was concerned with the sense of mastery, that is, the hopefulness, that these children had when they were faced with new situations. She writes, "All together, we can see that responses to newness often have foundations in the earliest infantile experiences of newness—the satisfactions, comfort, pain or frustration associated with these experiences and the residues or expectancies resulting from them (p. 57)." Later she writes,

> We can summarize this by saying that each experience of mastery and triumph sets the stage for better efforts in the next experience. Confidence, hope, and a sense of self-worth are increased along with the increase of cognitive and motor skills, which can contribute to a better use of resources. In this way the foundation is laid for spontaneous use of new potentialities made available by motivation as the child moves from one developmental stage to another (p. 367).

The benign circle is found also among adolescents. Silber, Hamberg, Coelho, Murphy, Rosenberg, and Pearlin (1961) studied a group of highly competent adolescents—those who were top students and active in extracurricular affairs. They reached out actively for new experiences and found pleasure in their mastery of them. The researchers report that one of the ways in which these students were able to maintain their sense of mastery in facing new situations was to refer to their successful coping in similar past situations.

Conversely, a vicious circle may start in which the organism fails at the start, avoids similar tasks in the expectation of failure, or, if he "must" perform, fails because of his expectation of failure. This hopelessness then spreads in a manner analogous to the benign circle; and a higher order schema—"I'm a failure at any task"—may develop and be applied to all new tasks, since they are exemplars of the constituent concept of "all tasks."

This reasoning gains support from experimental studies of the effects of infantile experiences of animals on their behavior as adults. Hall and Whiteman (1951) placed one group of infant mice in a tub and subjected them to painfully loud and inescapable noise for two minutes; another group was placed in the tub for the same length of time without noise. At age seventy or eighty days, the first group of mice were less likely to enter a U-shaped tube to get food than were the second group. These results were replicated by Lindzey, Lykken, and Winston (1960). The interpretation here is that the timidity of the traumatized rats derives from their inability to control, or escape, the pain of the noise, not the noise *per se*. Their lack of ability to escape leads to lower expectations of being able to master other tasks as well, probably through a kind of vicious cycle process occurring all through the period of time between the infantile trauma and the adult timidity test. This hypothesis could be tested by both systematic observations of the animals from birth to maturity and by experimentally varying their experiences in this period either to enhance or eradicate the effects of the early experience.

The benign or vicious circle interpretation is predicated on the organism's having coped or not coped with the pain inflicted in infancy. This assumption is supported by the findings of Stanley and Monkman (1956), who gave infant mice one of three types of experiences:

> (a) exposure to shock whose offset was contingent in *S*'s moving to the safe end of the apparatus (response-contingent group); (b) exposure to shock equal in duration in each specific trial to the amount of shock received by the matched litter mate in the response contingent group (arbitrary shock group); and (c) exposure to shock apparatus with matched trials duration but with shock turned off (the no-shock group) (p. 20).

When they became adults, these mice were tested for avoidance learning in an apparatus quite different from the one used on them as infants. The response contingent groups learned the avoidance task faster than either of the other two groups. The former group of mice had successfully coped with a painful situation as infants and thus became better contenders as adults; pain alone is not the problem.

What happens when a person who expects success is faced with an undeniable failure? The answer lies, in part, in the degree of invocability of some schema of his that leads to an expectation of success. If this schema is highly invocable, he is more likely to continue to expect to succeed on subsequent tries than if it is of low invocability; and with highly invocable, hopeful schemas, his expectation of success should lead to a higher level of performance on the next opportunity to perform. According to Proposition VII, the invocability of a schema is a function of the number of previous experiences consistent with it. It follows, then, that the greater the number of previous successes, the more likely a person is to continue to perform well, even after he has experienced a failure. This conclusion is consistent with the general findings that resistance to extinction is greater among animals that have made a greater number of successful (reinforced) responses than among those who have made a lower number.

Bayton and Conley (1957) gave college students a series of manipulation tasks. One group was led to believe they had five successes and then fourteen failures; another ten successes and then nine failures; and another fifteen successes and then four failures. Although all groups were ostensibly failing on their later trials, the latter two groups actually improved more during these failure trials than did the first group. Lewin (1951) cites a study by Fajans concerning the determinants of persistence, or the tendency of the individual to continue to strive for a given goal in the face of obstacles. He writes, "Fajans (1933) found previous failure to decrease persistence in one- to six-year-old children when they were again confronted with the same type of difficulty. Success led to relative increase in persistence (p. 231)."

Suppose that an individual succeeds at a variety of different tasks rather than at one type. As indicated, he would then be highly likely to develop a higher order schema that he can succeed at all kinds of tasks, even tasks at which he has had no experience. The constituent concept—all kinds of tasks—would be an emergent concept, developed on the basis of the individual's perception of the variety of tasks in which he succeeded. Higher order schemas regarding the degree of success in a variety of situations are apparently the same type of cognitive structure as referred to by Rotter

(1954) as "generalized expectancies." As was pointed out in the previous chapter, such high order schemas are relatively high in invocability and are relatively seldom subject to change because of inconsistent perceptions. Accordingly, when faced with a failure in a given task, an individual who has succeeded in a variety of tasks is less likely to lower his level of expectations of success about another new task than a person who has been successful only with one type of task. The latter has not had a chance to develop a schema of general competence. This was exactly what was found in an experiment by Rychlak (1958). He also found that a person who has failed in a variety of tasks is less likely to raise his level of aspiration on a new task after a success than a person who has failed on only one. The former has developed a higher order schema of hopelessness. He is, therefore, less influenced by a success.

Thus far we have considered the effects of more or less consistent success or failure on an individual's persistence in the face of failure. Suppose, however, an individual has not had only successes but has had a number of experiences in which his successes follow his failures. He would then develop a schema that failures are temporary and successes will follow. A person who has developed this type of schema will be more persistent in the face of failure than one who has not had these experiences. Diggory (1966) compared human subjects whose performance levels were experimentally controlled to become steadily closer to the goal level to subjects whose levels of performance sometimes improved, but sometimes did not. For the latter group, lack of improvement was therefore followed by improvement. As the experiment drew to a close, both groups of subjects were led to believe that they would be unlikely to attain the goal level. The subjects who had sometimes not improved were more optimistic about attaining the goal than the other subjects. An argument similar to the present one has already been made by Mowrer (1960) and Feather (1962) as their explanations for the oft-found effect of partial reinforcement greatly delaying extinction. This effect really is the same phenomenon described here as persistence in the face of failure. The main difference between the present point of view and that of Mowrer and Feather is that, in their approach, the sequence of failure leading to success would be restricted to those particular behaviors and situations in which the failures and successes were experienced, and in the present approach, the person might develop a more general tendency to persist even on tasks with which he was inexperienced. The person might more readily acquire the schema of persistence if he had achieved success through persistence in a variety of different tasks, rather than in one; succeeding in a variety of tasks is likely to lead to the emergent concept in higher level schemas—a concept of "all sorts of tasks," not just those on which the person worked.

An approach to the training of animals in persistence by rewarding them for persistence in a variety of ways is found in the work of Zimmerman (1957). He established an almost nonextinguishable habit by first presenting a buzzer a number of times. After only a few buzzes, he gave water to the rats. Next, they were presented with the buzzer, but no water, if they pressed a bar. Here again, the buzzer sounded only some of the times that the bar was pressed. Zimmerman found that animals trained in this way displayed great resistance to extinction. They continued to press the bar long after they received neither buzzer nor water as a reward. They had learned, in two ways, that persistence pays off. However, a more direct test of the prediction that learning to persist in a variety of tasks leads to a general schema concerning persistence is not yet available.

An underlying implication of using a persistence formulation instead of the "resistance to extinction" is that the individual would be expected to attempt to achieve his goals, to attain success by a variety of different means rather than solely by repetition of previous responses. The organism may have a schema of a variety of different actions leading to success, or the schema may be that success is probable but there may be no specifications regarding the means. Thus a variety of means of attaining the goal may be used. In most animal studies no opportunity is given the subject to try multiple paths to the goal during extinction. Grosslight and Child

(1947) did a study in which some children were rewarded with candy every time they pulled a series of nine levers while others were not given candy on every trial. All of the latter group's unrewarded trials were followed by rewarded ones. As in other studies, the partially rewarded group extinguished much more slowly. In addition, they also showed more attempts to try different solutions to the problem when they received no candy. They kept pulling levers in different orders, pushed some, skipped some, and so on. They were persistently trying to reach the goal since their "failures" had previously been followed by successes.

The suggestion that a generalized tendency to persist, or a general schema of "persistence in the face of difficulty leads to goal attainment," is more likely to be acquired on the basis of persisting in a variety of situations does not preclude the possibility of acquiring such a higher order schema from a more limited range of experience. A schema of persistence might be acquired from partial reinforcement in only one task but may generalize to other tasks that are similar because they are presented to the organism in the same laboratory by the same researchers as the task that was partially reinforced. Bernstein (1957) trained rats to *avoid* shock if they turned a wheel *within* three seconds after hearing a buzzer, and to *escape* an existing shock if they turned the wheel *after* three seconds. Then, one group of rats was blocked from the wheel for two seconds after the buzzer sounded, and then were allowed to turn the wheel to avoid shock; they learned the value of persistence. A second group was blocked for four seconds, and could then escape shock by turning the wheel. A third group was blocked for eight seconds, and only then could escape the shock they had been suffering for five seconds. A fourth group was not blocked at all. Subsequently, he trained all the rats to run down a runway to a food box. All groups learned this equally well. He then gave all the rats extinction trials. The two- and four-second delay groups showed much more resistance to extinction on this quite different task than did the other two groups. Those who had not been blocked or had suffered much shock while blocked had never learned the value of persistence.

The learning of persistence in the face of frustration can also generalize to persistence in the face of shock. Berkun (1957) trained some animals on a 100 per cent reward schedule to run up an alley; others were put on an intermittent schedule. After they had learned the criterion, the rats in both groups were given shock at the food tray. The intermittently reinforced group took fewer trials to reach a new criterion of running up the alley three times than did the one hundred per cent group. Finally, with the shock turned off, the intermittent group approached the food box more closely than did the others. Similar results were obtained in an ingenious study by Brown and Wagner (1964). They gave one group of rats (C group) reinforcement of food pellets every time they ran a runway; a second group (M) was given food for only half their runs; a third group (P) received shock as well as food on every trial. Then, half of each group was given extinction trials of no food; the other half of each group received both food and shock on subsequent trials. The results were that in *both* the extinction and the food and shock test trials, the M and P groups slowed up less than did the C groups. The M group was slowed down less in running during the final shock and food trials than the C group. Furthermore, the P group was slowed down less by non-reinforcement than was the C. Thus, the partially reinforced groups and the punished group learned to persist in the face of frustrations quite different from the ones in which they were originally frustrated.

Thus, a number of experimental studies show that when an organism learns to persist in the face of one type of frustration or difficulty, it learns to persist in the face of others; it acquires a general schema. This general type of reasoning regarding persistence has been applied by Farber, Harlow, and West (1957) to explain why some American prisoners in North Korea survived as well as they did. They write:

> The role of DDD (Debility, Dependency and Disease) in the reinforcement process depends on the fact that it is not a constant. Instead, it may be assumed to fluctuate in time, partly as a result of spontaneous physiological processes, and partly as a result of deliberate manipulations designed to maintain its intermittent na-

> ture, thus preventing its fall to a baseline of permanent depression and hopelessness. . . .
> [O]ne may conceive of two consequences of the occasional mitigation of DDD. First is the conditioning of the "expectancy" that DDD will be alleviated. . . . Relief, whether due to spontaneous factors or deliberate manipulations, is intermittent, temporary, and unpredictable . . . this tends to maintain expectancy and renders it less susceptible to extinction. In non-technical language, this process serves to keep hope alive, permitting some degree of adaptive behavior, and inhibiting self-destructive tendencies (p. 276).

Since the strength of a schema is a result, in part, of the number of events perceived to be consistent with it, it would be expected that the greater the number of non-reinforced trials during acquisition, the greater the resistance to extinction. Lawrence and Festinger (1962) did a study in which they systematically varied the number of non-reinforced trials for rats, while holding constant the ratio of reinforced to non-reinforced trials. They found greater resistance to extinction to be a function of the number of non-reinforced trials rather than that of the ratio.

Another instance of a phenomenon in which a negative event can arouse a schema of persistence concerns electrically shocking animals. If an animal learns that persisting in the face of shock leads to rewards, it will continue to do so. But the problem is how to get it to persist long enough to learn that a reward will be forthcoming. This problem has been solved by starting the animal in with very low levels of shock, then gradually increasing the strength. Muenzinger, Brown, Crow, and Powloski (1952) trained some rats to run an alley despite being shocked while running, the intensity of the shock being gradually increased from threshold during the trials. Others were trained without shock. Next, all the rats were placed in a choice situation, some being shocked for making the right (rewarded) choice. The rats who had previously been trained in shock were better able to learn the "shock-for-right-choice" task than were those not previously trained on shock. It is interesting here that the effect was generalized from the alley to the choice situation; a more general schema appears to have been developed: that sustaining shock would lead to rewards.

The acquisition of such a schema should also lead the organism to persist even in the face of severe shock. Miller (1960) trained rats to run an alley for food. Some received shocks from the floor of the alley on the early trials, the intensity of the shock being gradually increased from trial to trial. Other rats were given the same training without shock. Then both groups of rats were given twenty trials with very severe shock at the food box. The gradually trained group ran much faster during these trials than did the other rats.

It is clear, then, that the theory of schemas does handle the data of persistence of responses in the face of pain, as well as the data of partial reinforcement. It should be pointed out that the value of the schema approach is most evident when the resistance to extinction occurs with respect to some situation other than the one in which the subject was partially reinforced.

In this chapter we have presented a wide variety of data that are consistent with schema theory. The interaction between performance level and expectation, the relationships of both to level of aspiration, the generalization of these interactions and relationships, so-called apathy deaths, persistence in the face of failure and pain, have all been treated in the context of the schema theory.

The central theme has been that failure and success tend to be cumulative. Studies of the effects of successes or failures early in life seem to show that they may have lifelong effects, so that a person is consistently optimistic and successful or pessimistic and failing. Even though this trend may be general, there obviously are people who are chronically optimistic failures or pessimistic successes. Some of the latter may be especially familiar to clinicians. The question, then, that must be answered is, how does the present theory deal with these exceptions?

In applying the theory of hope to day-to-day living, many, if not most, events that an individual encounters in his life are at least somewhat ambiguous with respect to their implications for the future. Since the future is not directly nor readily knowable, the implications that present events are perceived to have for future goal attainment are, to some degree, a matter of the schemas that the individual brings to bear on the events. A defeat may be viewed as a "learning experience"; a disaster, as a chance to start again; an "objective" success as a sign of future failure since the person "played himself out"; a promotion as a threat, since new, probably overwhelming, responsibilities are to be found. Needless to say, the argument here is not that schemas are all determining. Reality cannot easily be denied if it is clear and sharp, so that repeated failure will ultimately come to be seen as such. But life does not always consist of events that have clear, sharp, unequivocal implications. In short, then, one answer to the question of optimism in the face of failure and pessimism in the face of success is simply that the perception of an event as having hopeful or hopeless implications is, to some extent, a matter of perception guided by schemas.

Some of the dimensions along which individuals may differ in their interpretation of successes and failures have been implied in the present chapter. People may differ in the degree to which they perceive that they control their own fate as compared to being controlled by others (Heider, 1958; Lefcourt, 1966). If they feel they are responsible for their own fate, they may perceive more hopeful implications in a success than will those who do not feel responsible. People may differ in the degree to which they perceive their failures as preludes to success or *vice versa,* or in the degree to which they have a schema that persistence in the face of failure pays off. They may differ in the order of schema that is aroused so that a given event may be viewed with respect to a higher order hopeful or hopeless schema rather than to one tied more directly to the event.

Another factor that may lead to optimistic "failures" and pessimistic "successes" has to do with the nature of the goals. Often the observer may not know what another's goals really are, nor what time perspective he has for that attainment. Therefore, it is difficult to evaluate the degree of psychological success or failure.

Still another factor in sustaining optimism and minimizing

pessimism is that the individual is motivated to have high expectations because hope both leads to joy and avoids anxiety. Thus the actual process of setting goals and moving toward them may be quite attractive in its own right, and the consequent motivation may be strong enough to override other determinants of perception.

CHAPTER 6

Anxiety and Action

The focus of the previous chapter was on the interrelationships between the perceived consequences of instrumental behavior and the development of schemas. Hopefulness and hopelessness were related to overt behavior. We can now take the argument one step further and explicate the relationship between hopelessness and anxiety. In Chapter Three, Proposition III positively relating hopelessness and anxiety was presented, as well as data directly supporting it. In this chapter it will be shown that the schema theory can be used to understand more subtle causes of anxiety, causes related to the person's own actions. The main theme is that actions of all sorts, whether or not they are directed at attaining hopeless goals causing the anxiety, can reduce anxiety. Before that theme can be developed, it is first necessary to show that anxiety is a result of the arousal of hopeless schemas or the lack of arousal of those in which hope is based on action.

Proposition III indicates that anxiety is the result of a low perceived probability (low hopefulness) of attaining an important goal.* A question then arises about the degree of anxiety an individual experiences if several schemas involving different degrees of hopefulness about the same goal are aroused at the same time. For instance, a higher order schema may be more hopeful than a lower order one; compare "I can usually find work when I come to a new city" and "I haven't been able to find a job here in the last week." In such cases, the discrepancy between these schemas could be resolved in one of a number of ways: the individual could change the higher order schema; he could perceive the lower order schema as not relevant to the higher one ("This is no city; it's an overgrown village"); he could change his perception of the situation (I'll get a job Monday for certain").

In most cases, the resolution of the discrepancy will involve minimal changes of the higher order schema since it is generally the stronger. In our present example, the individual will have had more experiences that he interprets as consistent with his having gotten jobs in various cities than he has of not having done so in the city in question. Therefore, it is more likely that he will change his perception of the immediate situation, and come to believe, say, that he will get a job on Monday, or that if he went to the next city, which is not an overgrown village, he would get a job. In that case his anxiety level will be lower than if his higher order schema had changed. The higher order schema leads to a lower level of anxiety than would otherwise be the case.

On the other hand, if the higher order schema were the more negative, the individual might be more hopeless and anxious. The person might even feel anxious if he did get a job in the city. He might come to expect that his employer's business will fail, the

* Not all hopelessness leads to anxiety, only hopelessness that pertains to the attainment of important goals. Furthermore, in most of the studies cited here, the subjects could not avoid anxiety by simply rejecting the goals. Social, physical, "psychological" pressures to retain the goals made it difficult for the subjects to give them up.

town will have hard times, or he will "goof up" the job. The higher order schema of hopelessness might then have a negative effect.

In short, an individual with a *hopeful* higher order schema in a state of arousal generally would be in a good mood, would be energetic, oriented to the future, aggressive but not hostile. An individual with a *hopeless* higher order schema in a state of arousal generally would be in a bad mood, would lack energy, would be oriented to the present, would be hostile. A higher order schema may thus determine how the individual feels about many specific situations, about the "little things."

The possibility of having more than one schema in a state of arousal at one time bears on a distinction, made by some writers, between anxiety and fear. The latter has been defined, at times, as a negative affective reaction to a particular stimulus that the organism can identify; anxiety has been defined as a negative affective reaction to some unidentifiable or general stimulus. Empirically, this distinction might be found to correspond to the distinction made here between lower and higher order schemas. The anxiety resulting from the arousal of a higher order schema would be what these writers have termed *anxiety.* Since the schema is of a higher order it is more abstract, more general, and therefore its source may not be easily attributable to a single event or stimulus. On the other hand, what others have called *fear* might correspond to anxiety instigated by the arousal of a lower order schema. The lower order schema has less scope and is more specific about events consistent with it, that is, the source of the anxiety is more readily identifiable to the person.

Most people and animals develop schemas to the effect that action that leads to some change in the environment often leads to the attainment of goals. Action that has a predictable consequence on the environment has, for most persons and animals, been basic to the attainment of goals. This relationship between action, choice, or activity on the one hand, and goal achievement on the other, is a very elementary aspect of survival. When an individual is acting effectively, his acting on the environment invokes the schema of action leading to hopefulness, and thereby reduces anxiety. In addition to reducing anxiety in this direct fashion, the arousal of a higher order hopeful schema increases the likelihood of invoking hopeful lower order schemas, which would otherwise be too weak to be aroused.

On the other hand, when the individual cannot act on the environment effectively, he is less likely to have an aroused schema of hopefulness and is more likely to experience anxiety. Furthermore, he may have another schema—that inability to act leads to no goal attainment—and this schema would also be invoked by an inability to act.

The present thesis would seem to suggest the antithesis that if an organism is raised so that every time it does nothing, it attains its goals and that every time it is active, it does not attain any goals, it would become hopeless and anxious if in a situation in which it was forced to act. Additionally, such an organism would probably "freeze" and remain frozen in order to reduce anxiety. To the author's knowledge, this exact hypothesis has not been tested. One way of testing it might be to raise an animal that was fed and given water only if it did not move, in contrast to a normally raised animal.

If an individual is in a situation in which he is never able to act to achieve certain goals, he is apt to be experiencing either a high level of anxiety because the goals are so important or to have lowered the importance of the goals in order to escape this anxiety. On the other hand, if he is in a situation in which he has been able to attain his goals, he is unlikely to have reduced their importance. Thus, on the whole, goals tend to be of higher importance in situations in which the organism has been able to act to attain them than in those in which he has not been able to do so. Accordingly the individual in the successful situations is more vulnerable to anxiety, since he has important goals, a necessary condition for anxiety. One way in which he can come to experience anxiety is to lose the ability to act to attain these goals.

When the necessary discriminations needed to attain a goal

become inordinately difficult, loss of the ability to act results. Krasnogorski (1925) gave food to a hospitalized six-year-old child whenever a metronome beat at one rate and no food when it beat at another. The child learned to open his mouth when hearing the appropriate beat. Then, on subsequent days, the food beat and the no-food beat were made increasingly similar. At first, the latency of his opening his mouth increased. Then the child became irritable. As the experiment continued over a number of days, the child became very nervous.

In a well-controlled experiment, Johnson (1963) gave subjects in his experimental group a problem of moving their fingers to one tone but not to another. If they made either an error of commission or omission, they were shocked. After they had learned the discrimination well, the two tones were made increasingly similar. As a result the subjects began to make mistakes and received shocks. Each subject in the experimental group was paired with one in a control group; both listened to tones and received shocks at the same time, but the control subject did not have any discrimination task to perform. For the control subjects, no goal of avoiding shock was established; or they had reduced its importance to escape or avoid anxiety. The experimental subjects showed more physiological signs of arousal, such as increases in heart rate, than did the controls and, after the experiment, they reported more feelings of anxiety. Although Johnson did not interpret his results in terms of anxiety, it is difficult to avoid doing so since the self-ratings of the post-experimentals indicated higher anxiety. As Johnson points out, the pain of the shock itself was not severe enough to produce anxiety.

Studies of experimental neuroses in animals also exemplify this process. In one type of study, after the animals have made successful discriminations in a situation, the discriminations are made too difficult for them but they are not permitted to escape from the situation. They cannot easily give up the goals involved in making the discrimination. Anxiety ensues. Even though Pavlov's (1928) interpretation of experimental neuroses differs widely from the present one, his description of the actual phenomenon of experimental neuroses fits the present approach:

> A conditioned food reflex is elaborated in a dog to a circle of light projected on a screen in front of it. Differentiation of the circle from the ellipse of the same size and intensity was afterwards tried, *i.e.,* the circle was always accompanied by feeding; the ellipse never. Differentiation was thus elaborated. . . . The first ellipse tried was markedly different from the circle (the proportion of its axes was 2:1). Afterwards as the form of the ellipse was brought closer and closer to that of the circle, we obtained more or less quickly an increasingly delicate differentiation. But when we used an ellipse whose two axes were as 9:8, *i.e.,* an ellipse that was nearly circular, all this was changed. We obtained a new delicate differentiation, which always remained imperfect, lasted two weeks, and afterwards not only disappeared spontaneously, but caused the loss of all earlier differentiations, including even the less delicate ones. The dog which formerly stood quietly on his bench, now was constantly struggling and howling (p. 342).
>
> And in this dog there was after the experiments a marked alteration in the general conduct; he was no longer gentle and docile, but was very excited and irritable (nervous) (p. 459).

In their conclusions based on a long-term study of experimental neuroses in sheep and dogs in Liddell's laboratory, Anderson and Parmenter (1941) state that one of the main causes of breakdowns in the animals they studied was the increasing difficulty of a discrimination. In a typical study, they gave the animals shock after a number of beats on a metronome, then increased the number of beats till the animals could no longer accurately anticipate the time of the shock.

Kamin (1954) gave dogs a shock in intervals of five, ten, twenty, or forty seconds after a buzzer. If the dog jumped over a small barrier, it could avoid the shock. Kamin found that the longer the interval, the slower the acquisition; the group with intervals of forty seconds hardly learned the meaning of the signal at all. They simply made a high number of jumps, regardless of the signal, so many that no emotional upset could be observed. The group with intervals of twenty seconds learned the meaning of the signal but not well enough to avoid the shock every time. These dogs, more than any of the others, became agitated, attacked the apparatus, climbed the walls, whined, barked, and vomited. This behavior increased when the signal was presented. Contrastingly, the five-second group was very alert; it jumped just after the signal. Apparently, it was the twenty-second dogs' inability to make an accurate time discrimination that caused their difficulty. Gantt (1942) concludes from his long-term study of a neurosis in a dog that great anxiety, as indicated by cardiac and respiratory changes, is generated by a situation of difficult differentiation from which the animal cannot escape.

Dimmick, Ludlow, and Whiteman (1939) taught cats to open a food box on signal, and gave them food when the signal ceased. Then, they shocked the cats if they opened the food box at any time except while the signal was on or within six seconds after it had stopped. This last discrimination was one the cats could not make. They became confused at this point. If they tried to back away (to give up the goal), they were shocked. Then, the cats began to show anxiety; they appeared to be afraid of the food box; they growled at lights and bells even without any accompanying shock; they crouched, climbed walls, bit, clawed, became less friendly in their living quarters, and so on.

The difficulty of making necessary discriminations can occur in social situations as well, and can produce anxiety as in the studies described above. Cohen (1959) subjected telephone operators to supervision by someone who would evaluate their performance after giving very inconsistent and ambiguous instructions to one group of operators, clear instructions to the other group. Further, half of each of these two groups were given clear tasks, half ambiguous tasks. Those who were subjected to greater inconsistency of tasks and instructions felt less secure, had lower self-evaluations, and were less motivated. Dibner (1958) varied the degree of clarity with which a counselor gave directions to interviewees at initial interviews. He found that interviewees showed more anxiety, both physiologically and subjectively, when the directions were unclear than when they were clear. Mann and Mann (1959) studied the self-ratings of various desirable traits made by adults before and after participation in one of two types of group meetings. In one, the group task was highly structured; the subjects were instructed to discuss a certain book. In the other, the subjects were told to discuss anything they wanted. The authors report that the ambiguity and lack of structure of the task of the latter group led to a general lowering of self-ratings; there was a general rise in the more structured group.

The difficulty of discrimination can occur not only between two stimuli, but also between the presence or absence of a crucial stimulus. Dworkin, Baxt, and Dworkin (1942) presented cats with signals to lift the lid of a food container, but the signals were right at threshold for these cats. These very weak stimuli were presented a few each day for a long period of time. After a while, the cats began to develop neurosis: they scratched more, rolled over more, licked themselves more, and generally behaved in a highly exaggerated and restless way.

Lazarus (1966), in his review of the research on threat, concludes that a major factor enhancing anxiety when an individual is faced with some potential harm is the degree of ambiguity of the source of the harm. If the organism does not know exactly the source of harm or does not have any information about it, he will be unable to act, incompetent to cope. Anxiety follows. The studies above support Lazarus' conclusions but show that the point is more general, since anxiety can result from an ambiguity related to positive goal achievement, as well as to the goal of avoiding the potential harm.

Another way to make an organism experience an inability to deal with a situation is simply to make the requisite response too difficult for it. James (1943) taught dogs to pull in harness to avoid being shocked. On successive trials, he both made the shock stronger and the required pull harder. When the required pull became beyond the dogs' strength, they became highly emotional—biting, whining, trying to escape, and so on.

Another situation in which an organism has great difficulty in achieving its goals is one in which there is conflict between two or more goals—where the achievement of one goal physically precludes the achievement of the other. In the typical study of conflict (Miller, 1944), the organism is allowed to act to achieve one or the other of the goals or simply to escape the conflict by withdrawal. In fact, the typical study concentrates on which response the organism will make, which goal it will choose. The possibility of action to achieve one or the other of the goals or to escape from the conflict tends to reduce the level of anxiety. Therefore, to study the reactions of conflict *per se* it is necessary to examine such situations as unavoidable conflict. This examination can be done in a variety of ways: physically preventing escape from the conflict, making the two goals equally important and equally difficult to surrender, and so on.

A few studies have come close to studying the effects of conflict from which there is no escape, either physically or psychologically. Hunt and Schlosberg (1950) electrified the water that rats had to drink. Each day, the charge was increased at a constant rate. After about forty days, three of the rats developed "tantrums": they climbed the walls of their cages, fell down, threw food pellets around, gnawed at the bars. Masserman (1943) placed cats in an enclosure and trained them to open the lid of a box at one end of the enclosure to get food, after signals were given. If they subsequently received a strong blast of air as they were opening the box or as they were about to eat, the cats cowered in a corner and showed marked anxiety whenever a feeding signal went on. Their pulses were rapid and irregular; they trembled; they avoided food for long periods, even to the point of starvation. It is important to note that the cats could not escape the conflict by getting out of the box; there was no runway down which to escape. They were forced to remain close to the place of conflict. Maier and Glaser (1940)' forced rats to jump from a Lashley jumping stand by playing a jet of air on them. The rats would then jump onto one of two targets. On each trial, one of the targets was made rewarding, but if the rat jumped at the other he bumped his nose and fell into a box below. Which target was rewarding and which punishing was changed from trial to trial in a completely random fashion. This procedure was repeated a number of times each day for a number of days. Some of the animals developed severe neuroses, running wildly about the experimental room, "dancing," climbing the walls. After a while some of the animals suddenly shifted to a state of "waxy flexibility" as if they had given up, in a manner similar to Richter's rats.

Obviously, if an organism can avoid or escape a conflict it will be less likely to develop an experimental neurosis. Maier (1940) reports that if rats are given a chance to escape the conflict in the jumping situation, not only do they take that chance but they do not develop seizures. Specifically, some rats were sometimes given a chance to make what Maier calls "abortive" jumps, jumps that avoided hitting the critical cards. When rats were given a chance to make such abortive jumps, they did so, and accordingly did not develop seizures. They had avoided the conflict. Proposition IV indicates that organisms will attempt to escape from conflict situations, as Maier's rats did, since they generate anxiety. Likewise, Lichtenstein (1950) gave dogs kept in tight harnesses a shock just as food was presented to them or as they began to eat. This procedure was repeated a number of times until many of the dogs simply stopped eating while in harness. The present theory can also explain why animals do not just sit frozen forever at the point of equality of the motivational strengths to reach incompatible goals. The conflict-generated anxiety can be escaped by, say, jumping into the fire; further, the very act of jumping can reduce anxiety, as we shall see below. This explanation differs from Miller's (1944), which is based on the organism's leaving the conflict because of a relative increase in strength of one of the motivations. No doubt there are instances in which such increases occur, but the present explanation is superior because it is more parsimonious, since it does not have to explain the changes in motivation. Whiting and Child (1953), in applying Miller's conflict theory to anthropological data, had to assume such avoidance of conflict in order to make sense of cultural influences on personality dynamics.

Thus, there is evidence that anxiety results from situations that are hopeless because of the organism's inability to act effectively and thereby to control those aspects of the environment relevant to his goals. This reasoning would also lead to the expectation that even in painful situations, the amount of anxiety would be reduced if the organism could act, even when the actions may make no difference at all. Since action is a part of the schema of adequately adaptive behavior, the organism's perceiving that it is acting or moving in some way would tend to arouse a schema of hopefulness, thus reducing anxiety (Proposition VI). When the organism cannot act in even unconsequential ways, hopelessness and anxiety increase. It is, of course, needless to say that actions that are effective and do make a difference reduce anxiety even more.

It is very important to bear in mind that the schemas whose content is that hopefulness is based on action are of a higher order than the schemas related only to the situation that aroused anxiety. As pointed out in Chapter Four, higher order schemas are invocable to a greater extent and are stronger in general than lower order schemas. Therefore they are less vulnerable to being changed by the particular experience causing hopelessness. Hence, hopeful higher order schemas can be invoked to reduce hopelessness in an anxiety-arousing situation without being weakened or made less hopeful as a consequence. Invoking them would lead to a net gain in hopefulness.

Mandler and Watson (1966) had one group of subjects take tests in an order they chose and one group take tests in an order determined by the experimenters. Each of the latter (determined order) subjects was matched with one of the former (free order) subjects, taking the tests in the same sequence. The "non-choosing" subjects performed worse on the tests than did the others, presumably because they were less hopeful.

Haggard (1946) had subjects free associate to a series of words. After certain words the subjects received an electric shock.

For some subjects, the experimenter directly administered the shock. Other subjects, on a signal, administered the shock to themselves by pressing a button. The subjects to whom the experimenter administered shock showed a greater GSR than the others did. The latter subjects, acting effectively in one aspect of the situation, even the aspect of self-inflicted shock, kept their anxiety down.

Champion (1950) gave humans electric shock in three different experimental treatments. In the first, the subjects were instructed to move no part of their bodies. In the second, the subjects were told to clench their fists for one second while the shock was given. The third group also clenched their fists when the shock was administered, but they were told that this fist-clenching would shut off the shock. The last group showed a faster rate of recovery from an initial rise in basal skin conductance than did the other two groups. Slowest in recovery rate was the first group. What is most interesting in this study is that the subjects' *perception* of the effectiveness of their action led to lower arousal.

Mowrer and Viek (1955) trained rats to jump into the air in their cages in order to shut off a shock in the cage floors, which was turned on intermittently. Each of these rats was paired with another rat who received exactly the same amount of shock at the same time but had no control over the situation. The second group of rats developed a strong neurosis, refusing to eat and becoming generally disorganized in behavior.

In Masserman's study (1943), some of the cats were trained to manipulate switches that activated the light signals that preceded the giving of food. He writes:

> Frustration of goal-directed behavior to food by the interposition of a barrier between the cat and the food or by failing to feed the animal after it had depressed the switch produced significant effects: the animal showed neither rapid extinction of the response nor behavior indicative of anxiety, but instead continued for long periods to activate the signals, look up at the light and even reach for it as though by doing so it was attaining some substitute satisfaction. When, however, there was no barrier to feeding but the current was turned off so that manipulation of

> the switch did not activate the sound or light signals, the animal developed more marked behavioral disturbances; it refused to feed, vocalized almost continually, paced searchingly about between periods of energetic manipulation of the switch, or even attacked the latter with teeth and claws as though to vent its anger and frustration. When the current was again turned on so that the next compression of the switch worked the signals, the behavior disappeared immediately, and the animal resumed its normal feeding pattern (p. 81).

Masserman reports elsewhere:

> Significantly, a quite different series of reactions was produced when, instead of being mechanically thwarted in its ultimate goal or intermediate (symbolic) goals, the animal was permitted to work the signal switch and thereafter to open the food box, but was then given an air-blast or grid-shock at the moment of feeding. Such animals developed all the neurotic behavior (abnormalities noted previously—anxiety, signal phobia, regression, compulsion, etc.)—although generally in a milder form (p. 82).

In seeming contradiction to the trend found in the studies of the effect of action in reducing anxiety is the well-known "executive monkey" study by Brady (1948). He placed two monkeys in adjoining chairs, which were so built that both would receive electric shock simultaneously. One was trained to press a lever every time a signal was received, thereby preventing the shock. The trained or executive monkeys developed ulcers while the others did not. A close examination of the study, however, raises serious questions about the meanings of these findings. The executive monkeys produced gastric juice mostly when they were not "working," pressing the levers. One valid analysis, then, is that the work reduced the tension or anxiety.

In the Haggard, Mowrer and Viek, Champion, and Masserman studies, the subjects' actions were at least related to the pain. A schema of hopefulness can also be invoked by actions that are not related even to the source of pain. Any action that has any affect on the environment or on one's body appears to be enough to prevent the extreme anxiety and experimental neurosis. Thus, anxiety increases if the organism is unable to act in any way that has an influence on the environment or on the body.

Auer and Smith (1940) reported that rats who ran around were less likely to develop convulsions (audiogenic seizures) as a result of painful auditory stimulation. Likewise, Griffiths (1942) reports that audiogenic seizures are reduced by activity: "Some animals seemed to find an outlet for their nervous energy by engaging in violent face-washing behavior, backing against the corners of the room, flattening against the wall, hiding behind the photographic curtain, or wedging themselves into a crevice . . . behind a retaining wall. A number making such reactions never had a seizure (p. 18)."

In Maier and Klee's (1941) conflict situations, some of the rats developed fixations, that is, they consistently jumped, say, to the right or to the circle. Maier *et al.* report that fixated rats tended to have a lower rate of seizure than non-fixated rats.

Tinklepaugh and Hartman (1932) observed baby monkeys under a variety of situations in their laboratory. They write:

> In the course of our experiments with the three baby monkeys, they were subjected to various stimuli, such as loud sounds produced by clapping boards together, and suddenly appearing objects, such as coats or burlap bags dropped before them. So long as a subject was clinging to some object with both hands and feet these stimuli aroused no emotional responses. In the course of the work with them, however, we found that as soon as a subject was prevented from making its grasping, contact reaction, it cried and struggled in a manner indicating fear. If, on the other hand, it was thwarted in its movements by the observers or its mother, it responded by quick bodily jerks which were probably indication of either anger or rage (p. 281).

In an experimental approach consistent with the above data, Bitterman and Warden (1943) gave one group of rats shock for a long period. After some running around, these rats started to crouch, since crouching minimized the amount of pain they received from the electrified floor. These rats were then subjected to loud noise which had led to many audiogenic seizures in the control conditions. After again running around, these rats began to crouch and showed a great many less seizures than did the control group. In a similar study, Goodson and Marx (1953) matched two groups of rats for susceptibility to audiogenic seizures. One group learned to turn a wheel in order to shut off electric shock; the other group did not turn the wheel but did suffer the same shock. Both groups were then subjected to a treatment in which shock came on three seconds before a painfully loud whistle. The rats who did not turn the wheel showed more audiogenic seizures than the others.

Since irrelevant action has the effect of preventing a rise in anxiety, organisms would be expected to react with anxiety merely by being placed in a situation in which they soon perceive that even irrelevant action will not be possible. Lewin (1951) pointed out that the less an individual cognizes that he has "space of free movement" (less freedom to engage in a variety of activities), the higher his tension will be. Stotland and Blumenthal (1964) showed it is not necessary for the person actually to be unable to act within the situation for anxiety to arise; all that appears necessary is that the individual *expect* not to be able to act, even in ways that do not materially influence his fate in the situation. Subjects were told that they were about to take a series of important tests and that the order of taking the tests had no influence on their scores. Half the subjects were told that they were to take the tests in a fixed order; the other half that they could take them in any order they chose. The former group showed more palmar sweating than the latter while they were being given these instructions.

Furthermore, research on animals also shows that an animal becomes more anxious as a result of being in a situation in which no action at all is possible, not even action unrelated to the attainment of any goals.

Ganong (1960) immobilized dogs by confining them in a comfortable canvas sling. Putting the dogs in the sling produced marked increases in adrenocortical secretion. On the basis of data from other studies, he concluded that their secretion was "psychic" rather than a result of muscular activity or struggle. Obviously, these subjects did not have any important goals, such as escape from pain. If they had, the level of anxiety would probably have been higher. Nevertheless, even when there are no immediately demanding goals imposed by the experimenter, the passage of a sufficient length of time will of necessity lead to the arousal of needs by processes within the subjects themselves, such as hunger or urination. Almost inevitably confinement will lead to a low level of hopefulness of attaining the goals relevant to these needs and will lead to a rise in anxiety. In Ganong's situation, the animals were in confinement for two hours, thereby enhancing the likelihood of the occurrence of anxiety.

Anderson and Liddell (1936) ask why sheep who are given increasingly difficult discriminations between stimuli while harnessed in the experimental shed became emotionally upset while the same sheep showed no such upset when they made errors trying to solve mazes. In answer they point out that the sheep in the experimental shed had been trained not to move and would have found it difficult in any event because of the harness. In contrast, the sheep in a maze consisting of pathways in a field were able to back away from the error. They were mobile. Liddell, James, and Anderson (1936) make the same point. They describe how the sheep go through a process of increasing restriction of movements as they are brought in from the fields, first into the yard, then into the shed; and they finally have to stand perfectly still in the experimental harness, while the research is going on. From the present point of view, it would have been interesting to learn what would have occurred had the animals not been released to the pasture between experimental sessions.

The significance of confinement for arousing anxiety and causing experimental neuroses has been indicated in a number of other studies. Cook (1939) attempted to establish an experimental neurosis in three studies on rats, without success. In each, the animals were placed in a conflict situation but were able to move about. In the fourth study, however, the rats were strapped in a stand so that the only sizable limb movement possible was a flexion of the right foreleg. Under some intensities of light, such flexion was rewarded with a food pellet; under others, the flexion netted an electric shock. When the discrimination between the two intensities was made more difficult, the animals began to squeal, lost any inhibitions of the flexion, became hypersensitive to being touched, stopped eating, struggled, became sleepy. Cook concludes that confinement is an important factor in generating neuroses.

Bijou (1943) placed rats in a harness that permitted very few free movements. The rats were trained to press a bar with their heads to receive food when two widely separated lights were flashed. When two closer lights were flashed, they received no food but did get a pinprick on their noses. Then half the rats had their hind legs bound; half had them left free. The discrimination between the two types of lights was made increasingly difficult in a series of trials. The bound rats showed experimental neuroses much more than the unbound ones: the former struggled, squealed, bit, attacked the box, broke away from the holder, urinated, defecated.

Masserman (1943) sometimes forced his cats close to the area of conflict between food and the blast of air. He reports that the manifestations of the neurosis increased if the barrier had side guards to prevent escape. If the barrier was made more "psychologically" confining by being opaque, the cats showed reactions suggestive of extreme claustrophobia and responded to the feeding signals with states of almost uncontrollable panic. Masserman further reports that the anxiety was alleviated when the barrier was moved further away from the area of conflict, *even when the cat itself did not change position.*

At an entirely different level, White and Lippitt (1960) studied the effects of placing social barriers on the "space of free movement" of children. In a classic study, they subjected some children to adult authoritarian leaders who were highly directive, told the children in great detail what they were to do, and allowed little initiative to the children. Other children were placed under democratic leaders who encouraged organized decision making and individual initiative. Under democratic leadership, the children were less tense, friendlier with one another, displayed more signs of liking the work they were doing. They continued working on their tasks even when the leader left the room temporarily; those children under the authoritarian leader did not. Of course, the freedom had to be commensurate with the children's ability. Giving a person freedom in a situation in which he does not have the competence to act is not really giving him freedom. Accordingly, in a third situation, the adult leader behaved in a laissez-faire manner—he gave the children no help, did not organize the group so that decisions could be made as did the democratic leader. Under the laissez-faire leader, the children were also quite tense.

Thus, there is experimental evidence that in painful situations, the organism will experience anxiety if it is unable to act, or even if it only thinks it is unable to act. Anxiety-reducing action can range from actions related to the source of pain but ineffective for reducing it, to actions effective for changing aspects of the situation but completely unrelated to the source of pain, and to movements not necessarily effective for changing anything.

The same phenomenon has been found in situations outside the laboratory, concerning both action in general and action relevant to the main goals in the situation. Zander and Quinn (1962) review a variety of studies in industrial settings and conclude that "Satisfaction is greater when a worker has some share in the process of making decisions that will influence his work, or when he has freedom and autonomy on the job (p. 55)." They also infer that affect is more positive when the person is able to control his own fate and has opportunities for independent action. Foremen who do not tell workers how to perform each minute detail of their job but allow them freedom to work things out on their own are preferred to the more directive ones and maintain higher levels of production in their crews. The same conclusions have been reached by Likert (1961) and Katz and Kahn (1952) in their reviews of the literature in industrial social psychology. Of course, these conclusions hold only if the workers are given tasks within their perceived levels of competence. If they are not, then their freedom is not real and there is an increment rather than a decrease in anxiety.

Heslin and Dunphy (1964) found that of the factors in small-group processes that are most related to member satisfaction, freedom to participate in the group process was one factor most frequently mentioned in the 240 studies they reviewed. Similar findings have been reported from military settings. Grinker and Speigel (1945a) report as follows about soldiers in World War II: "Prolonged periods of enforced inactivity while the men are still exposed to danger has a similar negative effect. This is especially true of men pinned down in foxholes under heavy enemy artillery fire or dive bombing (p. 69)."

Shaffer (1947) interviewed World War II pilots about their fear reactions in combat. He writes:

> Helplessness and hopelessness increased most often. Being attacked when one could not fight back or take any effective action, being idle while in danger, or being insecure of the future, seem to be elements that aggravated fear in combat. . . .
>
> Among factors that assist courage . . . The effects of confidence and morale were most conspicuous. Having confidence in one's equipment, crew, and leaders was the most frequent response. The second most notable condition for courage was effective activity. Keeping busy, concentrating on the job at hand, taking evasive action, or making a good hit reduced fear tensions by substituting constructive efforts (p. 141).

Erwin (1963) comments that he has noticed great anxiety in a number of his patients in the confinement of a barber's chair. He argues that the source of the anxiety is some other aspect of the person's life but that it is aroused in situations that involve confinement.

In his studies of surgical patients, Janis (1958) reports that they frequently react with anxiety to the severe restriction in their movements, perceptions, and cognitive activity imposed by surgical necessity in the operating room. Such anxiety occurs despite the knowledge that such restrictions are necessary for a successful operation.

Bettelheim (1960) writes as follows about his experiences in the concentration camps:

> . . . [W]hether or not one survived may have depended on one's ability to arrange to preserve some areas of independent action, to keep control of some important aspects of one's life despite an environment that seemed overwhelming and total. . . . By contrast, it was the senseless tasks, the lack of almost any time to oneself, the inability to plan ahead because of sudden changes in the camp policies, that was so deeply destructive (pp. 147, 148).

Later he refers to the loss of the "basis of hope" as a consequence of unpredictable changes in the camp experience.

These are the many indications from a variety of settings that the lack of ability to act, to act in any way, enhances anxiety. This general point is relevant to a conclusion drawn by Lazarus (1966) in his study of reactions to danger. He argues that the more sudden a threat of harm, the more likely it is to cause anxiety. In the present context, his point would be valid to the extent that the shortened time period deters action of any sort. This interpretation fits another point made by Lazarus—that anxiety is lower when the organism is actually confronting a potential harm than during the waiting period. In the actual confrontation, the person probably is acting in some way rather than waiting helplessly.

At this point, it is appropriate to raise and answer the question concerning the validity of the relationship between hopelessness and anxiety in such situations as ordinary extinction procedures in laboratory studies. The organism no longer acquires a reward as a consequence of making some response or engaging in some activity. Does not the lack of reward reduce his hopefulness? Why is it that, even after repeated extinction trials, the organism does not manifest many indications of anxiety? There are several answers.

It is not altogether certain that no anxiety is experienced by animals and humans when their usual behavior does not lead to the usual, rewarding outcomes. Extinction procedures may cause some anxiety. As shall be discussed fully in Chapter Eight, some learning theorists such as Marx (1956), Amsel (1958), and Brown and Farber (1951) have pointed out the drive-enhancing qualities of frustration (extinction). The data they present to support their view can, however, be interpreted in terms of the present theory. The question is, why is the anxiety not greater than it is usually found to be? Why does the repetition of the extinction trials not lead to greater hopelessness? This question brings us to our next point.

Hopelessness about attaining action goals does not result simply from failure in a given situation. It is also a matter of higher order schemas, higher, that is, than any schema referring to the organism's experience in the extinction situation. These higher order schemas may be both more hopeful and stronger. Most organisms have, for example, a long history of obtaining food; their very survival attests to it. Therefore, an organism is unlikely to be made hopeless easily during extinction trials. The long history of receiving food adequately thus makes this higher order schema both more hopeful and more invocable than a schema based on the situation itself.

Anxiety is, therefore, most likely to be generated in the laboratory by goals that are both very important and very new in the animal's experience. Escape from or avoidance of electric shock is just such a goal, and, it is clear from a perusal of the literature, it is one of the most frequently used means of generating anxiety.

Third, in most laboratory studies, the animal is free to move around after or during the extinction trials. He may move around the Skinner box, he may be returned to his home cage; he may be able to retreat from the area of the goal box in a maze; he may simply do something else instead of attempting to attain his goal. The last section of this chapter clearly indicates that these possibilities of movement and action have a strong tendency to reduce anxiety. In addition, many of these activities permit the organism to avoid being close to the exact place associated with his frustration.

CHAPTER 7

Other People and Anxiety

The two previous chapters focused on the influence on behavior and anxiety of schemas derived from an individual's direct experience. Now we shift our focus to schemas based on the individual's relationships with other individuals. Schemas can be derived not only experientially but also by communications from other people. Communication is not, however, the only relationship that can influence schemas. Mere perception of other people, who may or may not communicate with the individual, is also sufficient to influence schemas. Within the present theoretical system, such perceptions would be considered simply perceived events. Nevertheless, the perception of others stands as an event intermediate between communication from others and perception of one's own behavior.

In the present chapter, both types of relationships with other people will be examined with respect to their influence on the individual's own behavior and on his anxiety. Both types of social relations have effects much like those of the person's perceptions of his own actions. The effects of others' expectations on the individual's own expectations of performance, on his actual performance level, on his persistence in the face of failure, and on his very own existence will be shown to parallel the effects of his self-perception. Furthermore, an individual's expectations, performance, and anxiety level have been found to be influenced, under certain circumstances, by his perceptions of others' expectations, performances, and anxiety just as they are influenced by his perceptions of his own experiences. Other people are not merely *relevant* to an individual's expectations about his own actions; their very actions may determine the individual's potential for attaining his goals. Thus, the person's level of anxiety can be influenced by the perceived effectiveness of groups and others on whom he is dependent, just as his level of anxiety is influenced by his perception of his own effectiveness. Furthermore, just as an individual can maintain a low level of anxiety by acting on the environment, so also can he do so by being in the presence of some other person who has been associated with goal attainment.

We turn first to the influences of other people's communications and expectations. Since schemas can be derived from communications with others, the level of hopefulness a person has about attaining a particular goal can then be influenced by the expectations others communicate about goal attainment. Videbeck (1960) had subjects read poems aloud before an expert who approved or disapproved of their performance. Subjects whose performance was disapproved shifted their self-ratings downward but no change was found for the approved subjects. Maehr, Mensing, and Nafzger (1962) had an expert evaluate high school students' abilities to do simple tasks, either praising or derogating them. The subjects' self-ratings went down after derogation, up after praise. Haas and Maehr (1965) replicated these findings but with the additional determination that these changes in self-ratings endured for at least six weeks. Although these studies are compatible with the present theory, they are ambiguous because the self-reports were obtained in the same general social milieu as the one in which the expectations were communicated. The subjects may have been reporting back to the researcher what they thought they were expected to say. It would be useful to do a study in which the self-reports were obtained from someone completely divorced from the evaluator.

The present theory predicts that people strive harder for goals that others expect them to attain than they do for goals for which there is no such expectation. There are, of course, several qualifications to this general prediction. First, the effect of communicated expectations is maximal when there is minimal influence from the individual's own previous experience with the particular task or goal. This observation follows from Proposition IV, which maintains that schemas are a function both of communications from other people and of the individual's experience, with the further qualification that a communication can influence the significance the individual gives his successes or failures. It would be expected that, on the whole, children, having less direct experience than adults, would be more susceptible than adults to influence from others.

The second qualification concerns some of the studies cited below. The subjects are given a test or task and the experimenter then gives them an evaluation of their performances. This experimental procedure should not be taken as a contradiction of what was said in the previous paragraph, since the purpose of giving tests prior to evaluation is to provide a plausible basis for the communication of expectations to the subjects. In some cases, the subjects had no other way to evaluate their performance on these tests except through the experimenter's comments, so that the influence of their direct knowledge of their efficacy on these tests was minimal.

It is most important to note that in other studies the expectations of future attainment communicated to the subjects are sometimes directly contradictory to the levels of previous performance that are known to the subject. It is here that the efficiency of communicated expectations is most dramatic, if more difficult to demonstrate. The subject's past performance provides the basis for making the experimenter's communications credible, but the content of the communication may contradict what the subject believes about his past performance.

The third qualification is that the power of the communications from others to establish schemas in a person is, in part, a function of their expertness or status. Therefore, it is not surprising that in some of the studies, the children are influenced by communications from adults rather than from other children. In studies on adults, the communications of expectations often come from the "expert" experimenter.

To determine how communicated expectations affected performance, Sarason and Sarason (1957) gave adult male subjects a paired associates task using nonsense syllables. After the first fifteen trials, half the subjects were told:

> Mr. Jones, you seem to be having trouble with your test. Is anything wrong? Can you see the syllables clearly? How do you feel? You've been doing worse than the other people who have worked on this task. In fact, yours is the lowest score I've gotten so far, and you are the first person I've had who has not reached the college level on this test. That's why I asked if anything was the matter. You've only gotten eighteen right. Usually people get that many right in half the time it has taken you.

The other half of the subjects were engaged in neutral conversation during the same interval. The subjects were then given another trial, in which the failure group did worse than the control group. It is important to remark that, first, the task was new to the subjects so as to maximize the experimenter's influence; and second, the experimenter did not indicate to the failure subjects that he expected them to do better on subsequent trials. If anything, the communication to these subjects was that they were lacking in the required ability.

Hurlock (1925) gave children an arithmetic test. The next day she gave them more tests and: (a) praised them in front of other children and encouraged them to do better work; or (b) scolded them in front of other children for poor and careless work and for their failure to improve over the previous day's work; or (c) neither praised nor scolded them. The children then took more tests. Those that had been praised and encouraged improved more than either of the other groups. The reason that the group that was scolded did no worse than the group that was neither praised nor scolded may be that the scolding also communicated to the children expectations of improved performance. Hurlock's implications were that the children might do better since their mistakes were careless ones and since she had expected them to improve on the second day.

This explanation for the absence of a decrement in the scolded group is supported by another study by Hurlock (1924). She gave children subtests of intelligence tests. She then told some of the children that they had done very well so far; that they would receive another test on which they might do even better. Other subjects were told that they should be ashamed of their poor performances; that they hadn't tried; that the experimenter did not know if they always did badly; that they had another chance on the subsequent test, though she doubted they could improve. (Since she had just proclaimed her ignorance of their usual performance, the "doubt" was not that of a genuine expert.) Still other subjects were simply given the subsequent test. Both the praised and the scolded group went up in performance on the next task, as compared to the control group. The scolded children again were told implicitly that they had the ability but had not used it and they might not always do badly. Thus, their scores increased as much as the praised groups.

Zeller (1950) gave his subjects first a paired associates task with nonsense syllables. Next, they took a test consisting of tapping the same colored block as the experimenter. The subjects were then divided into four groups. Group I was given an easy version of the task and was told that they did "all right." Group II was given hard tasks at which they failed badly, but was told that the experimenter was surprised because they had done so well on the other tasks and each subject was advised "to get hold of himself." Consistent with the present theory, the subjects in Group II then improved their performance on the block-tapping task, even though they continued to be told they were failing. Furthermore, Zeller reports little emotional upset among these subjects. Group III was also given hard tasks on which they failed. They were told of their "stupidity" and were made to feel inadequate in every possible way. At first the subjects tried harder, but then they deteriorated, as would be expected. Group IV was treated the same as Group III except that they were told that their failure was predictable on the basis of their syllable performance. In the third phase of the experiment, subjects in all the groups were again given the paired associates task. Groups I and II did better on it than did Groups III and IV. (Group I was not different from II nor was III from IV.) Notice that the experimenter's expectation of better performance by Group II on the block tapping determined the subjects' subsequent performance on the paired associates test, even in the face of actual failure on the block tapping.

Moreover, in Groups II, III, and IV, the experimenter's evaluations of performance on the tapping did not directly affect the subjects' performance on the paired associates test. Not once did he mention any relationship between the two tasks. The fact that the influence occurred solely as a result of the experimenter's general expectations about the subject can be interpreted to indicate that the experimenter established a higher order schema in the subjects about their competence or incompetence, at least on tasks given in this situation. The subsequent performance on the paired associate task is then a case of a lower order schema being influenced by one of a higher order.

In several of the above studies, being given another chance

was emphasized. If the subjects then failed on this second chance—with no supportive expectations from the experimenter—it was predicted that their performance would deteriorate. Lazarus and Ericson (1952) told adult subjects that they were about to take an IQ test, the results of which could influence their later careers. They were given the digit-symbol test of the Wechsler-Bellevue and a group Rorschach. Half the subjects were then told that they had done poorly, as a group, in the digit-symbol task, that they did not seem to appreciate the task, but that they could have one more chance. During this second administration, the experimenter apprised the group of norms (false) that were impossible for them to attain. The other half of the subjects were told that they had done well on the digit-symbol test but that it was necessary to get further measures. The experimenter was friendly and encouraging. During the second administration, he called out norms that were more easily attainable. It was found that the first group of subjects increased their errors while the second group had a decrease, confirming our theoretical anticipations. It is important to note that unlike the previous studies, giving the criticized subjects a "second chance" did not lead to better scores. The reason is, clearly, that the subjects were led to believe that they were continuing to fail during this "second chance" by the communication of false norms.

Rosenthal (1966) reports on some research in which he told grade school teachers that certain of their pupils were expected to improve in IQ. In the lower grades especially, the pupils who were expected to improve did so, some of the changes being as high as twenty points. Of course, in such a study, it is difficult to determine whether the effects were an outcome of the expectations communicated in some way to the pupils themselves, or an outcome of changes in the teacher's behavior toward these pupils, or a combination of these reasons. Nevertheless, the results are consistent with the present formulation.

Not only is the level of performance affected by others' expectations, but persistence in the face of failure is also influenced. Lefcourt and Ladwig (1965) told some Negro prison inmates that they had skill necessary to do well at a game. Then each played against a white man and continuously "failed." They persisted longer at the game than any other Negro inmates who had not been told they had relevant skills.

On the basis of the above studies, one can conclude that when other people communicate expectation that a person will perform a given task at a given level, that person will do so. This communication can be effective both in the context of failure and of success on the first attempts at the task, provided that the failure is not interpreted as an indication of persistent failure to the performer. Further, the data suggest that other people's expectations of an individual's performance on one task appear to carry over into other tasks in the same situation.

The theory would also lead to the prediction that communication of expectations of failure to achieve goals that are important to an individual would cause him anxiety. However, little relevant experimental work has been done, probably for humane reasons.

To be clear about the conclusions, it is necessary to distinguish the studies cited above from those in which the effects of "social reinforcement" have been investigated, usually from a behavioristic orientation. In these studies, usually done with children, the experimenter typically says, when the children make the appropriate response, such things as "That's fine," "Very good." He does not *explicitly* communicate expectations about future performances. From the present point of view, it would be difficult to make predictions about what the subjects would do without much more detailed knowledge of the situation, far more detailed than is ordinarily given in a journal. In the first place, it would be valuable to know whether the experimenter did or did not somehow communicate his expectations of the subjects' performances to them *implicitly* without explicitly intending to do so. Rosenthal (1966) has amply documented the power and the subtlety of such inadvertent communications.

Another underlying factor may be that the exact goals of the subjects are not what the experimenters intend them to be. The subjects may simply be motivated to relate to the experimenter. This point is nicely illustrated in a study by Stevenson and Cruse (1961). They gave children the rather dull task of putting marbles in a box. The subjects worked up to thirty minutes on five successive days, being given permission to quit at any time during a session. The children in the "R" (response) condition heard the same comments from the experimenter and also observed him smile and nod. The children in the "Ab" (absence of response) condition had the experimenter present but found him silent and unwilling to respond to talk. The subjects in both the R and Ab conditions declined in performance from day to day (which raises the question about the appropriateness of the term "reinforcement"), but the subjects in the R condition stayed at the task longer and put more marbles in the box than did the others. The reason they did becomes clear from the following account:

> On the first day, the socially reinforced normal subjects were very responsive, smiled, and reacted to E's comments with pleasure. They attempted to engage E in conversation during the task. . . . After the first day, all the normal Ss showed a marked decrease in interest in the game and in the E. They talked less to E and became increasingly eager to leave the situation. On the first day, the normal Ss in group Ab attempted to interact with E and engage in conversation. When these attempts met with no response, they rather quickly lost interest and wanted to leave. . . . [In the Ab condition] When E left the room, the normal children played the game in a routine fashion and left (p. 129).

Clearly, this study can hardly be interpreted as showing that social reinforcement leads to an increased performance on a motor task.

Parton and Ross (1965) reviewed studies of children's reactions to social reinforcement and concluded that the results were not very strong or consistent in showing the effectiveness of such reinforcement. It is probable that confusion with respect to communicated expectations and to the subjects' goals are the nuclei of the lack of strength or consistency.

There is evidence that other people's expectations have effects even more profound than their influence on the individual's performances. If the other person is sufficiently important, prestigeful, authoritative for the individual, the former's expectations appear to influence even the person's very motivation to live. Cannon (1957)' quotes the anthropologist, Leonard, in his reports on parts of Africa:

> I have seen more than one hardened old Haussa soldier dying steadily and by inches because he believed himself to be bewitched; no nourishment or medication that were given to him had the slightest effect either to check the mischief or to improve his condition in any way, and nothing was able to divert him from a fate which he considered inevitable. In the same way, and under similar conditions, I have seen Kru-men and others die in spite of every effort that was made to save them, simply because they had made up their minds, not (as we thought at the time) to die, but that being in the clutch of the malignant demons they were bound to die (p. 182).

Cannon also cites incidents in Africa and New Zealand in which people died after having accidentally eaten a forbidden food. He quotes Australian doctors who have seen aborigines die as a result of bone-pointing.*

Thus far we have considered the influence other people have on an individual's hopefulness through communication of their expectations of the individual. However, the opening paragraphs of this chapter implied that the individual's perception of other persons might arouse certain types of schemas that influence his expectations even when there is no communication from other persons, that is, even when no expectations are communicated. The schemas these perceptions invoke are schemas that the individual may have acquired through the perception of a variety of events that are consistent with the schemas. We will consider two such schemas, one dealing with the individual's perceived similarity to another person, the other dealing with his perception of his membership in a group.

* Other reports cited by Cannon and by anthropologists are difficult to interpret in terms of hopefulness, since it is not unreasonable to assume that in many of these reports the people died of fright.

An individual often perceives that people who are similar in one respect are similar in others. People of the same sex tend to have more like interests and aspirations than people of opposite sex. Hence, if the individual perceives that others are in some way similar to himself, he will infer that he can be as hopeful about his behavior as they are about theirs. In many cases, this inference may have a reasonable basis. Conversely, an individual may perceive that someone similar to himself in level of training is doubtful of his ability to master a given task, for example, a skier being apprehensive of a given slope. Another skier of like ability may become fearful as well. Hertzman and Festinger (1940) told college students what level of performance on a test was expected by other college students. They found that the students shifted their predictions of their own level of performance toward that expected by the other students, regardless of whether it was above or below their own level of expectations. Information about the levels of expectations of groups different from themselves affected them less.

The individual will be influenced not only by the expectations other, similar persons have for themselves, but also by their levels of performance. Chapman and Volkmann (1939) found that subjects' levels of expected performance on a new task were consistent with the ostensible performance levels of people like themselves, but not of people who were different. Festinger (1942) told students that they had been performing either above or below the performance level of graduate students, other college students, and high school students. When they were asked to predict their levels of performance on the next trials of the task, they tended to shift their prediction down if they were above graduate students, up if they were below high school students, down if they were above other college students, up if they were below. In short, they moved their expectations closer to the performance levels of a group most like themselves.

Even further, an individual may invoke a schema of generalizing his similarity to others, even when there is no reasonable basis for so doing. Stotland and Hillmer (1962) led some subjects to believe that they had been arbitrarily and accidentally assigned the same tasks in an experiment as had some fictitious person. Others were led to believe that they had been assigned different tasks. The subjects were then told that this fictitious person was either very good or very poor at clerical tasks. The subjects then rated their own clerical ability. Those who were told that this fictitious person had the same tasks as they did rated their performance consistently with his level of clerical ability; those who were told their tasks were different were not affected. Diggory (1966) cites a study by Cutick in which subjects were introduced to another "subject" who was either similar to or different from them with respect to characteristics that had nothing to do with their experimental task. The latter subject also was presented as doing well or poorly on the task. Subjects introduced to the similar subject changed their estimates of their own probability of succeeding on the task consistently with his performance. Subjects introduced to the different subject changed less.

It could also be anticipated that the individual's level of performance on a task would be influenced by the level of expectations derived from his perceptions of similar others. Stotland and Dunn (1962) employed the same basic design as Stotland and Hillmer (1962) and discovered that the subjects' actual levels of performance paralleled their performance ratings as influenced in the latter study.

If a person sees another person similar to himself, in a similar circumstance, suffer anxiety, he will become less hopeful and more anxious. In her classic study, Jones (1924) describes the following incident:

> Vincent showed no fear of the rabbit, even when it was pushed against his hands and face. His only response was to laugh and reach for the rabbit's fur. On the same day, he was taken into the pen with Rosey, who cried at the sight of the rabbit. Vincent immediately developed a fear response. . . . The fear transferred in this way persisted for over two weeks (p. 390).

Grinker and Speigel (1945a) review some of the causes of

breakdown among soldiers in World War II. They write: "The sight of friends injured and killed, and the intense grief over the loss of good buddies, have a powerful destructive effect on an individual's resistance. Repeatedly we have heard the statement, 'I was all right until they killed my buddy' (p. 69)."

Although more than similarity is involved in the loss of a buddy, part of the process must have been influence by identification. Nardini (1952) tells of his experiences as a medical officer in the Japanese prisoner of war camps. One of the factors, he declares, leading prisoners to give up both hope and life was the sight of other prisoners dying. On the more positive side, Hamberg, Hamberg, and de Goza (1953) found that one of the main sources of hopefulness among severely burned patients was their witnessing the recovery of other severely burned patients.

In addition to generalizing from other persons similar to themselves, people may also contrast themselves with others. They may acquire schemas asserting that if they are very different or opposite from some other person or group in one respect, they tend to be opposite and different in other respects as well. This tendency to contrast is implicit in Newcomb's (1958) idea of negative reference groups, groups whose attitudes the person consistently rejects. No data are available with respect to the influence of negative reference groups on anxiety, expectations, or performance.

Another type of schema influencing an individual's level of hopefulness is based on his perception that he is part of a unified group. Often in life, an individual will experience situations in which his fate, his ability to achieve goals, is bound up with the degree of success of the group of which he is a part. If he is part of a successful group, he is successful; and *vice versa.* Therefore, an individual tends to acquire schemas that the degree of success of a group determines the ability of its members to attain their individual goals. If the group is "successful," he may develop a high estimate of his own abilities, even when these abilities are not relevant. Zander, Stotland, and Wolfe (1960) created highly unified groups of college students—they had a name, sat close to one another, were called a group, and so on. Other students were formed into groups of low unity without any unifying experiences. Then members of both types of groups worked on group tasks, half of them ostensibly doing well, half poorly. Thereupon, the subjects rated their abilities in a variety of areas, some relevant to the group task, some not. In both types of failing groups, subjects rated their group-task-relevant abilities as being lower than those in groups that had succeeded. However, subjects in highly unified groups that failed rated their non-group-task abilities as being lower than the subjects in any of the other three types of groups.

Being part of a failing group might seem to lead to an increase in anxiety if the goals of the group are sufficiently important to the person. Very few, if any, laboratory tests have explored this problem. Grinker and Speigel (1945a) report the following about soldiers in World War II:

> Many factors contribute to this inability to "take it." Loss of morale within the combat outfit is one of the principal forces destroying the resistance of the individual. In time of victory, morale is usually high. When the fighting is uncertain or defeat imminent, the morale of the group assumes great importance for the individual, sustaining him if it is good, further weakening his resistance if it is low (p. 69).

Thus far, the concern has been for the influence that others have on a person's estimated level of ability to achieve goals through his own behavior. However, the person may have experienced many situations in which his achievement of goals is dependent on the actions of other people. No documentation is really necessary for this point and it is raised here to distinguish it from other sources of hopefulness. When he is dependent on others, his hopefulness will be contingent on the others' motivations and ability to aid him. Cartwright (1950) has defined a person's sense of security, that is, his perception of the attainability of his goals, as being, in part, a function of the power and friendliness of other people in the situation.

How anxious a person becomes in a threatening or painful

situation often depends, in large measure, on the presence of effective and friendly others, others who share the same goals or who are, or have been, competent to achieve these and other goals. This effect of others' presence has been shown in situations whether the others have or have not the potentiality of acting to help the person. There are various examples of situations of the first type, where the potentiality of assistance is present. Arsenian (1943) has shown that children are less upset in new situations when a friendly adult is present.

Murphy (1962) writes:

> In our group, the child who felt anxiety at separation usually succeeded in holding the mother's support until he secured sufficient footing and sufficient security in the new situation and with new people to let his mother go, confident that he would rejoin her. [At separation] the feelings which overwhelm a child are not due simply to loss of love object, and to feelings of abandonment as such. They involve feelings of uncertainty about many aspects of ability to handle a new situation (p. 42).

Visotsky, Hamberg, Goss, and Leibowitz (1961) report that for victims of polio, hope is often a function of "specific and genuine reassurance about the course of illness" from a person of high status in the hospital who knows the patient. Janis (1958) states that a surgical patient's degree of anxiety prior to an operation is, in part, a function of his confidence in the surgeons.

The importance of confidence in others has been emphasized in military studies as well. Pilots interviewed by Shaffer (1947) report that fear is minimal when they have confidence in their equipment, crew, and leaders. Grinker and Speigel (1945a) summarize their psychiatric impressions they garnered during World War II: "Bad leadership and lack of faith in the commanding officers have an immensely deteriorating effect upon morale (p. 69)." Bartemeir, Kubic, Menninger, Ramano, and Whitehorn (1946) also survey psychiatric experience during World War II and report that the disruption of the unity of the group increased the number of psychological casualties.

Some studies have shown that the presence of "friendly" others, others who have previously been associated with goal attainment, can have anxiety-reducing effects even when they cannot take any action in the situation. Their mere presence seems to invoke a schema of hopefulness. Liddell (1950) developed a procedure for generating experimental neuroses in goats. The animal was repeatedly given shock to a foreleg after the lights in the laboratory were turned off for ten minutes. The neurosis was manifest in a rigidity of the shocked foreleg (sometimes persisting until the goat limped out of the laboratory); rigidity of posture; loss of ability to move the head freely; gasping respiration; slow, regular heartbeat; and absence of micturition and defecation in the laboratory room. Normal sheep and goats defecate and urinate during the test periods. Liddell placed one of a pair of twin kids in a room by itself while being subjected to this treatment. The other kid was subjected to the same procedure but in the presence of its mother. The isolated kid developed a neurosis; the one with its mother did not. In fact, the latter kid continued to romp around the laboratory. It is interesting to note that the prophylactic effect of mother's presence occurred regardless of what the mother did. Most often she was utterly indifferent to the kid, who might get close to her when the signal was turned on.

Mason and Berkson (1962) separated baby chimpanzees from their mothers at birth so that human beings became the mediators of goal attainment. Accordingly, if a baby chimpanzee was held in an experimenter's arms while receiving electric shock, the baby was much less likely to whimper or scream than if it received shock while lying on a table. Mason and Berkson also found that the threshold for whimpering and screaming was higher when the babies were held than when they were not.

The mere presence of others, especially friendly others, helps to keep anxiety low even in humans, as shown by Kissel (1965). He gave his subjects a series of insoluble perceptual reasoning tasks. Some of the subjects worked alone. Other subjects worked in the presence of another subject, a stranger, who was involved with an entirely different problem. The third group of subjects were treated the same as the second group, except that the other subject was a friend. It was established that subjects had a lower level of skin moisture (lower anxiety) when they worked on these insoluble tasks in the presence of another subject, particularly if that subject was a friend. Vernon, Foley, and Schulman (1967) found that children about to undergo anesthesia were more anxious if their mothers were not present than if they were.

Wrightsman (1960) told subjects that in a few minutes they would receive a shot of an experimental drug under rather frightening circumstances. The subjects then filled out a questionnaire about their feelings of anxiety. While awaiting the shot, some sat in a room alone; some sat with other subjects anticipating a shot and were permitted to talk; others sat in a room with others anticipating a shot but they were not permitted to talk. After five minutes of waiting, the subjects again filled out a questionnaire concerning anxiety. There was a general, but apparently not significant, trend for the self-ratings of anxiety to show a greater drop from the first to the second questionnaire in the two "together" conditions. However, if the subjects are divided according to birth order, firstborn and only children on the one hand, and later born on the other, the former groups show far more loss of anxiety in both "together" situations than in the solitary one. The later born do not show the difference. This disparity between the two groups can be understood as a consequence of their initial experiences with other people. Firstborn children tend to be involved primarily with parents who are supportive and nurturant. They then come to expect support and succor from others and gain hopefulness from their presence. On the other hand, those who are born later do not generally have initial experiences that are uniformly nurturant; obviously, siblings are not always supportive. In this way, they are less apt to have a schema of uniformly expecting sustenance from others.

CHAPTER 8

Reactions to Anxiety

How do people react to anxiety?

To answer this question, let us remember that an individual can develop schemas about his own behavior, and that he can develop them at several orders of abstraction. Individuals can develop higher order schemas about the various factors that can increase their hopefulness, and, accordingly, can reduce their levels of anxiety. These factors include effective activity, expectations held by other people, the perceived adequacy of other people, the perceived adequacy and motivation of persons on whom the individual is dependent, and so on. There are numerous occasions in which these factors have influenced hopefulness and anxiety. Thus, most individuals have developed schemas about the relationship between these factors and anxiety. Examples of these higher order schemas are: "Whenever I do something active, I feel better, less anxious";

"Whenever I talk to that optimistic person, I feel that things are going my way"; "Whenever I feel bad, I find that being with a group of people is helpful."

Since the individual is motivated to reduce or avoid anxiety, he is motivated to invoke one of these higher order hopeful schemas if he is in an anxiety-arousing situation. Furthermore, he is motivated to increase the invocability of these schemas even when he is not actually in a state of anxiety, if he expects that he might be in one at some future time.

The idea that humans and animals are motivated to increase the invocability of hopeful schemas is implicit in the oft-repeated assumption that they are motivated to increase their security. White (1959) has pointed out that a child first begins to act on its environment simply out of activity or curiosity motivation. The child then discovers that actions often bring desirable consequences; he thereby develops a schema that links action with goal attainment. According to White, the child then develops a higher order of motive, an efficacy motivation, which is the motivation simply to be effective. This is manifest in the child's actively coping with the world, practicing various activities, doing things in general, even when the goals of the actions are not immediately "need-satisfying" in the usual sense. The child, in White's terms, is increasing its sense of competence through these actions, its sense of its ability to cope with the world. In the present formulation, the child is acting to increase the invocability of a hopeful schema like "My actions lead to changes in the environment," or "I can do things effectively."

The stipulation of the present theory is that what White calls *efficacy motivation* would be enhanced by the anticipation of being in a potentially anxiety-producing situation. Since children have, of necessity, acquired a schema to the effect that "I frequently do not obtain my goals," they would in general be strongly motivated to increase invocability. Much of the behavior in the period from childhood to adulthood can be interpreted as activity to increase the invocability of certain schemas—making oneself feel secure.

Another form of behavior indicative of this type of motivation is the seeking out of other people, especially if they are effective and successful, reading about others like oneself who have been "successful," and so on. Lott and Lott (1965) reviewed the literature on attraction to groups and concluded, "It seems clear that members of successful groups tend to like one another more than do members of unsuccessful ones (p. 274)."

Which particular type of hopeful schema the individual attempts to make more invocable is a matter of his own particular history. The individual's history also determines the degree to which he anticipates being in anxiety-arousing situations in the future, and therefore the degree to which he acts to increase the invocability of the relevant schemas. These points are illustrated in the following study.

Solomon and Swanson (in Mowrer, 1960) deprived rats of water in their home cages for twenty-three hours. The rats were then put into small "water boxes" in which they could drink freely for half an hour. Then they were put in very distinctive-appearing compartments for half an hour; and then replaced in their home cages, the cages in which they experienced thirst. This procedure was repeated for ten days. On the eleventh day, half the group were placed in the home cages immediately after drinking but now had water available in these cages. Other rats were placed in the distinctive compartment where water was also available now. The first group drank significantly more water than the second. The former were evidently anxious about thirst since they were in the cages in which they had been thirsty. To reduce this anxiety, they drank even more than they needed. This phenomenon is probably closely related to hoarding in both humans and animals. The individual increases his hopefulness about future goal attainment or need reductions by "acting now," thereby reducing his anxiety.

The rewarding qualities of secondary reinforcements may also be explicable in these terms; the secondary reinforcement may be part of a hopeful schema, that is, it has usually been followed by the primary reinforcement. In a behavioristic context, Mowrer

(1960) has presented precisely the same explanation of secondary reinforcement as the one given here. It would be interesting to determine whether the organisms are more likely to act to gain secondary reinforcement when they are in states of anxiety, even when the anxiety is caused by experiences not directly related to the acquisition of the secondary reinforcement.

Now that we have seen how individuals act to avoid anxiety, we can examine how they react once their anxiety has been aroused. If an individual is in a state of hopelessness and anxiety, one way to reduce his anxiety is to withdraw from the task or problem. Withdrawal has already been shown to be a common reaction to hopeless situations. However, in some cases, such withdrawal is not possible for a number of reasons: withdrawing may be physically impossible; the goal may be so important to the person that he cannot withdraw physically without great loss; the goal may be so important that even if he withdrew physically, it remains with him symbolically; there may be strong social pressures against withdrawal; withdrawal may be a blow to his self-esteem; and so forth. When the person cannot withdraw, the only type of hopeful schema that could remain aroused would be one that would not immediately lose its state of arousal because of the perceived failure to attain the important goal. Among such schemas would be the hopeful schemas mentioned in the opening paragraphs of this chapter. They could remain aroused in the face of the failure because they are higher order schemas. As pointed out in the chapters on theory, higher order schemas are generally more invocable than lower order schemas; they have received more support from a wider range of the individual's experience. A single instance of failure will not readily lead to a loss of arousal. The arousal of the hopeful higher schema directly reduces anxiety. In addition, the state of arousal of the hopeful higher order schema increases the chance that a hopeful but more specific lower order schema will remain in a state of arousal. The latter schema may be too weak to do so otherwise.

One general, abstract schema the individual might act to invoke is that "action leads to goal attainment." The importance of this schema in preventing the arousal of anxiety has been shown in previous chapters. One way to invoke this hopeful schema is simply to act in some way, even in trivial ways. Of course, anxiety would be reduced more by action that is effective in accomplishing some change in the environment, but action alone may be enough to invoke a hopeful schema and to reduce anxiety. Sherman and Jost (1942) led children to believe that after they had succeeded on a number of trials of a task, they were failing and doing more poorly than other people. The children exhibited more hand and facial movements during the failures than they had previously. Zander (1944) did a study in which children worked on a problem for a number of days, the problem obviously becoming easier. However, the children were made to perceive that they were failing more and more. Those children who did not persist at trying to solve the problem and who, therefore, probably were anxious, showed more "neurotic mannerisms" than did children who persisted. Lewin (1951) cites a study by Dembo to the effect that, after failure, "all combinations of undirected expression, such as restlessness and purposeless behavior, occur." Masserman's (1943) studies of experimental neuroses in cats show parallel findings. Some of the disturbed cats frequently licked and cleaned themselves continually, but especially after the occurrence of the signals that preceded the conflict situation.

Ullman (1951) taught rats to eat small pellets of food in a grid. After four days during which the amount eaten was recorded, electric shock of moderate intensity was introduced for five seconds of each minute during which the rats were at the grid. This treatment led to a reduction in eating in the first two days, followed by an increase in eating, especially during the five seconds when the shock was on. Then the intensity of the shock was increased for four more days. During this period, eating activity increased markedly, with a large increase during shock. For the last four days of the experiment, the animals were satiated prior to being placed in the apparatus, and the procedure was carried out the same as before. During this time, total eating activity decreased, but of the eating that did occur, most was done while the electric shock was on. Ullman notes that "The adjustive act available to the animal in the situation was eating. The increase in eating becomes a generalized tension-reducing response in the situation (p. 531)."

In a follow-up study, Ullman (1952) put rats in a feed box for twenty minutes a day for one day or five days. Next, while the animals were in the box, they were given shock for five seconds at the beginning of each minute for twenty minutes, half of them on high shock, half on low. There was some tendency for those on high shock to eat more during this period. Next, the animals were satiated before being put into the box to receive high or low shock. The high shock group ate significantly more than the others during this period. The one- and five-day groups did not differ.

These data can provide another explanation for the "icebox neurosis"; the tendency to eat when anxious. Instead of the Freudian explanation—regression to an oral level of behavior—a simplistic explanation can be offered: for all organisms, eating has led to the reduction of hunger innumerable times in their lives; thus, eating is closely integrated with a higher order schema of action leading to goal attainment, and therefore eating is frequently used as a way of invoking a hopeful schema.

The theory would maintain that these actions are not pointless but serve to reduce anxiety. The value of action, in and of itself, was indicated in a study by Haggard and Freeman (1945). Palmar skin conductance and directed and nondirected restless movements were measured in twenty boys before, during, and after an experimentally induced frustration involving failure and loss of a previously attained reward. The boys who made more restless movements during the period returned more quickly to their prefrustration levels of palmar skin conductance.

The same phenomenon was noticed by Freeman and Pathman (1942). Their subjects lay on air mattresses so that their skeletal movements could be recorded at the same time that their palmar skin conductance was measured. Then they were subjected to stress. They heard guns go off; they were faced with a conflict in which they received contradictory instructions regarding which way to move their fingers; they were given a free association test, being told that the experimenter would be able to discover the true nature of their mental conflicts. The subjects who wiggled more showed a quicker return to their basal skin conductance levels.

On the basis of his observation of infant chimpanzees, McCulloch (1939) describes their behavior when they are emotionally disturbed by some noxious stimulus. At first they become excited, and then they try to clasp anything. After they find something to clasp, especially something hard, they become much more calm.

As indicated above, actions are more likely to invoke hopeful schemas if the actions are effective in accomplishing some change in the environment, even if that change does not help the individual attain his goal. In the Haggard and Freeman study, it was found that "those subjects who directed aroused energies on a relevant problem tended to recover [physically] more rapidly than those whose overt expression was less specifically directed (p. 581)."

It should be possible to reduce anxiety by changing the organism's environment in such a way that actions become more effective in controlling the environment. This can be accomplished by arranging things so that actions have predictable and regular consequences. Despite their behavioristic interpretation of what they accomplished, Wolf, Risley, and Mees (1964) appear to have been very successful at curing a case of severe temper tantrums in a boy. It is plausible to assume that any boy who has a temper tantrum is suffering some degree of anxiety. The boy in question had to wear glasses but would not. He had severe temper outbursts during which he would throw his glasses away. Wolf *et al.* waited until the child did something in which they were "interested" and then either rewarded him with food or punished him with confinement to a room. After a period of such regular and dependable consequences for his actions, he became less upset and gradually came to tolerate his glasses.

We have thus seen how action of almost any sort can abate anxiety, at least to some degree. Even aggression could be viewed, in the present context, as an effort to reduce anxiety through effective action. The more frequently an organism has attained its goals as a consequence of aggressive, hostile acts, the more likely it is that its acting aggressively will reduce its anxiety, even when this aggression is not immediately instrumental to attainment of any goals. Since males in American society are permitted more physical aggression than females are, males generally are more likely to have had experiences in which aggression leads to goal attainment. In support of this contention, Hokanson and Edelman (1966) found that the blood pressure of males was reduced by physical aggression against the source of frustration; this finding was not true of females.

Feshbach (1964) and Worchel (1961) have argued that some of the aggression that follows failure is an effort to restore self-esteem, or a sense of adequacy. Feshbach points out that not all aggression is motivated in this way, since some of it is simply instrumental to the attainment of goals; but when a failure or a painful experience is perceived to have some implications for the individual's sense of adequacy (his hopefulness), he will aggress in an attempt to raise his self-esteem. Feshbach's and Worchel's argument is that an individual restores self-esteem after an insult by derogating the source of the insult so that the source no longer has any great significance for the individual. Although their reasoning is probably valid for many cases of aggression, it is doubtful that it describes the only cause of aggression. The leap from their argument to the present one is not a big leap, since the present one implies that any aggressive act that is effective would result, to some extent, in restoring self-esteem, or hopefulness based on one's own competence. Horwitz (1958) has also argued that hostility occurs in response to a reduction in a person's power, his ability to control his own fate, and that only restoration of power can reduce hostility. White and Lippitt (1960) draw parallel conclusions from their study of children's reactions to autocratic leadership from adults, leadership that limited the children's freedom. These authors comment that "Aggression is a major manifestation, but only one manifestation, of more fundamental ego needs, the goals of which are importance in the eyes of others and an inner sense of power to cope with the environment (p. 164)."

In keeping with the hypothesis that aggression can reduce anxiety when it restores a sense of adequacy or hopefulness are the findings of Rothaus and Worchel (1964). They administered an intelligence test to groups of students, but badgered and insulted the students throughout the administration. Then the administrators of the test left the room temporarily, turning the group over to an assistant. Confederates were planted in the group as well. What occurred during these periods was experimentally varied. In the catharsis condition, the assistant accepted, reflected, and restated whatever spontaneous feelings were expressed by the subjects. The confederates remained silent. In the ego-support condition, the assistant did the same as in the catharsis situation but, in addition, the confederates made a statement designed to be very ego-supportive of the other subjects. In the instrumental communications condition, the assistant did the same as in the other conditions but one of the confederates said he would tell the administrator on his return about the unfairness of the test. He did, in fact, do so. In the control condition, the subjects filled out questionnaires administered by the assistant. When the administrator returned, he gave some further tests in normal fashion. Therefore, only in the instrumental condition did his change of behavior appear to be a consequence of some action of the group. This group (in the instrumental condition) was the only one in which subjects expressed less hostility than in the control condition. Although it is necessary to assume that restoration of hopefulness was accomplished vicariously through the actions of the confederate, the results fit both the present formulation and Horwitz's.

Berkowitz's (1962) conception of frustration as a cause of aggression also fits into this paradigm. He pointed out that frustration occurs when "a response sequence is blocked," when the individual loses hope of attaining the goal he is striving for. Furthermore, he argues that a state of "rage" is the immediate effect of frustration. Since rage and anxiety are not physiologically distinct, the actual processes referred to by the two terms may overlap to a large degree. This anxiety or "physiological tension" is reduced if the individual can inflict some pain on the source of the frustration, provided the person does not fear retaliation from the target of his aggression (Hokanson and Burgess, 1962; Hokanson and Shetler, 1961; Hokanson and Edelman, 1966).

It would be interesting to determine whether taking any actions that have a clear and marked effect on the environment (even if they are not effective in relation to the sources of the loss of hope) not only reduce anxiety but also reduce the tendency to aggress against the source of the frustration. We then might have a clue to the conditions for catharsis to occur when the aggression is directed at some target other than, perhaps not even similar to, the source of the frustration. In studies of catharsis, the perceived effect of the "displaced" aggression on its target usually is not experimentally varied or controlled. If the subjects were informed that the target of their displaced aggression "really hurt," they might then experience greater catharsis or reduction of tension, just at Hokanson *et al.* have found with respect to aggression directed at the source of the frustration.

In addition to directing actions either at physical objects or at other people, the individual can reduce anxiety by invoking schemas having to do with his dependency on other people. In the previous chapters we have seen how the mere presence of an effective and friendly other prevents the rise in anxiety. Accordingly, the individual may be able to reduce anxiety by invoking some such schema as "In the presence of other people, my goals have been attained." Hence, an individual might seek out others when in an anxiety-producing situation, even if the other cannot help the individual attain his goals.

Schachter (1957) informed subjects that they would receive a shot of a drug in a few minutes under quite frightening conditions. He asked them whether they preferred to wait for the shot alone, or in a room with other people. Other subjects were treated similarly but the frightening quality of the situation had been reduced by eliminating certain "electrical looking gadgets." In the more frightening environment, the number preferring to wait with other people was significantly greater than in the less frightening one. Correlating this preference with birth order, we find that those subjects who were firstborn or only children much preferred the company of others, while later born children did not. This effect of birth order is consistent with the data of Wrightsman (1965), cited in Chapter Seven, which also stated that the firstborn child and the only child experience greater reduction in anxiety in the presence of others than do children who are the younger siblings. The difference was explained as an outcome of the firstborn and only children's initial experiences being with their parents, who are generally nurturant, while those born later into the family structure do not have consistently supportive initial experiences. These differences lead to the development of different schemas about other people.

Lanzetta (1955) placed different groups under varying degrees of stress while working on a group task. High stresses consisted of badgering by the experimenter, setting unreasonably short time limits, restriction of work space, and so on. Compared with control groups with less or no stress, the experimental groups showed more affiliative types of behavior: more collaboration, cooperation, mediation; less aggression, arguing, disagreement. Evidently, the subjects sought to reduce their anxiety by being closer to people. Lott and Lott (1965), in their review of research on interpersonal attraction in groups, concluded, ". . . under certain conditions inter-member liking follows shared failure, especially, we suggest, where the failure is perceived as arbitrarily imposed by an outside source (p. 279)."

Harlow (Harlow and Zimmerman, 1959; Harlow, 1960) has presented many data indicating that for monkey babies, cloth-covered objects shaped like mothers appear to satisfy a need for contact and closeness; the babies cling to these mother surrogates while they do not cling to those built of uncovered wire. Thus, it would be expected that when baby monkeys are in anxiety-arousing situations, their anxiety will be reduced by the presence of a cloth mother surrogate. Harlow's work dramatically confirms this expectation. He raised two groups of monkey babies, one being given much access to a cloth mother surrogate, the other, to none at all. In a situation in which a cloth mother surrogate was available, he then confronted each monkey baby with large, strange objects, such as dolls and toys, which normally cause great fear. Full of fear, the baby monkeys who had been raised with cloth mothers ran up to the surrogate and clung tightly to "her." In a few moments, their fear subsided, while ordinarily they would remain fearfully in a corner. Some of the monkeys then climbed down the mother and actually began to "attack" the dolls. In Harlow's words, they had become more secure. The other group, raised with no mother surrogate, did not approach the cloth mother when confronting the strange objects, nor did their fear subside. In other words, if the cloth mother had been previously associated with goal attainment, it could serve the function of reducing anxiety. Harlow also found that whether the monkey baby received milk from the mother surrogate made little difference in the degree to which the baby clung to her in a fear-arousing situation. This result, which is contrary to the present theory, may be due to the fact, also established by Harlow, that receiving milk seems to be a much less powerful incentive for the babies than the clinging to the "mother." In fact, he found that for only a limited period in the babies' life are "lactating" cloth mothers more attractive than non-lactating ones, while cloth mothers are always preferred to wire ones.

There should be little question about the generality of Harlow's results. Mason (1964) reviewed both the experimental and field observation literature on sociability among monkeys and wrote, ". . . it is clear that the mother comes to occupy a central place in the emotional life of the young primate. She is sought when danger threatens, and her presence is a source of comfort and security (p. 283)."

Additional examples of socially oriented ways of seeking hopefulness are not uncommon in "real life" anxiety-provoking situations—the person who "regresses" to a more dependent form of behavior, the person who pulls out his "lucky charm," the person who reads about successful people similar to himself, or the one who becomes very loyal to a successful group.

People generally seek out others who are most likely to increase hopefulness; these others are often those who are not themselves anxious. Contact with anxious others would increase an individual's hopelessness for a variety of reasons; he could not depend on them to help with the source of anxiety; he might perceive himself as similar in some respect and consequently generalize from thee to me (see Chapter Seven). Rabbie (1963) showed that subjects who are under stress are more likely to prefer the company of less anxious other subjects to the company of more anxious others. Mulder and Stemerding (1963) assembled groups of small shopkeepers. Some of them were told they were about to suffer a very threatening invasion of supermarkets. Others were told that the threat was not very great. In each of these groups, one confederate was trained to act in a highly self-confident and effective way, manifesting many of the traits of strong leadership. Another confederate acted just like other members. The subjects then rated their desire to have a strong leader, and their relative preferences for the two confederates in that role. The highly threatened groups were more likely to prefer a strong leader than the low threat groups. Furthermore, the high threat groups' preference was for having the strong confederate as leader.

We have reviewed the various ways of reducing anxiety while in an anxiety-arousing situation, such as acting in a hostile way, or being close to others. We now turn to the more complex case in which the individual has physically left the situation in which he failed to attain his goals, but, because the goals were so important, he remains psychologically in that situation or readily returns to it psychologically.

One reason that an individual may psychologically return to an anxiety-laden situation is that the goals were so important that he cannot ignore his failure to attain them even after he has left. He may return to the situation symbolically and attempt symbolically to overcome this failure. Freud described this phenomenon in terms of "belated mastery." One such type of belated mastery is documented by Kardiner (1946) in his description of the symbolic return of some war veterans to situations in which they were traumatized. Kardiner writes that one of the symptoms of a war neurosis is a defensive ritual. He describes it as follows:

> . . . [T]he defensive rituals are the most circumscribed and the most highly organized of the war neurotic symptoms. The defensive ritual usually consists of some spasmodic gesture, ticlike movement, or more complicated ritual which when studied proves to be a motion, gesture, or action which would have spared the patient the traumatic experience had it been done at the time of the trauma. Thus, a soldier had a sleep ritual of sleeping in a prone position with his hands over his head. This, on examination, proved to be a gesture of adjusting a gas mask which had been dislocated during a gas attack, as a result of which the man lost consciousness and later acquired his symptoms (p. 196).

The action that the individual might take to reduce anxiety when he enters a physically new situation after failing in another one does not have to be, even symbolically, a way of successfully overcoming his failure. Any effective action can help to restore hopefulness and reduce anxiety. One such way of acting is to draw conclusions rapidly about some ambiguous aspect of the environment. Dittes (1959) made some subjects feel rejected by other group members during a discussion; others felt accepted. Both groups of subjects were then presented with a vague story, an inconsistent description of a person, and an ambiguous speech. They were instructed to determine what each really meant, but were not told specifically to make their determinations rapidly. The rejected subjects drew their conclusions faster than the accepted ones did. In another study, Dittes (1961) was able to repeat these findings. Half his subjects failed and half succeeded at a space relations test; half of each of these groups were told that the test was very important, since it measured important abilities, while the other half were told that the test was not very valid. The subjects were again given the task of drawing conclusions from ambiguous material. The subjects who had experienced ego-involving failure again drew conclusions most quickly. Non-ego-involving failures showed some of the same effects but to a lesser degree. Dittes explains these results as reflecting the efforts of the subject to rebuild his somewhat deflated self-esteem. The "premature closure" leads to an increment in self-esteem, he argues. His reasoning is very close, if not identical, to the present argument.

A conception parallel to the present one has developed among animal-oriented learning theorists. This conception also leads to the prediction that the organism's activity level will increase after the organism has physically left a situation in which it has failed to attain its goals.

Brown and Farber (1951), Marx (1956), and Amsel (1958) have theorized essentially that if an organism's responses are frustrated or blocked for any reason, or if an organism is not rewarded for a response for which it had previously been rewarded, the organism's general drive level would increase. It will perform any post-frustration behavior with greater vigor. These authors differ primarily in their degree of emphasis on the cue property of frustration. Marx appears to emphasize the idea that behavior that has in the organism's experience been successful in overcoming frustrations will be likely to occur after frustration. Marx argues that, in most cases, increased vigor of responses has been associated with overcoming frustration; therefore there is an increment in the vigor of post-frustration responses. This position is most compatible with the present one, obviously. Brown and Farber (1951) and Amsel (1958) argue that the increased vigor of post-frustration behavior is the result of both its cue and its drive properties. They do not, however, systematically treat the question of why frustration does have drive properties. Their main concern is to demonstrate empirically that it does have these properties. Clearly, the present theory would argue that the increased drive properties stem from the organism's motivation to do something effective immediately after a frustration in order to restore hopefulness. In line with Marx's reasoning, action is the most commonly learned way of increasing the probability of goal achievement.

Amsel and his students (Amsel and Roussel, 1952; Wagner, 1959) have devised an experimental technique in which rats are trained to go down a runway for food in a box placed in the middle of the runway, then to go on for some more food in a box placed at the far end. After they have completed their learning, they no longer receive food at the first box. Typically, the rats run faster from the first box to the second than they do during the first leg of the trip. Wagner showed that this increment in speed could not be explained by the lack of reduction of the hunger drive. Rats that were as hungry as the "disappointed" ones did not run as fast as the latter. One difficulty inherent in this research model is that the animal accomplishes at least two things by running faster: (1) he gets to the food sooner, and (2) he gets away from the place of frustration sooner. If we assume that animals are motivated to avoid places (stimuli) associated with frustration, as Amsel (1962) does, then there is no need to postulate any "frustration effect" of increased drive level consequent on frustration in the instance where the box was set up at midpoint. The same problem also occurs in interpreting the results of Holder, Marx, Holder, and Collier (1957). They varied the length of delay at a box halfway down a runway leading to food. They also found that delay increased the post-delay speed of running. In line with this avoidance interpretation, the post-delay speed of running became greater with each additional trial. Also, the present avoidance interpretation is consistent with Amsel and Hancock's (1957) finding that the greater the similarity between the runways before and after the first goal box, the greater the speed of running away from the box. The runway stimuli leading from the box (the point of frustration) were similar to those leading to the box, and therefore became additionally aversive to the rat. This criticism of Amsel's mid-box set-up should not be taken to imply a rejection of his theory; the criticism is purely methodological.

The present argument that anxiety-producing failure leads

to heightened action should not be construed as contradictory to the earlier argument that failure leads to lower expectations and thereby to less effort. The difference is that in order to reduce anxiety after a frustration, the organism will attempt to act in a way that is easy and where success is readily predictable and accessible. In Dittes' studies, for example, the subjects did not aspire to do a very good job of explicating the ambiguous stories; that would have taken more effort and would have invited failure. Instead, they took the "easy way out." It would be valuable to do a study in which the subjects had to choose between easy and difficult tasks while in a state of anxiety.

Needless to say, there are any number of additional ways in which the individual can reduce anxiety after physically leaving the anxiety-arousing situation: he can seek the company of friendly or non-anxious others, seek supportive statements from others, study the successes of other people like himself, join successful groups. These ways of reducing anxiety have not yet been studied enough.

CHAPTER 9

Help from Other People

The ways that other people can help in reducing anxiety, even when reducing others' anxiety is not their primary motivation, were discussed in Chapter Eight. In this chapter, we discuss the reduction of anxiety through the help of people whose job is therapy; and we limit our discussion to therapy for "normal" people, reserving for a later chapter therapy for the acutely disturbed. The processes that determine the effectiveness of therapy parallel those processes of anxiety reduction described in preceding chapters, including the action-oriented processes, observational processes, group processes, and communications from other people.

We have already seen how anxiety can be reduced by action. However, the present theory does not require that the individual inspire himself to action and thus restore hopefulness and reduce anxiety; other persons can influence, direct, or even force the person to act. And such action can then invoke a hopeful schema. However, the action of the other person in instigating action is also a communication. As we shall see and have seen, this communicative aspect can have an influence on the person's hopefulness independently of the effect of the action itself. In some cases, the instigated action and the communication can be directed toward both the reduction of anxiety and the increase of hope. Furthermore, the action that is instigated does not necessarily have to be action directed at the solution of the person's problems or at overcoming the person's previous failures. The individual's action invokes a broader, more abstract schema of hopefulness, which reduces anxiety and can lead to the arousal of lower order schemas that are more hopeful about the specific problem. The latter schemas were part of the person's cognitive structure even before the higher order schemas were invoked, but the lower order ones were too weak to be aroused without the invocation of the higher order schemas.

Nardini (1952), in reporting on his experience in Japanese prisoner of war camps, points out that many of the deaths were the result of hopelessness, apathy, and depression. He writes that one way of preventing imminent death among the prisoners was to provoke them to anger. Similarly, Stressman, Thaler, and Schein (1955) report that apathy deaths among American prisoners in the Korean War could be prevented by "getting them on their feet doing something, no matter how trivial, and getting them interested in some current or future problem." Grinker and Speigel (1945a) indicate that giving the war-neurotic patients work around the hospital was therapeutic, particularly if it had some meaning to it and even more so if there was some relationship between the work and the war effort.

The reactions of children to disasters also appear to fit this paradigm. A group of researchers studied the effects on children of having their schoolhouse destroyed by a tornado, with a number of casualties (Perry and Perry, 1959). The researchers were impressed by the low number of emotional difficulties that ensued, especially since the destruction of a movie theatre in another town, Vicksburg, had led to a high proportion of such difficulties among the children there (Perry, Silber, and Bloch, 1956). Perry and Perry cite as one of the reasons for this difference:

> *The child* [in the school disaster] *has a role of responsibility in the household in these communities.* In the two communities studied, the child seems to gain self-esteem in the household through his responsibilities as a member of the family. . . . By contrast, in the middle-class families studied in Vicksburg, the child is not considered important in the functioning of the family; he is more in the position of a valued possession ([p. 12] italics supplied).

Some of the effects of therapy on emotional problems can be interpreted consistently with the present approach, even those forms of therapy whose theoretical orientation is quite different from the present one. In order to make this reinterpretation, it is necessary to make the simple assumption that a person can view his psychological difficulties as something separate from the rest of himself. Of course, this assumption does not mean that somchow a "problem" is really separate, or that the individual can be completely compartmentalized; it does mean, however, that the individual is not *wholly* sick when he has a problem. Even a schizophrenic is likely to have lucid, rational periods. The person may refer to his "problem," his phobia; he perceives his own behavior, his sick as well as his healthy behavior. The same assumption that was made in Chapter Five, namely, that the individual can perceive his own behavior and develop schemas about it, has its parallel here. The individual perceives his "sick" behavior and develops a schema, such as "I feel frightened every time I look someone in the face."

Accordingly, the process of therapy can be seen in part as the individual's acting to solve his "problem." This very statement, which is implicit, if not explicit, in many interpretations of psychotherapy, implies that there is some sort of a dichotomy—the acting (healthy) part of the person and the part that is acted upon (the problem). This dichotomy is also implied in the recent trend toward emphasizing the strengths of patients, instead of their psychopathology only. The therapist relies on the patient's strengths to help overcome the pathology.

The acts, covert or overt, symbolic or muscular, that the individual must perform to attain the goal of overcoming his problem are varied: restraining himself, examining his own motivations, acting constructively, approaching or avoiding certain activities or places, and so on. He is more likely to engage in those actions about which he feels hopeful. This point has been made by Frank (1961), who emphasized the social sources of such hopefulness; and by French (1958), who pointed out that bringing the patient's anxiety-laden impulses out into the open can be therapeutic only if it is done in a hopeful context, a context in which the person has some hope of satisfying those impulses in a realistic and appropriate way.

It has been remarked that one of the ways to invoke a hopeful schema is to do something effective. A broad, abstract hopeful schema is aroused and has an influence on the schemas that pertain to the particular problem. As we have established in the chapter on theory, the broader schema can influence those subsumed under it.

Masserman (1943) reports that cats, which had learned to manipulate switches that controlled the signals for dropping food into the box, put this learning to good use after they had developed an experimental neurosis. He writes:

> . . . [A]nimals trained in the use of the switch and then made neurotic by the air in a shock technique possessed a definite advantage over others not so trained, in that the former, either spontaneously or under additional pressure from increased hunger or spatial constriction, began once again to approach the switch, to re-explore its possibilities and to manipulate it with increasing confidence until they had re-established their individual signal sounding and feeding patterns. When this occurred, their neurotic abnormalties rapidly diminished and their normal behavior returned (p. 82).

It follows that if a person is acting in some way effectively while he is facing his problem, he is likely to approach the problem without anxiety, to deal with it so as to achieve his goals. Some of the forms of so-called behavior therapy appear to capitalize on this influence of effective action, although this influence is hardly the only factor in treatment.* Jones (1924) relied on this influence in her studies of the elimination of childhood fears. She says:

> During a period of craving for food, the fearful child is placed in a high chair and given something to eat. The fear object is brought in, starting a negative response. It is then moved away gradually until it is at a sufficient distance not to interfere with the child's eating . . . While the child is eating, the object is slowly brought nearer to the table, then placed upon the table, and finally as tolerance increases it is brought close enough to be touched (p. 388).

Bevan (1960) describes a case of a woman who suffered from an obsessional fear about the atom bomb and other world problems. Her successful treatment consisted, in part, of the reading aloud of newspapers with bad news. If she became anxious or upset, she stopped. Each day she managed to read more.

Clark (1963a) successfully treated a married man who had a fetish of wearing a woman's girdle and stockings. He was made nauseous by drugs and vomited while handling and looking at pictures of his fetish objects. He also had to keep up a verbal report on how he felt while he was vomiting.

Wolpe's (1958) approach to psychotherapy also appears to capitalize on this relationship, even though his interpretation is quite different from the present one. One of the forms of treatment he recommends is systematic desensitization. In this treatment, the

* In the following pages, a number of studies dealing with the outcome of therapy of people in emotional difficulties will be described. These studies generally are not those in which the results were measured by a verbal measure such as a test questionnaire. The reason for omitting studies using a verbal measure is that the problems of response set—of the patient's perceiving the test as a means of communicating, to the therapist or his surrogate, the expected or the previously rewarded—have not yet been surmounted in the studies using these verbal measures.

individual is confronted, either symbolically or actually, with a hierarchy of objects or situations that he fears, starting with the least feared one and moving up through the "fear gradients" to the most feared, provided that the patient is not overwhelmed in the process. The patient is confronted with these sources of anxiety while he is in a state of relaxation resulting from previous training in Jacobson's (1929) method of progressive relaxation. Crucial to an understanding of Wolpe's effectiveness is an examination of Jacobson's method.

Jacobson's basic objective is to teach the person to relax generally in three stages:

> (1) The patient relaxes a group [of muscles] further and further each minute. (2) He learns consecutively to relax the principal muscle groups of his body. With each new group he simultaneously relaxes such parts as have previously received practice. (3) As he practices from day to day, according to my experience, he progresses toward a habit of repose, tends toward a state in which quiet is automatically maintained (p. 34).

Jacobson's actual method of teaching people to relax progressively is, however, a highly demanding one. A successful student is almost a minor yogi. His students must learn to become highly observant of their own muscle tensions, to use their own initiative in relaxing tension away, and to become more and more adept at relaxing. The extent to which this ability is a major achievement is suggested by Jacobson's own comment: "From the outset, the learner does everything for himself. If he fails, he may be scolded and made to try again . . . (p. 52)."

The individual is taught to relax part of his musculature in everyday situations, as much as he can without interfering with his regular activities. In this way, his anxieties will be reduced. It is clear that any individual who can achieve this level of proficiency must consider it a major achievement, for when he partially relaxes his musculature in the course of his everyday activities, he is practicing a great skill. Even though the action of relaxing is not directed to the environment, it is effective nevertheless. A person invokes a hopeful schema by his achievement.

When a patient is treated by Wolpe's method of systematic desensitization, he is in effect invoking a very hopeful schema. He faces his problem while a hopeful schema is in a state of arousal. Each anxiety-producing situation is faced in this condition.* The effectiveness of this form of therapy has been experimentally demonstrated by Lazarus (1961) who placed people in groups sharing the same type of phobias and constructed "group" hierarchies of fear-arousing situations. They then engaged in group desensitization, in which, after being trained to relax, they were instructed to imagine increasingly more fearful situations. These patients were compared to a group who had received traditional forms of group psychotherapy, emphasizing insight into one's problems in a permissive atmosphere. The desensitized group showed a much greater loss of symptoms, even in a follow-up study about nine months later. Moreover, Lang and Lazowik (1963) showed that group-administered desensitization to a fear of snakes was more effective than mere passage of time for getting people to pick up harmless snakes.

Following Jacobson's original suggestion, the patients are also instructed to relax in everyday situations in which they begin to become anxious, in addition to relaxing during the actual therapy sessions. Clark (1963b), who uses Wolpe's approach, treated a woman for spasms of the jaw. To augment other forms of treatment, Clark trained her in relaxation and then engaged in a discussion of her areas of anxiety. She was instructed that if a spasm was feared, she should smile in a set way. As she smiled, progressive relaxation was again instituted. Clark (1963c) gave similar instructions to a woman who had great fear of birds. She had, among other forms of treatment, instructions that, when she faced anxiety-arousing situations in everyday life, she should count and breathe as she had in the doctor's office when he had gotten her to relax.

* Other factors involved in this form of therapy will be cited later.

When the patients cannot be made to relax by Jacobson's method or by hypnosis, drugs are occasionally used. In these cases, the subject clearly is less likely to invoke a hopeful schema based on his own action. The effectiveness of treatment should therefore be lowered. For example, Walton and Mather (1963) describe a woman who had a whole series of problems: fear of faces; compulsive changing of clothes after bowel movements; fear of men; fear of going out in public. To get her to relax, drugs were necessary. Her treatment was only partially successful: she lost some of her fear of men, but none of the other problems was resolved. From the case reports, it is difficult to determine whether such instances are characteristic. However, Freund (1960) reports on a series of cases of homosexuality that he treated by showing the patients, after they had taken an emetic drug, pictures of men; then showing them, after they had received an injection of male hormone, pictures of women. They were therefore not especially active during this treatment. Freund makes a rather modest claim for the effectiveness of this treatment—that it is no more nor less effective than other ways of treating homosexuality. His report is one of the few instances in which behavior therapists have not been able to claim a higher rate of cure than those who practice other forms of psychotherapy.

There is another aspect of systematic desensitization that helps to account for its effectiveness. In their state of relaxation, the patients first face the least fearful of the fearful stimuli; they discover they can face it without great anxiety. Then they face the next least fearful stimulus, again discovering that they can do so calmly. The patient in systematic desensitization must then come to develop, as he goes up the hierarchy, a schema that he is successful in overcoming increasingly intense anxieties. This schema is, in itself, a hopeful schema and thus makes the whole therapeutic process a benign circle of hopefulness leading to greater success in facing subsequent frightening stimuli.

Many years ago Keister (1943) took children who, when faced with failure, gave up, asked for help, and became hostile or emotionally upset. She gave them a series of puzzles of increasing difficulty, but encouraged them to work and to succeed on their own. When they returned to the situation of the original failure, they were less upset with their failures and persisted more than did a control group that originally behaved the same but received no training. Keister's study suggests that training in persistence or assertion can generalize to other situations, provided that the training involves performing well on increasingly difficult tasks. The subjects became more hopeful in general and therefore persisted longer. The implication for desensitization procedure is obvious.

Another method behavior therapists employ is direct action. They have the patient actually practice the "technique" he needs in order to function more adequately in society. Wolpe (1958) speaks of training his patients in "assertive responses," especially when the patient's problems appear to stem from a lack of aggressiveness on his part. He goes so far as to role-play assertive behavior with his patients. Wolpe's interpretation of the effectiveness of such training is that it counteracts anxiety at the physiological level. However, it also is a straightforward way of training subjects to improve performances, to become more hopeful and more capable in dealing with the environment. There is no need to delineate any physiological interpretation.

The action of the person does not necessarily have to be assertive or aggressive in order to be effective in solving his emotional problem; even Wolpe does not use assertiveness unless the lack of it appears to be a problem for the patient. If the individual has learned straightforwardly to master the problem, this in itself constitutes an even more effectively direct form of action and its effect on an individual's hopefulness is very straight and true. Taylor (1963) describes a woman who for years had plucked out her eyebrows by hand, hair by hair, as she was reading. Since all other forms of therapy failed, he ". . . decided that the best hope of success lay in putting on her the responsibility of opposing the impulse every time it arose (p. 242)." Since she was instructed to perceive that the source of action was herself, her degree of success directly effected whatever hopefulness was based on her own competence. The patient was instructed that every time she saw her hand beginning to move to her head for the purpose of plucking, she was to say, "No, stay where you are," or words to that effect. This treatment was highly successful. The significance for hopefulness of her perceptions of her own behavior and of its success is indicated in Taylor's comment, "Evidently the pleasure she experienced in at last being able to control her behavior was going to provide powerful reinforcement of the response of saying no to the moving hand (p. 243)."

To sum up: much of the effectiveness of behavior therapy can be understood in terms of the present theory because of the great emphasis behavior therapists place on the patient's *acting* in some effective way. The patient's perception of his own effectiveness appears to be a highly significant factor in this form of therapy. We can turn now to the effect on a person's anxiety of his perceptions of others in therapeutic situations.

Chapter Seven has demonstrated that an individual's degree of hopefulness and anxiety can be influenced by his perception of other people as similar to himself in some way. Because one perceived similarity to another person can lead the individual to perceive additional similarities, the individual who becomes anxious and perceives a similar other who is not anxious would tend to have his own anxiety allayed. This process appears to have occurred in Jones' (1924) study of the reduction of fear in children. A boy who had a fear of furry objects was playing with two girls when a rabbit in a basket was placed near them. At first the boy was upset and tried to have the rabbit removed, but when he saw that the girls were interested in the rabbit, he followed them to observe it more closely.

Jones (1960) also noted the same sort of effect in the classic study of Peter, who had a fear of rabbits. Among other procedures used to reduce Peter's fear, she tells that the presence of other children who were unafraid of rabbits reduced his fears. She reports the following in her observation notes.

> Lawrence and Peter sitting near together in their high chairs eating candy. Rabbit in cage put down twelve feet away. Peter began to cry. Lawrence said, "Oh, rabbit." Clambered down; ran over and looked in the cage at him. Peter followed close and watched (p. 49).

On a later occasion she reports:

> Peter with candy in high chair. Experimenter brought in rabbit and sat down in front of tray with it. Peter cried out, "I don't want him," and withdrew. Rabbit was given to another child sitting near to hold. His holding the rabbit served as a powerful suggestion; Peter watched the rabbit in his lap and held it for an instant (p. 49).

A question must be raised as to why the anxious children's fears were alleviated, why the other children did not acquire the fears of the anxious children. In fact, the previous chapter made a point of people's tendency to acquire one another's fears. There is no ready answer to the question, but such factors as the amount of previous experience with the object of fear, the nature of this experience, the motivations to reduce anxiety, the relationship between the children, and the personalities of the children would influence the direction of influence.

The effect of perceiving anxiety, or lack of it, in similar others helps to explain the success that Lazarus (1961) had in using systematic desensitization in a group therapy session to reduce phobias. He assembled groups of patients with the same type of fears—acrophobia, for example. While in a state of relaxation, they were asked to imagine fear-arousing situations, starting at the least fear-arousing and then moving on to the next in the "fear hierarchy" when all of the patients indicated that they could imagine the situation without excess fright. Since the subjects communicated their fear, or lack of it, publicly as each situation was presented, each of them knew how every other member of the group was reacting. The success of this treatment could have resulted in part from the subjects' perceiving that everyone in the groups was making progress, albeit at different rates.

We thus have evidence that perceiving the good fate of similar others reduces anxiety. Other people can influence a person's hopefulness and anxiety also through membership in a close-knit and hopeful group. If an individual who is suffering anxiety can be reassured of his membership in the group—provided the group is one that is itself hopeful—he will experience a reduction of anxiety. In describing war neuroses during World War II, Grinker and Speigel (1945a) write: "Among the factors which enable the soldier successfully to withstand the onslaught of anxiety in the war situation is his identification with the group. The identification with the group is powerfully protective to the individual (p. 117)."

Bartemeir *et al.* (1946) conducted a survey of the treatment of combat exhaustion in World War II. They report that sending an exhausted soldier to the rear leads to greater passivity and to a lesser chance of recovery. If the soldier is treated by his battalion surgeon, and his group identification is thereby retained, he probably will return to the front in forty-eight hours.

In his survey "Psychotherapy in the Combat Zone," Glass (1954) also concludes that soldiers were more likely to overcome their anxiety if they were treated near the front by a medical officer of their own unit. He argues that they can thereby maintain a closer identification with their group. Those who were evacuated to the rear had a tendency to develop into chronic cases.

Another way in which other people can influence one's hopefulness and anxiety is by communication of positive expectations, by exhibiting, verbally and non-verbally, their confidence that one will overcome difficulties. Nardini (1952), who spent several years as a doctor in a Japanese prison camp, believes that one of the factors that could prevent death resulting from depression and apathy is praise from a friend. Stressman, Thaler, and Schein (1955) report that in the North Korean prisoner of war camps, a prisoner could be saved from apathy death through the "effort of a friend who maternally and insistently motivated the individual toward realistic goals, or the realization of ties to loved ones at home . . . (p. 999)."

Kobler and Stotland (1964) have shown that the research literature on suicide is most readily interpreted as indicating that people who decide to go on to suicide are those who have been reduced to a state of near-hopelessness. However, in this state of near-hopelessness, they had some hope (at a higher order of schema) of finding hope through the communicated expectations of others. They had turned to these others, asked for help, for hope in some way. They had asked by verbal communications, abortive suicide attempts, and had received a fearful reaction from others, signifying little hope. After they had received this communication, they went on to suicide. If they did not receive an anxious, hopeless response from others, they were unlikely to go on to suicide. Kobler and Stotland's (1964) study of an epidemic of suicides among mental hospital patients illustrated this interpretation.

The power of expectations in psychotherapy has been emphasized by a number of theorists. Despite his emphasis on more "psychodynamic" processes in psychotherapy, Freud (1953) wrote as follows:

> In Lowenfeld's instructive work many of the methods of primitive and ancient medical science are described. The majority of them must be classified under the head of psychotherapy; in order to effect a cure, a condition of "expectant faith" was induced in the sick person, the same condition which answers a similar purpose for us today (p. 250).

Rosenthal and Frank (1956), Frank (1961), French (1958), and Goldstein (1962) have all emphasized the power of the therapist's expectations. Frank has argued that the hopeful expectations of the therapist are crucial for the patient's improvement. Although unequivocal research data to support this point are rare (*cf.* Goldstein's review, 1962), there is little doubt that it is operative.

Honigfeld (1962) measured the attitude of therapists having four or more patients toward their patients' ability to assume responsibility and toward their general adequacy. Therapists who had more positive valuations of patients in general on these dimensions had patients who were less likely to become agitated, excited, and hostile (thereby strengthening the therapists' schemas!).

Stevenson and Fisher (1954) worked with unemployed, highly dependent, neurotic outpatients who had stopped looking for work. As soon as physical disabilities could be realistically rejected as a cause of unemployment, the therapists stressed how much the patient had improved, spoke of his skill and intelligence, and hence of his potential employability and proof of his ability as evidenced by past work records. A social worker was highly instrumental in securing jobs, while the therapists threatened to cut off welfare payments. Although the patients were obviously anxious about their new jobs, they did well and were praised for their performances. Of twenty-five cases, twenty were working six months to three years later, with high morale, fewer symptoms, and a rise in self-esteem. Only seven continued to have any contact with the clinic.

An objection to this general line of reasoning might be raised in that it seems to suggest that patients in psychotherapy almost inevitably become dependent on their therapists. However, a close examination of the reasoning indicates that this is not necessarily the case at all. The therapist can communicate hopeful expectations regarding the patient's own ability to overcome his difficulties. The patients may be dependent on the therapist for this hopeful evaluation of his abilities, but the abilities are his own. If this communication then leads the patient to act, and to act more confidently, then other sources of support for a hopeful schema are established, and the patient loses his exclusive dependency on the therapist. For persons in acute difficulties, the only source of hope may be the therapist, and the latter's hopefulness about his own ability to help the person may then be the only significant hopefulness available to the patient. Even though this type of communication does not as readily lead to the person's trying out his own abilities, the therapist's hopefulness may prevent the person's completely withdrawing in the face of anxiety. This situation should not be confused with the therapist's communicating confidence about the patient's ability to act effectively, as described above. This situation is one in which the therapist's, or other powerful person's, ability to act effectively in the person's behalf is the basis of hope and thus the person might become dependent on the therapist.

Moreover, the theory suggests at least one factor that militates to some extent against such dependency's becoming a serious problem. This factor is that a schema in which hopefulness is dependent on another person's action is, after all, a lower order hopeful schema. As such, it could in many cases invoke a higher order schema of hopefulness. For example, the person may be reminded by the therapist's hopefulness that hope in general is still a valid feeling, that hope is realistically possible. This more abstract schema, while aroused, could have an influence then on another lower order schema, the person's schemas concerning his own ability to act effectively. He may become more hopeful about his own ability, as well as about the other person's effectiveness. Of course, this process is contingent upon the person's having some basis for having at least a potentially arousable hopeful schema about his own abilities. If he has had little or no experience upon which to base such a schema, then it is unlikely that his dependency on a hopeful other will lead to his dependency on a hopeful self.

The influence of a powerful, friendly other person in reducing anxiety is sometimes so strong that his mere presence may have a mitigating effect. Jones (1960) reports that Peter, the boy who was afraid of rabbits, lost some of his fear in the presence of a Dr. S. She writes that

> Peter was very fond of Dr. S. whom he insisted was his "Papa." Although Dr. S. did not directly influence Peter by any overt suggestions, it may be that having him there contributed to Peter's general feeling of well-being and thus indirectly affected his reactions (p. 49).

There are a number of factors that can enhance the person's hopefulness when it is dependent on another person. The friendliness of the other is important because it indicates that the other's power will be used to help. Not only is the person's confidence in the therapist important; the therapist's confidence in his own ability is obviously crucial. Bandura (1956) found that therapists who were ranked by their supervisors to be high in psychotherapeutic competence were ranked by other psychotherapists as being low in anxiety as pertains to dependency, hostility, and sex. Part of the effectiveness of behavior therapists like Wolpe (1958) may stem from their telling the patients, directly and forcefully, that they will cure them and how they will do it.

This process occurs even among animals. Gantt (1942) reports that the presence of an experimenter and his petting of a neurotic dog helped to allay the disturbed behavior. Masserman (1943) also reports that neurotic cats would calm down in the presence of an experimenter who customarily fed and cared for them.

Sometimes the therapist's reliance is not so much in himself as on the tools that he employs. In that case, his confidence in these tools would be expected to influence the course of therapy. Honigfeld (1962) found that therapists who had more positive attitudes toward chemotherapy were more likely to have patients become less agitated, excited and hostile as a consequence of taking drugs. Also, Honigfeld (1963) found that among patients treated by a placebo, there was more improvement the more their therapists believed in chemotherapy.

Sometimes the therapist's confidence in a particular technique can be communicated directly to the patients. Clark (1963c) describes the case of a woman who had a great fear of birds. He writes that

> In the course of repeated exercises of dynamically induced relaxation during treatment sessions, the patient had been told that she would become progressively more relaxed and free of apprehension or anxiety as the psychologist counted from one to ten. She was asked simultaneously to breathe deeply and slowly. Latterly, Mrs. B. was trained to carry out this counting and breathing by herself at the psychologist's request. It was found that by so doing she was able to increase her skin resistance which had

> been previously reduced by an artificial stress stimulus. . . . the patient was also told to use this technique to enable her to relax should she ever be disturbed by a bird outside (p. 65).

Of course, the effectiveness of this therapy is also probably a function of Mrs. B's being actively involved in the therapy.

The parallel between all the various social psychological processes in psychotherapy cited above and the procedures of medicine men, shamans, and the like in more primitive societies has been illustrated by a number of authors, such as Frank (1961) and Kiev (1964). Since these authors have documented the parallels well and Frank has interpreted them in a way quite consistent with the present approach, it does not appear necessary to repeat their work. However, a few examples of the incidents that point out the similarities between primitive and modern therapy might help to clarify the issue, especially since anthropologists appear to be generally impressed by the effectiveness of the primitive forms of therapy.

Opler (1936) studied shamans among the Apache Indians. In this tribe, shamans are believed to be able to invoke supernatural power. They judge the cases they are to treat, picking the easier ones apparently in order to enhance and sustain their reputations and presumably their power as well. They refuse to treat sceptics. The patients they treat have to humble themselves before the shamans. Payment is demanded in advance, thus bringing additional pressure on the patients to "believe." The shaman explains to the patient and to his family how he came to acquire this supernatural power. Non-believers are asked to leave the ceremonial area. The shaman often knows much about the lives of his patients and can therefore direct his efforts appropriately.

Leighton and Leighton (1941) describe the work of the "singers" among the Navaho. Before a singer arrives at the family home of the patient, the family makes elaborate preparations for his coming. Upon arrival, the singer immediately tells the patient he will recover. Other people who are present, including the patient's family and all the important people in his life, join in the singing, reaffirming the singer's belief that the patient will recover. And the patient actively participates in the rather elaborate ceremonies. Murphy (1964), in her analysis of the effectiveness of shamans among the St. Lawrence Indians, states that their effectiveness seems to be due to suggestion, group participation in affirming their belief in the shaman's effectiveness, "focusing awe" upon the shaman, and having the patient do something "objective," such as penance. Prince (1964) describes psychotherapy among the Yoruba people of Africa. He points out that they rely on suggestion of the power and effectiveness of the healer, as communicated by "direct commands," similes, illustrative stories, songs; actively doing something by the way of a sacrifice, joining a protective and supportive group.

In sum, the experimentally demonstrated processes influencing hopefulness and anxiety described in the earlier chapters also appear to be important in the formal and informal help that people give one another when they are in emotional difficulties.

There is a danger of oversimplification of the practical implications of the thesis that hope is a basic aspect of helpful relationships. The oversimplification is that all that is needed in therapy is the therapist's communication of strongly, nay, *blindly* hopeful expectations. This implication must be qualified in several ways. A mechanical, sudden, or overwhelming communication of hopefulness could indicate to the patient that the therapist simply does not comprehend the seriousness of his problems and the failures of previous attempts to solve them; such a communication could imply a subtle rejection or derision of the patient, as well as provide doubts about the therapist's sensitivity and competence. Thus, the hopefulness of the therapist must be in the context of a clearly evident full understanding of, and appreciation for, the difficulties of the patient.

Another qualification of the effectiveness of the hopeful communication is that it should not be blind to the possibility that there will be failures, difficulties, frustrations before the goal of, let us say, relief from anxiety is attained. The communication of hopefulness should subsume an implication of ability to overcome the expected difficulties. We have already seen that the effect of a frustration or difficulty is determined by its perceived implications for future goal attainment; this has been illustrated in studies of partial reinforcement effects and of reactions to "you-can-do-better-than-that" kinds of "punishment." Thus, hopefulness with built-in buffers is what is needed, not hopefulness alone. The present argument implies that goals should not be set so high as to assure a failure of such proportions that it almost automatically implies poor expectations for future attainment. Briefly, the practical message is reasonable goals with reasonable expectations of failures that will be overcome.

Most difficult life situations are not beyond hope; the future is often more malleable than imagined. The argument that one needs to be "realistic" (not too hopeful) is literally unsound, since hope refers to the future, which is not yet a reality. It is impossible to be realistic about a non-reality. Hope is a subjective state that can strongly influence the realities-to-come; prophecies are often self-fulfilling.

CHAPTER 10

Hope and Psychosis

If the theory about hope as presented here has any validity, it can be applied to all areas of human endeavor and human problems. The value of such application would be twofold: one, the theory would be tested again; two, some practical benefits might result. But because it is impossible to present in one book an application of the theory to all areas of human endeavor and human problems, I had to choose only one. I decided on severe emotional disturbance or psychosis for several reasons: there is an extensive, relevant research literature; I have done some research on some of the pertinent issues; and the practical values of the approach seem obvious.

The application of the present approach to the problem of severe emotional disturbance is not intended as a total "answer" to the problem. It does not provide answers to such questions as why one person takes the schizophrenic route while another, confronted with the same difficulties, takes a "normal" or "depressive" or "character-disorder" route, or why one shows a given form of schizophrenic behavior or symptoms, while another shows a different one. Thus the present approach should be viewed within a more limited framework. This framework is mainly, but not exclusively, concerned with the secondary effects of using so-called "sick" solutions to the problems of living (Szasz, 1961), but not necessarily with the reasons for an individual's "choosing" that particular way out. Once the individual begins to withdraw, to hallucinate, to communicate poorly with others, to have delusions, there are additional consequences. He perceives that there are difficulties, "sick" behavior, either in himself or in the world about him. He tends to develop schemas of less hopefulness about any improvement in his life situation.

There is much presumptive evidence that the early experience of schizophrenics presented exceedingly difficult problems, often involving relationships with their parents. For present purposes, it is not necessary to choose among the various formulations that have appeared in the literature. All of these formulations indicate that the interpersonal relationships of potential schizophrenics are full of conflicts, ambiguities, inconsistencies, and harshness of a direct or indirect sort. These difficulties tend to have several diverse effects on the person. First, he develops a schema that other people are harsh, rejecting, hostile, demanding, and unsympathetic. Second, he develops a schema that he is worthless, weak, and incapable; and in this schema his own behavior provides little basis for hope. In his relationships with his parents, there is often little that he can do that is at all effective in gaining any important goal. He perceives his own ineffectiveness again and again and therefore develops this hopeless schema about his own actions.

What is the evidence relevant to this formulation? Myers and Roberts (1959) studied, intensively and extensively, families of schizophrenics and families that were similar in social class and other relevant variables. In summarizing their findings about the lowest socioeconomic class, "Class V" in their terminology, they report as follows:

> Presses found among more schizophrenics than neurotics in Class V, such as disorganized homes, parental neglect, lack of personal guidance and control, lack of familial affection, and harsh but inconsistent punishment, seemed conducive to the development of particular types of stress for the patients—feelings of defensiveness, isolation, neglect, rejection and fear. The Class V patients' lack of warm inter-familial feelings or guidance seemed related to their feelings of being lost and uncertain of their goals in life and whether they would achieve them (p. 89).

Myers and Roberts also report that in the lower middle class, the families with schizophrenic children were those who placed the heaviest demands on children, setting very high and often unattainable goals for them, regardless of their ability.

> In contrast, Class III [lower middle class] presses associated more strongly with schizophrenia than neurosis, seemed to give rise to other stresses. At the social level, the patients' anxieties appeared centered upon concern about their failure to realize the high goals set by their mothers and about their lack of respect for their fathers [because of father's general inadequacies and failure in life, and his subordinate role in the home]. Such feelings apparently caused severe guilt because they were contrary to Class III values (p. 90).

Lu (1962) interviewed families in which there was one schizophrenic and one non-schizophrenic child. She found that the parents demanded a higher level of general achievement and assumption of responsibility by the schizophrenic-to-be, and at the same time instilled more submissiveness and emotional dependency on them. The non-schizophrenic siblings had lower, more easily achievable goals set for them and thus could become more independent. On the other hand, the schizophrenics felt they were failures and incompetent, especially when they compared themselves to their siblings.

Bateson, Jackson, Haley and Weakland (1956) have suggested—on the basis of their studies of schizophrenic families—that one situation faced by a youthful schizophrenic-to-be, in his relations with his family, is the so-called "double-bind." Weakland writes (1960):

> 1. In a double-bind situation a person is faced with a significant communication involving a pair of messages, of different level or logical type which are related but incongruent with each other.
>
> 2. Leaving the field is blocked. Such escape, presumably followed by the establishment of more satisfactory communications elsewhere, would be one potential avenue of natural and adequate response. Its unavailability is usually an outcome of dependence on the person (or persons) giving the contradictory messages. . . .
>
> 3. It is therefore important to respond adequately to the communication situation, which includes responding to its duality and contradiction. Two contradicting significant messages mean two incongruent behavioral injunctions because every message instigates behavioral response. . . .
>
> 4. An adequate response is difficult to achieve because of the concealment, denial and inhibition inherent in or added to the basic pair of messages . . . (pp. 376–377).

In summarizing the results of their study of the families of fifteen schizophrenics, Lidz, Cornilison, Fleck, and Terry (1958) state that ". . . our patients were not raised in families which adhered to culturally accepted ideas of causality and meanings, or respected the instrumental utility of their ideas and communications because one or both of the parents were forced to abandon rationality to defend their own precarious ego-structure (p. 315)."

Langner and Michael (1963) studied a cross section of the very diverse population of midtown Manhattan in New York City. Each subject in their study was comprehensively interviewed about any and all types of stresses to which he could have been subjected. Each person then received a score as to the total number of the following types of stresses he had experienced in both childhood and adult life:

1. Parents' poor mental health
2. Childhood economic deprivation

3. Childhood poor physical health
4. Childhood broken home
5. Parents' character negatively perceived
6. Parents quarreled
7. Adult poor health
8. Adult poor interpersonal affiliations
9. Work worries
10. Socioeconomic status worries

It was found that the greater the number of such stresses experienced in early life, in adult life, or in both early and adult life, the greater was the probability that the individual would experience some psychological difficulties later in life, schizophrenia being among these possibilities. It is interesting to note that, contrary to the expectations of those researchers, the particular types of difficulty did not appear to make any difference; the number of stresses was the determining variable. As the authors point out, a large part of the influence of these stresses is a circular, cumulative process of stress leading to more stress.

On the basis of these data, it is difficult to disagree with Arieti's (1959a) conclusions:

> [P]resumptive evidence indicates that a tremendous amount of conflict, tension,and anxiety exists, and has always existed in these families [of schizophrenics]. It does not matter whether the parents are overtly rejecting or overanxious or irrational and paranoid: the result is the same. They offer to the patient an environment saturated with anxiety, an environment where his attempts to grow psychologically will be thwarted (p. 469).

The stresses that lead to schizophrenia and other mental illness can be described at more sociological levels of analysis. It is patent that life in the lower socioeconomic class is more stressful than life in the higher classes. The stresses probably are not as subtle as those of the double-bind, but are embroiled mainly with the sheer difficulty of living. There is less realistic basis for hope, for a sense of movement and growth, for feeling able to cope with the world. And the very difficulty of life makes for cold, harsh attitudes and behavior. Hollingshead and Redlich (1958) found that the rate of occurrence of schizophrenia tripled as they went down the social class ladder. They based their data on an exhaustively thorough study of mental patients in New Haven, Connecticut. In their study of midtown Manhattan, Langner and Michael also found that the rate of psychological disturbance was greater in the lower classes. Leighton, Harding, Macklin, Macmillan, and Leighton (1963) studied in depth a county in the Maritime Provinces of Canada and again determined that lower occupational groups had a higher incidence of psychological disturbance. This class differential was found over and above the effects of the sheer number of stresses that were identified in each person's life.

The schizophrenic, then, has developed a schema that his own actions and communication can have little influence in achieving his goals. It is very important to note that for the purposes of the present theory, the particular source of hopelessness is not crucial. We are concerned here not with the type of disability or handicap that causes the low expectation, but with the circular process whereby the low expectations generalize and become self-strengthening. Thus, the present reasoning could apply even if the causes of the hopelessness were far different from what is proposed above, even if they were, let us say, of genetic origin. Nevertheless, the particular original source of the hopelessness is important in another respect. Any experience or stimulus that has been associated with the primary source is likely to arouse a schema of hopelessness. As will be pointed out, social schemas do in fact appear to have this effect for schizophrenics.

The present theory holds that people are motivated to avoid situations of hopelessness that bear upon major goals, schizophrenics being no exception. Their way of avoiding their completely hopeless situation is to create an autistic world. By so doing, they reduce the importance of real goals and thereby lower anxiety. Lidz and Fleck (1960) conclude that "through altering the world autistically, by changing his perception of himself and others, and by abandoning the logic of his culture, he finds some room for living and some semblance of self-esteem (p. 325)."

As we stated previously, autistic living is not the only solution possible for the problems faced by the schizophrenic. The "choice" of symptoms, however, is beyond the scope of the present theory. We do not pretend to answer the question of why the person does not become extremely neurotic, behaviorally disturbed, or manifest his problem in other symptoms.

The present theory would also predict that the hopelessness of the schizophrenic person would destroy any motivations to achieve goals in the real world. With little hope, there is little basis for actively dealing with the world. In turn, the failure consequent upon the lack of coping only confirms the hopelessness, in turn leading to even more withdrawal. The vicious circle has begun. Again, we quote Lidz and Fleck (1960):

> The thought disorder tends to be self-perpetuating because the patient no longer tests the usefulness of his ideas or behavior for meeting his environment or establishing communication. When the onset of the illness is acute, the abandonment of object relations is often precipitated by fear of loss of control over homosexual or homicidal impulses; and the ensuing panic increases disorganization and interpersonal disorientation (pp. 325–326).

Arieti (1959a) writes of schizophrenics:

> [At the time of puberty] He feels "pushed around," when environmental forces compel him to do things in spite of his detachment. On the one hand, reduction of his experiences in living has made him unprepared, hesitant, awkward, fearful. . . . At times the patient himself is not satisfied with his withdrawal and harbors strong desires to make excursions into life, but every time he tries, he is burdened with anxiety, is awkward and ineffective, and meets defeat. Defeat in turn reinforces his inferiority feelings, and a vicious circle is then perpetuated (p. 473).

Lane and Albee (1963) examined the IQ test scores from the early and late childhood of schizophrenic adults, and found a statistically significant loss between early and late childhood. Control groups of normal children showed little loss and some gains during the same period of time. In this way, the cumulative nature of the deterioration process becomes manifest.

The circular process of withdrawal and failure is often enhanced by the increasing difficulties of the life situation and problems the growing individual must face. Lu (1962) found that the conflicts between parental demands for achievement on the one hand and for dependency and submission on the other become increasingly difficult as the individual grows into adulthood and into more demanding roles in society. Lu found that the breaking point in the development of schizophrenia often occurs when a significant other person suddenly and explicitly expresses the opinion that the potential schizophrenic should assume concrete adult responsibility, or when there is sudden pressure on the person to assume increased adult responsibility because of, say, the death of his father, or when there is a sudden loss of intimate relations with members of a peer group upon whom he has leaned for support. The individual is then confronted by a very explicit, concrete, and awesome test of his abilities.

The research literature in the area of manic-depression is not nearly as extensive as that for schizophrenia. But what little has been done is consistent with the present point of view. Bebring (1953) examined a number of cases of depressive psychosis and writes:

> In all these instances, the individual felt either helplessly exposed to superior power, fatal organic disease, a recurrent neurosis, or to the seemingly inescapable fate of being lonely, isolated, or unloved, or unavoidably confronted with the apparent evidence of being weak, inferior or a failure. In all instances, the depression accompanied a feeling of being doomed, irrespective of what the conscious or unconscious background of this feeling may have been; in all of them a blow was dealt to the person's self-esteem, on whatever grounds each self-esteem may have been founded. From this point of view, depression can be defined as the emotion expression (indication) of a state of helplessness and powerlessness of the ego, irrespective of what may have caused

> the breakdown of the mechanisms which established his self-esteem (p. 24).

Mowrer (1960) gives a vivid description of the depressed patient:

> For hours he may sit virtually motionless; but he would tell you, upon questioning, that far from being unmotivated and comfortable, he is the most miserable and tortured of living mortals. If then asked why he does not *do* something about his discomfort and problems, he will reply (if he bothers to reply) that there is nothing that he *can* do, that he is in utter despair, and that he has no hope of *ever* being able to resolve his difficulties and feel well again. Here the term *hopelessness* is the key to the situation: it is not that the individual is unmotivated, driveless; it is rather that so far as he can see no action he can take will better the situation. So he just sits, immobile and miserable! (p. 197).

Similarly, Becker (1962) argues that depression is the result of loss of self-esteem consequent to the loss of self-concept-validating relationships with other people, when there are few other people or groups to replace the lost support from others. Lichtenberg (1957) presents a more differentiated picture. He theorizes: "We propose that depression be seen as a manifestation of felt hopelessness regarding the attainment of goals when responsibility for the hopelessness is attributed to one's personal defects (p. 519)." He then goes on to differentiate several types of depression in terms of the degree of generality of the goals involved. Arieti (1959b) argues that manic-depressive psychosis results from an excessive sense of guilt and of personal responsibility for any failure.

Grinker *et al.* (1961) had various psychiatric personnel rate patients diagnosed as depressives on many different rating scales. A factor analysis of the ratings produced the following as the first factor: "In general, the high loading of traits express a dismal affect, hopelessness, loss of self-esteem, and a self-image of badness. Shame and guilt feelings seem expressed as primary and secondary reactions to the nuclear concept of unworthiness (p. 135)."

At the same time that the individual is developing these

schemas of hopelessness, he is acquiring a schema that he has anxieties, hallucinations, obsessions, difficulties of all sorts. In other words, the individual perceives his own difficulties and develops schemas about them. This is not to say that all disturbed persons are always aware of their disturbance, but that the perception does occur in many, if not most, cases. The difficulties will come to mean that the individual has increasingly less basis for any hopefulness that he may have had. He is aware of his difficulties as well as of the hopelessness they engender. If he views these symptoms and anxieties as problems, his schema of general hopelessness about solving problems is aroused, and he would be expected to apply it to his own "difficulties." Paradoxically, he may be hopeless about overcoming the sources of his own hopelessness. Even further, however, this process of self-perception and development of schemas may lead him to become so hopeless about his ability to judge, and so uncertain of himself, that he will be uncertain about exactly *how* hopeless to be.

Since the behavior of other people often has been the source of his difficulties, he cannot easily turn to them for help and hope; approaching them might arouse a schema of hopelessness. He may then withdraw into his world of delusion and hallucination. But, in another sense, he cannot easily withdraw from others. Since he is hopeless, he does not feel that he can be judge of his own situation. The evaluation of others becomes paramount, as it does for many people with low self-esteem. Others' reaction may then determine exactly how hopeless to be. Furthermore, his own previous defeats in life may have put him in a lower-status position, reinforcing his lowered self-esteem. His defeats and hopelessness may make him dependent on others for the satisfaction of other—for example, physiological—needs, again lowering his self-esteem. Thus, his dependency on others and sensitivity to their reactions to him have many compound sources.

But the reactions of others to the disturbed person may be based on their own needs, fears, and anxieties, some "legitimate," some "sick." Arieti (1959c) summarized the reaction of a disturbed person's family as follows:

> At some point the deviant person can no longer be seen as normal, and a "break" occurs in the perception of and behavior toward the deviant. At this point a whole range of feelings, attitudes and interactions must, to some extent, be reordered, with consequent strain. The family now contains a "sick" member whom it is difficult to treat normally and who may be unable to fulfill his normal duties. Such a failure in normal living may lead to a demoralized state, and nearly all the family routines may suffer. Attempts to reorganize the family with different roles for the sick member, a new authority situation and new alliances may take place (p. 131).

If the family members reject him, have exaggerated fears of him, mistrust him, refuse to help him, he is bound to be even more hopeless. Even if they take the easy way out and deny that he has any problems at all, that he is just malingering, that if he had "will power" he could "straighten up," he still does not become any more hopeful. This kind of pseudo-hopeful communication also carries with it a denial of the validity of the person's problems. He is not to be helped and, furthermore, his ability even to perceive his own behavior accurately has been doubted by others. They deny he has a problem; "I really have a problem, or can't I even know *that* for certain?"

The individual's degree of hopefulness about overcoming his difficulties may also be influenced by the way he understands the causes of his illness. He may feel hopeless and despondent if he regards his illness as something that has burst upon him, as a terrible calamity that has been imposed on him by a cruel fate. His perception of his illness in these terms may be derived from a variety of culturally learned sources. On the one hand, he may regard his illness as an entity he cannot understand, cannot bring under control of his "will." On the other hand, if he is more psychiatrically knowledgeable, he may blame it on some such factor as his early family experience. He had, and has, no control over this experience and its effects. The more primitive approach, that the illness is caused by fate, and the more sophisticated one, that it is caused by early experience, have in common the attribution of illness to a single "thing" or entity. This approach has been called by Szasz (1961) "modern demonology." In this "illness" point of view, the patient is helpless; his illness is caused by an "it" (Mazer, 1960), about which he can do nothing.

The way in which the patient enters the hospital and his image of it may also influence his hopefulness. The patient learns of the hospital from his community (Greenblatt and Lidz, 1957). This image may vary. He may perceive the hospital as a place for rapid recovery and intensive treatment amid pleasant surroundings, both physical and social. This image is more likely among members of the upper social classes (*cf.* Hollingshead and Redlich, 1958). On the other hand, the hospital may be seen as a fearful place of impoverished living conditions, inadequate and possibly prolonged incarceration. If the latter image prevails, the new patient cannot help but be hopeless since the very conception of mental illness has already made him feel helpless.

The patient's hopefulness is also influenced by his family's attitude toward hospitalization. As Goffman (1961) points out, the patient may perceive hospitalization as an act of betrayal on the part of his family. His relatives seem to be telling him that he is no longer capable of controlling his fate, that he is helpless to handle his own destiny. If the patient does view hospitalization as a betrayal, his confidence in the family as a source of support will deteriorate or be destroyed. The loss of confidence in the family further aggravates his feelings of helplessness and hopelessness. Moreover, the feeling of being "tricked" into going to the hospital validates his helplessness and hopelessness in another way: he finds that his evaluations of other people's behavior have been erroneous.

If he enters the hospital through some agency of society—the police, the courts, a social agency—his humiliation is great. Society has told him that he can no longer take responsibilities for himself.

M. B. Cohen (1957) writes:

> The patient comes to the hospital feeling that he has lost control of the situation. It is reasonable to assume that this is basically true of every patient, regardless of his "diagnosis." He also comes

> feeling that he is a failure; he may blame the world and become quite paranoid, but deep down he feels he is a failure (p. 195).

If the mental patient comes to the hospital at the end of a series of defeats, he could be expected not only to have low self-esteem and a high level of anxiety, but also to be generally unmotivated to act toward achieving goals in the real world. His expectations of achievement are extremely low; he could not be expected to direct his efforts toward goal attainment.

Furthermore, the lack of motivation to act to attain his own goals, even the goal of overcoming the "illness," is enhanced by the very conception of the person as a mental patient. The mental patient is a type of medical patient and, as such, there may be some expectations that are associated with the role of patient. Parsons (1957) has pointed out that medical patients are supposed to be exempted from normal responsibilities, to be passive, dependent, helpless, and loyal to their doctors. These are hardly the traits of a person who is to develop some hope about his own ability to achieve his goals. Sobell and Ingalls (unpublished manuscript) developed a Likert-type questionnaire based on Parsons' description of the role of the patient. They determined that psychiatric patients in a state hospital had about the same conception of their role as medical patients had of theirs. Talbot, Miller, and White (1961) had patients and non-patients rate the concepts *me, baby, child, mental patient, worker, citizen,* and so on, on a semantic differential. One of the dimensions of this differential was responsibility. On this dimension, patients rated the concept *me* similar to their rating of *mental patient.*

Hopelessness may also be communicated within the hospital by the staff's perception of the patient as simply one of the unarticulated mass of patients. Hospitals are total institutions. The arrangements for existence in total institutions differ greatly from the general social arrangement, in which we tend to work, rest, and play in diverse places with diverse groups of people. Goffman (1960) writes:

> First, all aspects of life are conducted in the same place and under the same authority. Second, each phase of the member's daily activity will be carried out in the immediate company of a large batch of others, all of whom are treated alike and required to do the same thing together. Third, all phases of the day's activities are tightly scheduled . . . being imposed from above through a system of explicit formal rulings and a body of officials. Finally, the contents of the various enforced activities are brought together as part of a single over-all rational plan purportedly designed to fulfill the official aims of the institution (p. 451).

The resemblance to the restriction of response as a cause of experimental neurosis is striking. In one hospital, the following was reported (Dunham and Weinberg, 1960):

> Patients have their clothes and their money entrusted to hospital care; they are forbidden to telephone people outside the hospital; their letters are read before being mailed. "Fate has not been kind to me," remarked a patient. "Being locked up in this place gives me the feeling of being hopeless."
>
> In their relationship with the outside world, they learn, too, of their deprivation of some civilian rights and their complete dependence upon their custodians and guardians. The combination of these factors prompted a patient to say, "You soon learn your place, and it's low."
>
> An agitated patient, apprehensive about her belongings wrote the following excited note to the doctors:
>
> "What is going to happen to my things while they're denied me? They are going to be destroyed by some other attendant who doesn't know what she's doing. They are going to be appropriated by this one and that one. Worse still, they will be given as 'rewards' to other inmates; those are the things that lower my morale."
>
> Their freedom restricted and their activities limited, the patients, in the process of institutionalization, learn to become reconciled to these pressures. One patient regarded his adaptation to this situation as follows:
>
> "They don't give you a chance to exert your own will. I'm always taking orders from a number of people. I have to do exactly what they tell me and when. That may be all well if you have no understanding of what goes on, but when you have understanding and know what is going on, I don't see any need of it. The attendant tells the other attendants, 'Don't let them have

their way or you won't be able to control them.' You have to follow orders so you won't get in wrong" (pp. 67–68).

The staff in some cases does not respect the patient as a responsible person, who has integrity and humanness, but sees him as one of "them"—patients beneath dignity. Descriptive of this phenomenon (Dunham and Weinberg, 1960) is the following:

> For in the attendant society it is necessary to know very well "what side one is on," and there is no greater violation of the customs of this group than to treat patients as persons who are entitled to some human considerations. One may treat them humanly but always with the tacit understanding that they must keep their places. It is analogous to one Southern attitude toward the Negro; namely, that he can have everything—education, economic opportunity and work—as long as he knows his place (p. 52).

A tendency may then arise for the ward staff to perceive all of the patient's behavior as evidence of illness, reducing hopefulness even more. Again, from Dunham and Weinberg (1960):

> The point is that the hospital organization has no flexibility in dealing with the unruly behavior of patients; all disapproved behavior is regarded as evidence of abnormality. And yet all such behavior is treated by what Thomas called the "ordering and forbidding" technique and this in an environment where behavior is not expected to be motivated by rational considerations (p. 40).
>
> Time after time in the course of this study situations came to our attention in which patients acted in ways which any reasonable person would judge as appropriate to the situation had it only been outside of the hospital. One female patient who had displayed a situational emotional upset and who was leaving the hospital after a short stay commented in this vein:
>
> "As soon as you start holding your own and trying to stand up for yourself, the attendants say you are disturbed and want to put you down on Ward 7 . . . acutely agitated patients. It hasn't happened to me but it has to some. I'm afraid to say anything but one has to stand up for oneself on some occasions" (p. 48).

The pressure on the patient to accept the staff's definition of them is extreme, since they are completely dependent on the hospital staff and are generally uncertain about themselves. Dunham and Weinberg again:

> Patients realize that conformity is essential for their welfare. They are aware of their few rights, their utter dependence upon others for their well-being, and their inability to resist effectively the hospital rules. Defiant patients are restrained or placed on a "strong" ward, or penalized in other ways (p. 67).

The implications of the administrative processes of the hospital, such as the designation of wards as "open" or "closed," are also of importance here. A feeling of hopefulness or hopelessness may be conveyed to the patients by the very nature of the administrative unit in which they are placed. Belknap (1956) reports from one hospital:

> In organizing their work, the physicians of this group defined their patients in three layers:
> (1) The convalescent and hopeful patients who show improvement and potentiality for discharge by adjustment to the realities of ward life. This adjustment is manifested in orderly conduct, willingness to do ward housekeeping and hospital maintenance chores, and a generally cooperative attitude on the ward.
> (2) The potentially hopeful group of patients who show general tendencies toward adjustment to the ward and are at least passively accommodated to hospital life.
> (3) The patients who have little prospect for improvement, who show little adjustment to the realities of ward life, who are uncooperative, often disturbed or excited, of little use in ward work, and sometimes dangerous to themselves or others (p. 143).

Similarly, wards are sometimes explicitly designated by the staff as "hopeful," "acute," and "hopeless." Such designation cannot help being communicated to the patients. From Dunham and Weinberg (1960):

> Another tradition of the hospital which is particularly pertinent to the doctor's role is the attitude that many patients are incura-

> ble and eventually become chronic hospitalized types. Individual doctors, of course, are aware of recoveries among patients who have been in the hospital for a long time and are familiar with the literature dealing with such cases. But in practice they tacitly accept the idea that all one can do for many patients is to furnish them with good custodial care. This tradition, which pervades all mental hospitals and which the staff doctors eventually if not immediately come to accept, has been strengthened by the Kraepelinian viewpoint concerning the poor prognosis for schizophrenia. About two-thirds of the doctors on the staff operate conceptually within this tradition. The remainder have adopted a psychological dynamic viewpoint toward the development of functional disorders (p. 41).

Staffs tend to concentrate their efforts on the most hopeful wards and to neglect others (Kennard, 1957). A patient placed in a closed ward, where he receives little attention from the staff, may easily perceive that the staff has given up hope for him, and may improve little; while a patient placed in a ward full of therapeutic activity and movement may see that the staff anticipates his upward movement, and respond positively. The self-fulfilling nature of the staff's hopefulness and hopelessness is obvious.

There are many ways in which patients attempt to interpret the staff's expectations of them through ward transfers (Goffman, 1961). If they come to feel that the transfers are made for trivial reasons, not genuinely related to improvement, they may not perceive these transfers as having any significance for their hopefulness, even when the staff sincerely wishes to communicate hopefulness.

It may be argued that it is only in large, crude, obsolete institutions, such as some state hospitals, that patients are relegated to the status of a mass of inferior beings. But the kinds of communications just described appear in the small, therapeutically-oriented hospital as well. A sympathetic staff, working under good therapeutic conditions, may communicate the same feelings to its patients as the staff of a poor one. The good intentions of staff do not necessarily render patients more hopeful. Caudill's (1958) observation of a small hospital bears this out. He found that the psychiatric nurses regarded their patients as rather helpless, as needing care, as dependent upon the hospital for their security. Their feelings toward patients were benign and salutary; they stemmed largely from the professional identity of the nurse, who is trained to "take care of" patients, and accordingly to view the patient as helpless and—in the case of the mental patient—very likely hopeless, outside the hospital. It is therefore not surprising that patients do not regard their contact with the nurses as highly therapeutic. Since the nurses *did* regard their interaction with patients as therapeutic, it becomes evident that nurses and patients do not agree on what constitutes good therapy.

Thus in small hospitals as well as large ones, the expectations of the staff may be communicated to the patients in direct face-to-face interactions, in the overtones of words, in the words themselves, or in any of the many nonverbal ways of communicating. These face-to-face interchanges may reflect an overall atmosphere or culture within the hospital, a set of norms of mental illness that the staff may hold.

The number of ways of communicating hopelessness and hopefulness to patients is too exhaustive and extensive for cataloging. The message comes through such things as the quality and attractiveness of the physical surroundings, the arrangements made for visits from relatives, the assignment of more or fewer hospital personnel to certain patients and wards. Since patients are desperately attempting to discover what to expect from themselves and from their future, everything they experience in the hospital is fraught with meaning.

If the analysis just presented is valid, then schizophrenic patients have very little hopefulness. The hopelessness of emotionally disturbed people is reflected in a variety of ways in their behavior in hospitals: in their withdrawal from anxiety-arousing situations, in their low self-evaluations, in their poor performances on tasks, and in their lack of any drive or internal pressures to overcome failure. Since in the life history of the schizophrenic other people have generally played a somewhat negative role, schizophrenics would also be expected to withdraw from others.

Schizophrenics can be expected to describe themselves as falling short of ideal and normally accepted goals. That patients are aware of the socially acceptable ideals for people in general in our society is indicated by a study by Kogan and Kogan reported by Edwards (1957). They obtained the judgments of the social desirability of items from the interpersonal checklist of 105 skid row, alcoholic, and tuberculosis patients and from forty-six neuropsychiatric patients. Their ratings correlated .94 and .95 with ratings given by college students. It is not surprising, therefore, that patients rate themselves low. Sperber and Spanner (1962) found that the correlation between the social desirability of an item on a personality inventory and the probability of endorsement was lower for patients than for normals. Taylor (1959) found that the correlation between patients' judgments of social desirability of an item on the Minnesota Multiphasic Personality Inventory (MMPI) and their attribution of the item to themselves was only .36, much lower than the correlation for normal populations as cited by Edwards (1957). Rapaport (1958) gave patients the MMPI first under standard instructions and then under ideal-self instructions. The results showed marked discrepancies between the patients' actual-self descriptions and their ideal-self descriptions. Grayson and Olinger (1957) also found such discrepancies. Cromwell, Rosenthal, Shakow and Zohn (1961) found that schizophrenic patients perceived less than normals that they could control their own fate. This perception was measured by the locus of control scale (*cf.* Lefcourt, 1966).

Schizophrenics manifest their hopelessness in a low level of motivation to perform on tasks, with resulting poor performances. This low level of performance has been found in a variety of studies. It should be pointed out that at least some, if not many, of the studies reported below were conducted in large state hospitals, some of them in the era preceding the present shift to more enlightened practices, so that the hopelessness might have been greater than it is under present circumstances.

In a classic paper, Hunt and Cofer (1944) examined the literature dealing with the poor performance of schizophrenic patients in a variety of tests. They concluded that the poor performance of the patients was the result of a motivational deficit rather than the result of any organic deterioration or any intrinsic inability to relate to the world the way that others do. As stated in Proposition I, this motivational deficit can be manifested in a number of ways. The person may not direct his efforts to achieve the goals appropriate to the situation and consequently may attend to irrelevancies in the task confronting him. He may simply think about something other than the situation before him. Or, if he does direct some effort to the task, he may find some rigid, stereotyped way of responding, so that he does not exert any additional effort in finding new or better ways of reacting. This stereotyping may then lead him to be indifferent to changes in the situation, to perseverate inappropriately.

This motivational interpretation of the schizophrenic's deficit encompasses other interpretations of the same sorts of data. For example, Buss and Lang (1965) maintain that the most parsimonious interpretation of deficit is that the schizophrenics are more easily disturbed, that they are unable to continue to attend to the relevant stimuli in a situation, that they are more susceptible to interference from other nonrelevant stimuli. However, in trying to explain why they are more distractible than normals, Buss and Lang rely specifically on a neurological deficiency. However, these researchers do not present any data to show that this neurological deficiency is more prevalent in schizophrenics than in normals.

Shakow (1962) argues that a schizophrenic cannot long maintain a segmental set—a set to direct his behavior to an appropriate goal. Other sets divert him. Shakow's argument is that the schizophrenic avoids certain kinds of anxieties by reacting more to peripheral stimuli, and by this means tries to satisfy more infantile needs. He presents no data, however, to support the idea that infantile needs are being satisfied. Thus, although Buss and Lang and Shakow all observe that schizophrenics cannot long keep themselves oriented toward a goal, they do not interpret this observation in terms of the relatively simple notion that the schizophrenics' failure is the result of low motivation. In the present formulation, their lower motivation results from their low hope of attaining almost any goal, a consequence of their history of failures and defeats.

There are a number of studies that support the motivational interpretation of schizophrenics' poor performances. In a series of sessions, Hunt (1936) had both normal and schizophrenic subjects perform a variety of tasks, such as dealing cards, sorting cards, substituting numbers and letters. After the first session, Hunt showed each subject his norms on, say, addition, and asked the subject whether he could better that. He was then given a test again. Hunt interviewed the subjects about how they felt and about what they were thinking during the tasks. Then he coded their replies in terms of the type of preparation for the tasks, both before and after he showed them their first set of scores. Schizophrenics were less likely than normals to report that they tried to outdo their previous performances, and that they wanted to do well; they were more likely to say that they were willing to perform better but "did not plan," that they were preoccupied, indifferent, or even antipathetic. About the actual performances, schizophrenics reported less than normals that they were pushing themselves to the limit; schizophrenics were more likely than normals to say that they were indifferent or grudging about their work, and that they were preoccupied with incidents irrelevant to the tasks, with problems, issues, and so on. In simplistic terms, the schizophrenics simply were not involved.

Huston, Shakow, and Riggs (1937) rated schizophrenics for their cooperativeness during a reaction-time study, and obtained a negative correlation between reaction time and cooperativeness. The schizophrenics who "cared" were much quicker. In a second part of the study, the subjects were to react to a yellow stimulus that was preceded sometimes by a red stimulus, sometimes by another yellow one. Compared to normals, the least cooperative patients showed a slower reaction time to the yellows that came after the reds than to those that followed the yellows. This difference was interpreted to be an effect of perseveration, or lack of sensitivity to changes in the environment. In a third part of the study, the procedure was changed to compare the patients' performance when warnings of the stimulus were presented at regular intervals to performance when they were presented at irregular intervals. The patients did not show better performances in the regular-interval procedure than in the irregular, whereas the normals did. The patients were not reacting to the environmental changes. Moreover, the patients did not do as well as the normals in the irregular periods, apparently because they could not get prepared and maintain their state of readiness. Rodnick and Shakow (1940) also found that in a reaction-time study normals showed more discrimination between conditions of regular and irregular warning intervals than did schizophrenics.

Rickers Ovsiankina (1937a) watched normals and schizophrenics while they were waiting in a room full of puzzles, toys, and games. While the normals actively worked with the puzzles, the schizophrenics only glanced at them. If a schizophrenic actually handled one of the puzzles, he appeared to "play" with it, while the normals appeared to be trying to, let us say, solve it. In another study (1937b), she gave normal and schizophrenic subjects some tasks that had different goals and some that were repetitious. She interrupted some of the goal-oriented tasks and put the subjects to work on repetitious ones, then left the room in order to observe the subjects from an adjacent room. The normals tended to grumble at being interrupted and to resume the goal-oriented tasks while schizophrenics tended neither to grumble nor to resume.

Malamud and Palmer (1938) gave psychotics the Stanford-Binet and examined the scatter of the scores on the subtests. They interpreted the scatter as a function of conation. "[Directive control of thought] is the application in the process of certain conative adjustments, mental attitudes, and motivational sets which facilitate adaptive thinking (p. 78)."

This conclusion is based, in part, on their finding that the schizophrenics did better on the vocabulary test—a test in which the subjects depended only on their memories and in which the experimenter kept the subject focused on the task because of the short trials. On the other hand, they performed more poorly on the weight-judging test, primarily because they seemed to become concerned with irrelevancies and to lose sight of the goal. They performed relatively poorly on the three-word task, which required them to integrate the words meaningfully. Their relatively poor performance on the absurdities test seemed a result of their inattention to essential aspects of the stimuli.

Rubin (1941) drew parallel conclusions after giving the Wechsler-Bellevue Scale to schizophrenics and normals. Here, too, the schizophrenics' verbal scores were higher than their other scores. He states that "the tests which do not hold up in schizophrenics require initiative in seeking and achieving an unknown goal (object assembly), abstracting ability (similarities), and speed in forming new associations (digit symbol). The tests which hold up tend to be largely reproductive in nature (p. 100)."

Wegrocki (1940) gave schizophrenics a variety of intellectual tasks, such as interpreting proverbs. He summarized his findings: ". . . *all* the high error score schizophrenics manifested some type of behavior disorder in the test situation, some showing a lack of ability to focus upon a problem, and others manifesting a powerful motivational arrest, while still others, although showing neither of these disturbances, exhibited a marked lack of appropriateness ([p. 50] italics supplied)." Wegrocki reports that the schizophrenics tended to be dominated by a particular set throughout the tests; that they appeared not to organize their thoughts because of preoccupation with irrelevancies in the situation, because of the interfering effect of internally preoccupying fantasies, or because of volitional inhibition, a total lack of drive and interest in the problem situation.

A number of the early studies cited above of poor performance of schizophrenics on intellectual tasks were interpreted as indicating that they tended to be nondirective in their efforts and inattentive toward the appropriate goal in the situation. More recently, this interpretation received more unequivocal verification from Chapman (1956). He found that the inferior performance of schizophrenics on concept-learning tasks was the result of their attending to irrelevancies in the situation. Normal and schizophrenic subjects were to sort cards containing four figures. The sorting was to be guided by three four-figured standard cards. One figure on each standard card was arbitrarily designated by instructions as correct for sorting; the other figures were incorrect. Each response card had one figure which showed some commonality with the correct figure on one standard card. In addition, some of the cards shared common concepts with incorrect figures on a second standard card. The schizophrenic group, much more than the normal, used the incorrect commonalities as a basis for sorting. Again, the schizophrenics would not focus on the main goal in the situation.

The failure of schizophrenics to maintain a set in the face of distractions was also reported on in the early studies. This finding has been verified by Zahn, Shakow, and Rosenthal (1961), who gave their subjects a reaction-time test. They independently varied the intertrial interval and the preparation time (the time from the ready signal to the initial stimulus). They found that a long preparation time led to longer reaction times than did a short time, but that the variation in the intertrial interval did not influence performance. The ready signal effectively brought the subjects back into the field, but they would not stay in it for a long period.

Another interpretation of the schizophrenics' poor performance in the earlier studies was that they did not vary their behavior in accord with changes in the environment. Since they were less highly motivated, they were less likely to have chosen the path with the highest probability of success. This perseverative trend has recently been demonstrated more conclusively in a number of studies. Hutchinson and Azrin (1961) instructed schizophrenics to pull a knob to get candy and cigarettes. On each successive day that the subjects performed, the ratio of rewards to pulls would go down, leading the patients to respond faster and faster. However, even on days when the ratio was not changed, they would increase in speed of response. In a similar manner, Crumpton (1963) found that schizophrenics, compared to normals, were more apt to persist in making a response even after the situation had changed so that the response was no longer adaptive. For example, subjects were first rewarded each time they guided a toy car across a map on the same route. Then they were punished for following this route. The schizophrenics were slower to change than the normals. Jost (1965) had schizophrenics and normals state their levels of aspiration on a series of trials on a Rotter Aspiration Board. He found that the schizophrenics were less likely than the normals to shift their levels of aspiration up after a success and down after a failure.

In short, there is ample evidence that schizophrenics do not cope with situations but take the "easy way out." Coping requires some hope that their efforts will be successful—and hope about success in the practical world of non-schizophrenics is what the schizophrenics lack. More than that, this hopelessness of schizophrenics would be most apparent after they have failed in a given task. It would be expected that they would be more likely to give up, to withdraw, since they would have little hope of reversing the failure. Rosenzweig (1945) gave schizophrenics and normals two jig-saw puzzles in a competitive situation, allowing them to complete one puzzle but interrupting the other in a manner indicating to the subjects that they had failed. The subjects then were asked which they would like to do again; the schizophrenics preferred the successful puzzle while the normals preferred the failed one.

If schizophrenics thus withdraw from situations of failure, their performance level on a series of tasks could be expected to go down as a consequence of failure on their first experience with the tasks. Wilensky (1952) gave some schizophrenics and normals a series of tasks and led them to fail early in the series. Others were permitted to go on with the tasks. The schizophrenics who failed performed less well than those who did not fail; the normals who failed showed a smaller decrement. Webb (1955) gave some subjects the similarities test of the Wechsler-Bellevue Scale twice, telling them before they worked on it the second time that they had failed badly on the first attempt. These subjects' performance deteriorated in comparison to a control group that had worked on another task in between the first and second administration, confirming that schizophrenics do more poorly after failure. With little hope of overcoming their failure, they stop directing their behavior toward the achievement of the goal.

Why, then, has success not led to higher performances? The answer lies partly in the history of failure. As was pointed out in the theoretical discussion, the probability of the arousal of a schema is a function of the number of experiences the person has had consistent with it. If this proposition is valid, then the schizophrenics—or mental patients in general—would be less likely to develop schemas of success. A series of successes is less likely to lead to the arousal of a schema of hopefulness among schizophrenics than among normals. It is the arousal of such a schema that would lead a person to react to one success by expecting further successes and therefore being motivated to achieve them. However, as will be pointed out, it is not impossible for schizophrenics to develop such schemas. The development of such schemas appears to require a more concentrated, intense experience, usually with social supports.

Another reason for the relative ineffectiveness of success in leading schizophrenics to higher levels of performance is the nature of the communication of success in the experimental situation. Often, the experimenter will tell the subject, "You're doing fine." A communication of this sort does not necessarily imply that the subject is expected to improve.

In summary, then, there is sufficient evidence to conclude that the schizophrenic's poor performance on tasks is, in large part, a matter of motivational deficit.

The hopelessness of schizophrenics, as pointed out, appears to stem in part from the treatment they have received from other people. Accordingly, it would be expected that any experience in which the focus is on social stimuli would arouse schemas of hopelessness and preclude active engagement with the situation. Whiteman (1954) gave schizophrenics and normals a verbal analogies test and a picture reasoning test and had them select cards that illustrated some social feature. The normals did better than the schizophrenics on all tasks, but the greatest disparity was on the social tasks. This decrement in the social learning task was evident when the scores on the first two tasks were controlled. Davis and Harrington (1957) gave schizophrenics and normals a task of selecting an example of a specified category, going from broader to narrower categories. Some of the categories concerned humans, others did not. The schizophrenics did relatively more poorly on the human tasks than on the non-human, while the normals showed no difference in their performance on both kinds of tasks.

Johannsen (1961) gave schizophrenics and normals a repeated double alternation problem, with feedback on their performance that came either from an experimenter in the room who said only "right" or "wrong," or from a light that indicated right or wrong. The schizophrenics did worse in the experimenter condition than in the light condition; for normals, the reverse was true. Note that the experimenter neither encouraged them to do better if they were wrong nor instructed them to make the right response. Brodsky (1963) gave patients and normals five sorting tasks. Three of them contained pictures of people and concerned aggression, authority, and sexual identification. The other two tasks involved geometric figures or impersonal aggression (lightning). The schizophrenics did worse on the social tasks than on the impersonal tasks, and they did worse than the normals did on the social tasks.

The withdrawal of schizophrenics in social situations is also indicated in a study by Schooler and Spohn (1960) who found that some schizophrenics who performed well in judging the relative lengths of lines when alone deteriorated in their judgments when they were placed in an Asch-type situation (in which they were exposed to others' erroneous judgments). They neither conformed to the group's erroneous judgments nor did they make accurate judgments. Rather, they simply made errors that were different from the group's. They neither reacted appropriately to the physical stimuli nor sought to determine what the stimuli were by referring to their peer group.

If social situations arouse schemas of hopelessness in schizophrenics, they would be expected to avoid interactions with other people. Schooler (1963) found that schizophrenics, more than normals, disliked working with another person in situations in which there was an exchange of both positive and negative affect. This avoidance of close relationships with others is also reflected in Gill's (1963) finding that schizophrenics made fewer conforming responses than normals did in an Asch-type situation. However, part of this withdrawal from others may be attributable to something more than a general schema of hopelessness. It may be due to a more specific schema of hopelessness about being able to cope with and respond to others.

The schizophrenics' hopelessness about interpersonal relations is a function of factors stemming from both their past and their present situations. In hospital settings, their withdrawal may result in part from their perception that other patients are generally anxious, hostile, unpredictable in behavior (which makes them difficult for anyone, let alone other patients). Singer and Feshbach (1962) found that psychotic patients attributed more anxiety and hostility to persons described as having been mentally ill than to persons not so described. If the schizophrenic's withdrawal is partly a function of the anxious, hostile, or unpredictable behavior of another patient, patients should prefer to socialize with patients who are healthier, less anxious and more predictable. Schooler and Spohn (1960) showed that healthier patients were more likely to receive social overtures from other patients than were the more regressed ones. The latter tended in fact to be rebuffed. The patients told the researchers that among the reasons for this preference for the healthier patients was that the latter were more likely to respond reasonably.

In short, then, there is much evidence that the poor performance of schizophrenics, especially in social situations, is more likely due to low expectations of goal attainment than to more complex factors, such as neurological disorders.

Obviously, not all schizophrenics have had equally hopeless lives before entering hospitals. Thus far, we have ignored these differences, mostly for reasons of exposition. Now we will turn to the issue of variation in the degree of hopelessness. We can approach this issue through a differentiation among schizophrenics that has been given a number of names: good *versus* poor premorbid; acute *versus* chronic; reactive *versus* process. Heron (1962) examined all of these different dichotomous descriptions and concluded that all these formulations of the dichotomy refer, more or less, to the same underlying dimension. Johannsen, Freidman, Leitschuk, and Ammons (1963) found extremely high correlations among three methods of classifying patients: (1) acute–chronic, the former having been hospitalized for under six months and having had no hospitalization prior to one year before the study; (2) high and low social competence, as measured by the Phillips scale (Zigler and Phillips, 1962); and (3) process–reactive schizophrenia as measured by clinician's judgments.

This dimension appears to be correlated with differences in a multiplicity of differing situations, and has been shown to have more predictive validity than the classical descriptions in terms of patterns of symptomology. For present purposes, the dichotomy will be referred to in terms of good *versus* poor premorbid, usually, but not always, as defined by the Phillips scale. The Phillips scale is intended as a measure of a patient's premorbid level of social competence; but we can as easily and as accurately call it an index of hopefulness. The raw material used for scoring is derived from the patient's case history rather than from any questionnaire. There are six variables that are taken as indices of social competence: age, intelligence, education, occupation, employment history, and marital status. The categories of each variable and the order of variables from low to high are as follows:

1. Age: 24 and below; 25–44; 45 and above.

2. Intelligence (IQ obtained on a standard intelligence test): 84 or less; 85–115; 116 and above.

3. Education: none or some grades; finished grade school, some high school, or high school; some college or more.

4. Occupation: unskilled or semiskilled; skilled and service; clerical and sales; professional or management.

5. Employment History: usually unemployed; seasonal, fluctuating, frequent shifts; part-time employment; regularly employed.

6. Marital Status: single, separated, divorced, remarried, widowed, single continuous marriage.

Although the scale is termed "a measure of social competence," the variables it comprises permit one to describe the scale in slightly different terms. The last four variables can be regarded as measures of an individual's level of success in life, of his economic, marital, and educational status. Whether he is competent or not is a matter of inference, since the authors of the scale assumed that the attainment of such status is the result of personal ability; it may or may not be. A high level of educational attainment may be the result of high parental socioeconomic status. A high level of economic attainment may also be ascribed to parental social class. Marital status is, obviously, also a matter of the partner's competence and motivation. Maintenance of continuous employment may, especially of older people, be a matter of the business cycle, local economic conditions, and other variables.

The arguments for including age in the scale are unclear. It is hard to see how a long-term repressed schizophrenic can score higher simply by having vegetated a few more years. Intelligence comes closest to a measure of competence, but the scale is purported to be more than a measure of IQ. Furthermore, IQ is affected by economic attainment, educational level, and other influences.

The scale thus appears to measure an individual's success in achieving socially valued goals. But, as Kogan and Kogan (1957) have shown, patients do not differ from normal in their perceptions of the valued ways and attributes of our society. Thus, it is implicit that scores on the scale are correlated with the schizophrenics' perception of their own level of success or failure as measured by society's standards.

The present theory is not diagnostically directed nor concerned with why some people have a poor premorbid history. Whatever the original cause of this type of schizophrenia, the concern here is with its secondary consequences. If the disability leads to a failure early in life, as it does for poor premorbids, then the cyclical process of failure begetting more failure has a long time in which to occur. The end product would be a high state of hopelessness among poor premorbids.

On the other hand, the good premorbids have had a history of some success in life prior to the onset of illness. They have some basis for having hopeful schemas, and there has been less opportunity for the circular process of failure enhancing failure to operate. If with the Phillips scale the criterion for the dichotomy is chronicity *versus* sudden onset of schizophrenia, the reasoning is the same. A long period in a mental hospital is hardly a basis for a hopeful schema; however, the period of success prior to onset would be the basis for a hopeful schema for the acutes. Thus, it would be expected that poor premorbids would be more hopeless than good premorbids, and that good premorbids would be more like normals. Generally, the data support these expectations.

Rodnick and Garmezy (1957) cite a study by Ussing, who gave Thematic Apperception Tests to both good and poor premorbids. The good premorbids told more stories involving strivings for independence; the poor premorbids told more stories of a dependent person making no effort to alter his situation or actively to seek help.

Long (1961) gave chronic and acute schizophrenics a task of placing marbles in correct boxes. He praised some, told others that they were doing poorly, and made no comment at all to others. He found some, nonsignificant tendency for the acutes receiving the failure comments to increase performance more than the other subjects did. The acutes evidently felt somewhat hopeful of overcoming their deficiency in performances. Long then gave his subjects a task of choosing the correct button after each of several lights went on. The acute schizophrenics who had been criticized on the first task performed better on the second task than did those who had been praised or told nothing. The different instructions had no effect on the performance of the chronic schizophrenics. The acute who failed had more expectation of being able to compensate for poor performance on the first task by showing the experimenter that he could do well on the second.

The greater tendency of poor premorbids to avoid painful experiences or failure situations is indicated in a study by Alvarez, cited by Rodnick and Garmezy (1957). First, subjects rated twelve facial photographs of men and women in order of preference. Then each subject was presented with four of the six pictures in his middle range of preference and had to choose one of two possible answers the persons in the pictures had given to a series of questions. The subject was told that he was wrong on two pictures, right on two. He was not presented with the remaining two. Then the subject was asked to rate the preferences for all six pictures. The poor premorbids showed more decrement of preference on the "wrong" picture than did the good premorbids.

Another way this greater hopelessness of poor premorbids could be expressed is by their tending to avoid situations of interpersonal significance. Baxter and Becker (1962) gave good and poor premorbids the parent-child cards of the Thematic Apperception Test (TAT) and measured their tendency to avoid the test. This measure was based on the subjects' proneness to avoid talking objectively about the figures in the cards, to produce little verbally, to produce stories with no affective content, and to displace persons in time and space in the stories. There was more avoidance by the poor premorbids than by the good.

Rodnick and Garmezy (1957) cite a study by Mollet in which he found that poor premorbids tended to omit stimulus figures from their stories, to show errors of personalized intrusions, and to perseverate story contents. Garmezy and Rodnick also cite findings by Ussing that good premorbids produce more on heterosexual TAT cards, produce more in general when working on the cards, and reflect fewer personal inadequacies in the story content.

Moriarty and Kates (1962) matched normals and the two types of schizophrenics on conceptual ability in formal tasks. The subjects then worked on concept learning, using cards portraying interpersonal situations. The poor premorbids made more redundant card choices, needed a greater number of cards per concept, and took more time than the good premorbids, who, in turn, were less competent than the normals.

Dunn (1964) gave schizophrenics a mosaic task, telling some that their mosaic would be shown to "others" as part of a design made by a group of patients. Some were told that their mosaics would be shown individually. He also told some subjects in each of the above groups that their showings were to be formally evaluated; some that no such evaluation would occur. All the subjects then filled out rating scales of attraction to the situation after having worked on the mosaics. The poor premorbids rated the group situations lower than did the good; the poor also tended to rate evaluative situations lower than nonevaluative.

Clearly, then, the evidence indicates that good and poor premorbids differ greatly in their level of hopefulness, especially with respect to social situations. Although the present theory does not purport to explain why some people become disturbed early in life while others become so later, there can be little doubt that these groups differ in their degree of hopefulness.

CHAPTER 11

Hope for Mental Patients

If the reason for the poor performance of patients on most tasks is, in large part, motivational, it should in principle be possible to improve performance by raising their motivational levels by reducing their hopelessness and, as a concomitant, increasing their hopefulness. Such increases in hopefulness are not easily accomplished; but they are not impossible. The therapist may take three possible avenues: the first depends on the schizophrenic's susceptibility to the influence of pressure from persons in positions of authority; the second depends on a prolonged series of successes, which might create a new, hopeful schema for the schizophrenic; the third is not so much a matter of increasing hopefulness as of taking advantage of the one "hopeful" schema that schizophrenics generally have, that is, of "successful" withdrawal from painful situations. The schizophrenic typically does have a high expectation of attaining the goal of withdrawing psychologically (and, perhaps, physically) from any difficulty. This withdrawal has been the most characteristic theme of his life—so that he has a strong schema of being able to withdraw from difficulties.

Accordingly, schizophrenics would be expected to perform well in situations in which the adaptive response is to escape or withdraw. One such situation is sheer physical pain. Pain not only gives rise to avoidance or escape schemas, but also demands the attention of the person so strongly that his tendency to withdraw from the situation is overcome. Thus, the schizophrenic must attend at first, but then can avoid pain.

Pascal and Swenson (1952) gave schizophrenic subjects a complex discriminative reaction-time task. At the end of the four trials, some of them were subjected to a loud, annoying sound until they reacted. These subjects showed a marked increase in performance as compared to those who did not hear the noise. Cohen (1956) gave schizophrenics a series of three tasks in which they had to move a handle in the direction indicated by a stimulus. After a training period during which they were encouraged and praised, half the subjects received a shock until they made the right response. The other half simply responded to the stimuli. The shock group did better than the others, these differences increasing with time. In a reaction-time study, Rosenbaum, Mackavey, and Grisell (1957) told normal and schizophrenic subjects to depress a key on a signal from a light and to release it as soon as possible at the sound of a buzzer. Half of each group was given a shock through the key as soon as the buzzer sounded. Before the shock condition was introduced the patients were slower than the normals, but the patients who then received shock improved in performance until they were at the same level as the normals. The schizophrenics' poor performances thus could be raised under the appropriate conditions.

In a concept-formation study, Cavanaugh (1958) gave half of the schizophrenic subjects and half of his normals a dose of painful white noise until they had successfully completed each item on the test. The other half of each group were simply informed that they had not achieved the correct solution. The schizophrenics who received noise did better than those who didn't and even approached the level of performance of the normals.

In another reaction-time study, Lang (1959) had both normal and schizophrenic subjects which he then divided into five experimental conditions: (1) control (no painful noise was presented); (2) escape (nearly painful noise was turned on with the critical stimulus and off by a response); (3) excitation (the noise was turned on for an arbitrary period after the critical stimulus); (4) avoidance (the subjects could avoid the noise by reacting quickly enough); and (5) information (the noise was presented at a low intensity a short period after the critical stimulus). The normals did not show any condition differences, but the patients in the escape, excitation, and information conditions did significantly better than the controls, while the avoidance subjects did somewhat better, but not significantly. The effects of the stimulation appear to be partly the result of its attention-holding quality (in the excitation and information conditions), and partly a result of withdrawal in the face of pain (in the escape condition). The nonsignificant results in the avoidance condition may be attributed to the fact that the subjects could avoid the noise even if they delayed their response up to their median response on the warm-up trials.

In sum, there is ample evidence that schizophrenics' performances are increased if their inattentiveness is overcome by some very strong stimulation and if the performances demand behavior consistent with a schema of avoidance. It is interesting to note that in the Rosenbaum *et al.*, Cavanaugh, and Lang studies, the patients did as well as the normals under the proper conditions. This equality confirms Hunt and Cofer's (1944) argument that the relatively poor performances of patients is a result of motivational deficit, rather than of an intrinsic inability. And, of course, these data conform to the present theory in that the schizophrenic has a high expectancy of being able to withdraw "successfully." In each of the studies, the experimenter told the subjects exactly how to avoid the pain, making the way out obvious. Furthermore, it is noteworthy that all but one of the studies used reaction-time tasks, which place a minimal demand for goal-oriented, complex behaviors over a relatively long period of time. Meeting such a demand would entail an ability to withstand the *en route* failures and frustrations attendant on any goal-oriented behavior. It is doubtful that the schizophrenic would improve as readily in performances on the more complex tasks.

The tendency of schizophrenics to learn easily to avoid a pain can be used therapeutically. Lovaas, Schaeffer, and Simmons (1965) gave two schizophrenic children an electric shock if they showed some pathological behavior or if they did not approach an adult. They quickly learned to escape shock by stopping the pathological behavior and by approaching adults. They also learned to avoid the shock, since they continued to behave in these positive ways even during extinction trials. However, after a number of sessions, they reverted to their withdrawn behavior. But if their reversion led to another shock, they returned to the more positive behavior.

In short, the data show that schizophrenics can react better if the behavioral demands of a situation are clear, if the stimuli are strong enough to force attention, and if the demands fit the schizophrenic's schema of withdrawal.

A second way to stimulate schizophrenics' hopefulness and higher performance is to rely on their low self-estimates and their consequent susceptibility to influence from authoritative other people. In the studies cited in the previous chapter concerning schizophrenics' reactions to other people, the other people were people of equal status—other patients. Suppose, however, the other people were of higher status than the patients. The patients' low self-esteem would lead them to accept the direction and influence of these others, presumably. The patient may have such low self-esteem that he is unable even to know, for example, how right or wrong he is in a given line of action.

The schizophrenic's lack of conformity in the studies cited in the previous chapter may be due not only to the peer-group aspect of the situation, but to the fact that no one was actually directing the patient to act in a specific way. The patient was not told exactly what to do. He was simply presented with certain physical and social stimuli. His reactions to them were his own decision, and, with his tendency to be hopeless, there is small wonder that he could not develop an appropriate reaction. It will be recalled that in the pain-avoidance experiments, the experimenter told the subjects how they could avoid the pain—and they did so.

It would then be expected that schizophrenics would conform more in situations in which they were low in status and in which they were told by a person of higher status exactly what to do. Janis and Rife (1959) administered a persuasibility test to adolescent mental patients. In the first session of the study, each patient was brought to the examiner's office and, there, filled out an opinion questionnaire, read five persuasive articles, and then answered the questions again. One week later the patients were brought back to the examining room. They read five articles that took positions opposite from those at the first session. The subjects again answered the questions. It is important to note that the messages were given to them by a high-status person, the examiner, and were quite explicit in what they advocated. The findings were that the patients conformed more than a group of high school students. Since Janis and Rife also found that mental patients score lower in self-esteem, this finding is in line with the present theory. Furthermore, they found a .66 correlation ($p. < .01$) between self-esteem and persuasibility.

In Janis and Rife, the material in the persuasibility test was directly and overtly intended to persuade. However, if the patient is presented with a message from a type of person who has, in the patient's past experience, been a powerful and directive person, the persuasive intent of the message need not be made obvious for it to be effective. Hypothesizing thus, Clarke (1964) had his schizophrenic and normal subjects make choices between pairs of vocations in terms of which vocation they would recommend to a boy. They then learned of the choices that were made by a cold, domineering mother for her son and then made their choices again. The schizophrenics, more than the normals, changed their choices toward the mother's choices.

If schizophrenics are susceptible to influence from persons higher in some hierarchy than themselves, this influence can be used to increase their expectations of achievement of their goals. Whether the influence leads to the acquisition of a new hopeful schema or to the arousal of a previously acquired more hopeful one would of course depend on the schizophrenic's previous history. In the studies to be described in this section, it is not possible to distinguish between acquisition and arousal, although later, in the examination of the difference between good and poor premorbids, this distinction will be somewhat easier to make. In any case, it does not make a great deal of difference for the present theory whether the effects reported below are interpreted in terms of acquisition or arousal.

Stotsky (1957) gave schizophrenics a reaction-time task and a pegboard task. Between sets of trials, some of the subjects met with their therapists, who encouraged them and urged them to do better. Only therapists who said they had a positive relationship with the patients were used. A control group simply had a rest period between the sets of trials. After the break, the encouraged group improved their performance on both the reaction-time and pegboard tasks more than the control group did.

Benton, Jentsch, and Wahler (1960) gave schizophrenics a visual choice reaction-time task. After a baseline rate had been established some of the subjects were told:

> This time I want to see just how very fast you can make the reactions. . . . You should do better than you did last time. This time after each reaction, I will tell you in hundredths of a second just how long it took you to react. Try to adjust reactions

so as to continually do better. Knowing how you are doing each time should help you. Let's have a few warm-ups first (p. 27).

During actual performances, the experimenter gave the subjects accurate feedback, saying "too slow," or "OK" (if there was no change), or "good" or "fine" (if there was improvement) while urging the subject to do even better. A control group was simply told to work the task again. The experimental group improved much more than the control group.

D'Alessio and Spence (1963) gave normal and schizophrenic subjects a task of placing brass pins in holes as fast as possible. In the intervals between trials, all of the subjects were reminded of the instructions and the proper procedure of placing the pins. In addition, the experimenter encouraged half the subjects during the intervals with such comments as, "That's good," "Fastest I've seen," "That's still fine!" *"See if you can't go even faster next time"* (italics supplied). Furthermore, the subjects who received the encouragement were treated by the experimenter in a warmer and friendlier manner than the others. Both the normals and the schizophrenics did better when encouraged than when not. It should be noted that the encouragement was very specific; at the same time that they were encouraged, the subjects were told exactly what to do.

Wing and Freudenberg (1961) gave patients manual tasks in a group situation. Some of the time, the experimenter-therapist supervised "passively"—just took care of the allocation of work and made certain it was done properly. Some of the time, the supervision was "active"—encouraging the slower, poorer workers, praising the others, urging them to do better. The patients were divided into two groups; both groups received passive supervision for two weeks. Then, for a period, one group received active, encouraging supervision. The actively supervised group increased markedly in level of performance; the other remained constant. Then both groups received passive supervision, with the result that the previously actively treated group reverted to the other group's level. Then both groups received active supervision and both groups' rates of production increased. The complete dependency on the encouragement of supervisors is striking, but it could be expected on the basis of the relative absence of any hopeful schemas in the patients.

The previous chapter pointed out that the schizophrenic's characteristic reaction to failure is lowered performance. However, the patients' failures were communicated to them in such a way that they were given little hope of overcoming them. They simply discovered that they were "wrong" and had not achieved a goal. Since there is little basis of hope in their own schemas for their assuming that they could overcome failure, it is no wonder that they deteriorated. Suppose, however, that the schizophrenics fail but are also told how to overcome their failure and are encouraged to do so by some person in authority. According to the present theory, and to the data just cited, they would be expected to improve. This reasoning helps to explain some of the studies cited below, in which it was found that "positive reinforcement" did not lead to an increased level of performance or did not lead to as much increase as did "negative." Some "positive reinforcements" do not involve communicating expectations of improvement to the subjects. The subject may be told simply that he is doing well. This might very well mean that he is doing well enough. Without a schema of hopefulness, the schizophrenics would not go on from this point to expect to achieve even higher goals. They are doing well enough in the eyes of the experimenter and that is what matters. Conversely, telling the subject that he has failed, but can be expected to improve, is quite a different matter from telling him only that he has failed.

This line of reasoning was tested by Losen (1961). Schizophrenics and normals were given arithmetical reasoning and digit span tests. Losen selected these tasks because of the susceptibility of performance on them to variations in attentiveness. Some of the subjects were censured for their errors as follows: "No, that was wrong. Now listen carefully to this one." Other subjects received either no censure or were simply told what the correct answer was. The schizophrenics who received censure did better on both tasks than the other groups did. This is especially striking since some of the subjects in the other groups were informed by implication that they were in error. As Losen suggests, the difference appears to lie in the suggestion that the subject might do better on the next trial. He reports that some of the subjects reported that the censure was helpful. The normals, on the other hand, were not so sensitive to censure.

Cavanaugh, Cohen, and Lang (1960) gave chronic schizophrenics a reaction-time test. After their base rates had been established, some were told that they would hear a voice or a tone "to help them respond more quickly by providing information about their performance." The voice ("That was bad—too slow——") or tone would be heard if they did not press the response lever in time. Other control subjects were given no such instructions or treatments. The subjects who received either the voice or tone improved more than did the control subjects.

Fisher (1963) gave schizophrenics two series of trials on a task in which they were to match each of several stimuli by pulling the appropriate lever. One group of subjects was told in the interval between the series that they had done poorly and that their responses were too slow. A second group of subjects was told the same thing after some of the trials during the second series on which they had performed poorly. A third group was given some form of praise, unspecified in Fisher's report, after some good performances on the second series of tasks. A fourth group was given no evaluation at all. In the first two groups, the subjects were told not only that they were doing poorly, but also what was wrong with their performances. Furthermore, the experimenter gave them further trials, thus communicating to them his belief that they might perform better. The latter possibility would be especially evident to the second group of subjects, who were censured for some of their worst performances; the subjects could contrast these performances to their other, better performances. Not surprisingly, the groups receiving criticism did better than the group receiving no evaluation. The praised group performed on an intermediate level, but the results for this group are difficult to evaluate since it is not clear whether these subjects were encouraged to do better or not.

If an experimenter has already indicated to a schizophrenic subject that he has confidence that the subject can improve in performance, he need not state his confidence every time he points out an error in order to obtain an increment in performance. Olson (1958) trained schizophrenics and normals on a digit-symbol substitution task. He first had the subjects learn the substitution code to two correct trials by oral repetition of the code. That is, he worked with these subjects until they mastered the task, a sign of his confidence in them. Then, he administered a series of untimed adaptation trials. Errors occurring during the adaptation trials were pointed out by the experimenter and corrected by the subject. Again, he communicated his confidence and told them just what to do better. Then he administered three blocks of trials, telling the subjects one of the following between the first and second blocks as well as between the second and third:

> 1. Positive condition: "I've scored your paper and see that so far you are doing very well. As a matter of fact, you are doing much better than most men of your age and background. Let us try it again and see what happens."
>
> 2. Negative condition: The same as the positive, except that the words "not very well" and "very poorly as compared to" were substituted for the appropriate words.
>
> 3. Non-evaluative: "We've scored your paper—but we have more to do, so give me just a second or two to get the material arranged" (p. 311).

For the schizophrenics, both the positive and negative conditions produced better performances than the non-evaluative. In the negative condition, the subject was told he had done poorly but was being given another chance by an experimenter who had been supportive and encouraging during the adaptation period. The results for the positive condition simply duplicate the findings in the previous studies cited.

An apparent contradiction of the interpretation of Olson's work appears in a study by Berkowitz (1964). He measured the subjects' reaction times after having established three different types of relationships between subject and experimenter prior to the measurement of reaction time. In the warmth condition, the subjects met with the experimenter for three meetings prior to the testing. During those meetings the experimenter tried to get better acquainted with the subject, acted in a warm, friendly manner, encouraged the patient to talk, sympathized with him, praised him. In the rebuff condition, there were also three meetings, but in these meetings the experimenter told the patient that he really was not interested in getting to know him nor was he concerned about him; the experimenter then answered patient's questions about the experiment succinctly or remained silent; and when he spoke his tone was flat and aloof. In the no-contact condition, there were no meetings between patient and experimenter prior to the reaction-time phase. During the reaction-time measurements, the experimenter behaved the same for all groups, attempting to maintain an equally friendly attitude toward all. Twenty-four training trials were administered.

> In order to induce a set for improvement on the following thirty-six test trials, subjects were praised for their performances on the training trials and were encouraged to attempt to improve the trials to come. . . . If the subject improved upon or maintained the level of performance manifested in the preceding block of trials, he was praised. . . . If the subject's performance deteriorated, he was praised, but was reminded to improve his performance (p. 514).

Berkowitz found that the performance of the warmth groups was significantly lower than that of the other two groups both during training and test trials, although all groups tended to improve from trial to trial. Berkowitz interprets the difference among the conditions in terms of satiation of a social drive; the warmth groups had received so much warmth during the three meetings that they did not need any more from the experimenter and therefore did not respond faster in order to obtain some positive reaction from him. In the other conditions, no such social satiation prior to the testing would have occurred. However, this interpretation is sharply contradicted by another bit of evidence from his study: the subjects in the warmth conditions made significantly more requests at the end of the study to have further meetings with the experimenter.

An interpretation consistent with the present approach takes into account the fact that almost all of the differences between the warmth and the other conditions occurred between the first four and the second four trials during training. The rebuff and the no-contact subjects sharply increased their performances between these sets of trials, while the warm group improved much less. After the eighth trial, all these groups appear to improve from trial to trial at pretty much the same rate. Clearly, then, the differences among the conditions occurred early in the study, when the rebuff and no-contact subjects suddenly found the experimenter friendly and supportive. For the rebuff subjects he had been cold; the no-contact subjects no doubt had a generally skeptical attitude toward the experimenter before entering the experimental room. Thus, these subjects might very well have reacted to this very pleasant surprise by attending more closely to the experimenter's instructions. Furthermore, the rebuff subjects might have interpreted the shift in the experimenter's behavior as a result of their having broken down the experimenter's reserve—a hopeful experience. Plainly, Berkowitz's study does not necessarily contradict Olson's.

One of the communications to the subjects in Olson's study was the idea that they had better or worse scores than other people who were like them. If the subjects were told that they were doing worse than people like themselves and were then given another trial, this communication was one of expected improvement, since people tend to generalize their similarities with others. Accordingly, Johannsen (1962) gave schizophrenics and normals a task of canceling out *e*'s on a page of type. Between trials the subjects were told one of the following: (1) that their performances were inadequate and below the standard achieved by most subjects; (2) that they were performing above the standard; or (3) no communication. Both schizophrenics and normals did better in the first condition than in the latter two, although the second was slightly above the last.

Interestingly, Johannsen comments: "The use of the simple letter cancellation task . . . appears to have led to a situation in which the clearest escape was for a schizophrenic subject to avoid further punishment is to act in an adaptive and productive way (p. 266)."

Another way in which the expectations of high performance by patients can be communicated is to increase the responsibility given them. Lerner and Fairweather (1963) set up groups of five patients to work up housekeeping tasks in their dormitory. The experimenter placed some of the groups under maximal supervision, indicating his lack of confidence in them. He acted as the integrator of the patients' work, continually making suggestions as to what the patients might do to perform better on such commonplace tasks as mopping, making beds, and the like. In other groups, the experimenter first told them about their tasks and equipment, and then withdrew to a doorway. A sign was left in the room listing the tasks. Although the experimenter was available for information and advice, he seldom appeared to have any to give. This absence of explicit instructions was not a serious problem here because the tasks were familiar to the patients. The less supervised groups did a better job at housekeeping the dormitory and became more cohesive. The better performance of these patients appears to be due in part to the experimenter's confidence in them. In addition, the increased cohesiveness of the less supervised groups may have been the result of the fact that they developed stable role relationships around the tasks, leading to predictable and reasonable behavior. Compatible with the discussion on page 122, these more predictable relationships might have led to less withdrawal from others and less hopelessness in general.

In sum, then, the second avenue of reducing the schizophrenic's hopelessness—relying on his susceptibility to influence from authority—has been shown to be effective. The schizophrenics respond well to the expectations of good performance communicated by experimenter-therapist-authority.

The third avenue relies on an extended series of successes to raise levels of expectations and of performance. In the studies quoted so far, subjects responded to success with higher performances if the experimenter encouraged them. However, it is possible that an extended series of successes, even without encouragement from the experimenter, under powerful enough conditions would lead to better performances.

Loeb, Feshbach, Beck, and Wolf (1964) gathered subjects in groups of three and gave them word-completion tasks. Unknown to the subjects, the difficulty of the tasks varied, so that one subject in each group perceived that he had done better than the other two, while one perceived that he did worse. Afterward, the top performance subjects were much more willing to volunteer to work on a similar but harder task in a competitive situation than were the inferior performers. (The relative ease with which the higher motivational levels were induced might be a result of the fact that the subjects in the study were predominantly paranoid schizophrenic, with relatively few chronics. Paranoids are frequently better integrated than other schizophrenics.)

Hopefulness might even be built up in interpersonal relations, the area in which the schizophrenic experiences the most anxiety. Spohn and Wolk (1963) obtained a baseline of social interactive behavior by giving four-man groups of chronic patients a series of tasks, some requiring verbal interaction, some not. The patients' social behavior was observed and rated while they were working on these tasks. Then, half of the subjects participated in three group problem-solving sessions per week for four consecutive weeks. Working with the same four-man groups for the entire "experience" period, subjects were instructed at each session to solve five group problems in succession. These problems required little or no verbal communication. The other half of the subjects received no such treatment. At the end of the "experience" period, all the subjects were given the same tasks that they had worked on at the beginning of the experiment, sometimes working in groups of "strangers" (subjects who never participated together before), sometimes in groups of "familiars." In both the "familiar" and "stranger" groups, the "experience" subjects showed more social participation than the others. This difference held both for the tasks requiring verbal interaction and for the one that did not.

A lessening of withdrawal in social situations can also be obtained by giving the patients success experience on words that are most likely to be used in a social situation. Ullman, Krasner, and Collins (1961) had subjects tell stories to TAT cards under one of the following conditions: first, the experimenter nodded his head and said, "mmm-humm" every time the patient used an emotional word; second, a counter would click every time the patient used an emotional word; third, the experimenter did nothing in response to the subjects' words. The first subjects showed a greater increase in adequacy of interpersonal relations in group therapy than did the other two groups. Obviously, emotional words are the lifeblood of group therapy.

Since part of the schizophrenics' withdrawal from other patients is a result of the hopelessness caused by their unpredictable and unreasonable behavior, they should withdraw less in situations that are structured so that behavior is both predictable and reasonable; they should have less hopelessness about responding to others' behavior in a reasonable and predictable way. The lower level of withdrawal would also be expected to lead to a higher level of conformity to the behavior of others. Lerner (1963) first gave patients a task to work on alone, telling them to work either fast or slowly. Then some of the subjects were brought into a room where they met another subject-patient. They were told that one of them was the leader, one the follower, and to continue working on the task. Regardless of the amount of conversation between the two patients, they tended to become more alike in rates of performance, the slow one speeding up, the fast one slowing down. Control groups of subjects who worked together without having the situation structured in terms of leaders and followers showed no change, nor did control groups who did not meet with another subject.

The studies cited thus far have demonstrated the effectiveness of the authority-oriented task and the success-oriented task; that is, if a schizophrenic patient is strongly encouraged by someone in authority or is successful over a long period, even in interpersonal tasks, his level of performance will rise. Of course, the impact of this encouragement and success seems to have been contingent on the power of the experience, since it would have to overcome the patient's hopeless schemas. In part, the success of the encouragement and of the achievement must have been the result of the building up of schemas of hopefulness in the patients—hopefulness, that is, in achieving a particular goal in a particular situation. This way of viewing the findings raises the question of whether or not patients develop hopeful schemas about situations other than the particular one in which they were encouraged or were successful. In essence, this generalization is what therapy is all about. And, in a sense, such generalizing was accomplished to some limited degree in Spohn and Wolk's study of the effects of success in group problem solving. The subjects increased their social interactions with strangers as well as with the people with whom they had solved problems. However, no significant generalization to ward behavior occurred. Ullman *et al.* found the patients doing better in a group therapy situation, which is similar in many ways to the experimental situation, since both in this situation and in therapy, a person of high status reacts to their verbalizations. In both, the use of emotional words tends to be rewarded. The main problem is how to foster the acquisition of hopeful schemas, which can then be generalized to a variety of other situations, such as behavior on the ward.

The present theory suggests some of the conditions that enhance the probability of developing generally hopeful schemas. First, if a patient succeeds in achieving a variety of goals, rather than one, he is more likely to develop a schema that he can succeed at all sorts of goals. This schema would be based on the configuration of lower order schemas concerning his success in achieving each of the specific goals. He would realize that he "succeeds at all sorts of goals," and therefore would be more hopeful in new situations (see Chapter Five). Second, if the individual has succeeded at increasingly difficult problems, he will develop the schema of being more and more successful, and thus may approach new situations more hopefully (see Chapters Two and Five). A third condition is the consistent, persistent encouragement and expectations of authoritative others that the person can and will solve the problems.

There are at least two studies that show that experiences combining all three of these conditions do lead to a more effective behavior in situations differing from any in which the experiences occurred. Presumably, this more effective behavior was the result of more hopeful schemas. One of these studies is by Peters and Jenkins (1954). They divided chronic schizophrenics into three groups: Group I received the special learning treatment; Group II received some of the attention paid to the first group, but not the special learning; Group III experienced the usual ward routine.

> The eight patients of Groups I and II were separated from other ward patients at 7:00 every morning. While other patients were at breakfast, these remained on the ward where they received subshock doses of insulin (to make them even more hungry). Then, with the nurse and two aides, they walked to the O.T. [occupational therapy] building, one of the aides packing a food cart containing sandwiches, coffee, fruit juice, milk, and fudge . . . [These patients] were seated at a single table . . . [and] every weekday morning were given an especially intense form of O.T. One or two nurses, two aides, and two student nurses worked every day with these eight patients and, from time to time, an occupational therapist was present also. Thus, every one of these patients received more than the usual attention given in O.T. and had opportunity to show interest in a wide variety of constructive works. . . .
>
> At some time during their two hour O.T. period, these patients were taken in pairs, one of Group I and the other of Group II to another room where they had breakfast. . . . The Group II patients were immediately seated and given food. . . . The Group I patients were first conducted into an experimental room . . . where they spent 20 to 30 minutes at problem solving [described below] with fudge as a reward. This problem solv-

> ing was done individually, with only one patient and a psychologist present in the room at any one time. After the patient had completed learning, he had breakfast and returned to O.T. (pp. 86–87).
>
> The purpose of the insulin was to motivate patients, and since after several weeks, it seemed that they were habituated to the learning, it was stopped in the middle of the experimental period for all eight subjects. This seemed to have little effect on their problem-solving behavior (p. 87).

The problems worked on varied greatly from the most simple to the most complex. The patients started on the easiest—getting fudge (which they could then eat) out from the middle of a transparent tube by using rods. Problems of intermediate difficulty were stylus mazes, a variety of a Porteus maze, and a multiple choice task that involved choosing among ten levers. When the patient had been doing well on the other tasks, he was given various types of reasoning problems, such as the Binet Ingenuity problems. Finally, in the last three weeks of the three-month experimental period, the Group I patients met as a group to role-play simple interpersonal situations from "real life." Within each of these types of problems, from the fudge tubes to the interpersonal, the subjects were given increasingly difficult problems to work as they succeeded at each level of difficulty. Also, it should be noted that the subjects moved from motor problems to ideational to social. Also, the manner of receiving the fudge reward was made increasingly more indirect and no fudge was used in the social problem solving situation. Instead the leader "took pains to praise a patient for the least of efforts." During the problem solving, the experimenter would help and guide the subjects, at first only verbally. If this guidance failed, the experimenter would physically guide the subject's responses or would give him another, equally difficult, problem.

The results were that the Group I patients showed significantly more positive "Objective Ward Incidents" than the other two groups. The incidents were recorded from the hospital records and consisted of positive incidents, such as earning privileges and better jobs in the hospital, and negative incidents, such as having a fight or injuring oneself. A patient's score was the algebraic sum of the incidents. All of the Group I patients had zero or positive scores.

King, Armitage, and Tilton (1960) gave special treatment to an experimental group of chronic schizophrenic subjects for fifteen weeks, three times a week. In Phase I, the patients learned simple operant behavior, pressing a lever to obtain candy and cigarettes. The subjects were taught by demonstration, urging, or direct guidance of their responses. The experimenter greeted each successful lever press with "good," "good work," or similar comments. After the subjects began to respond voluntarily, they received nonreinforced trials. When any stopped, the therapist gave instructions and demonstrations until the subject started again.

In Phase II, the problem was made more complex, requiring the subject to select one of four possible directions of movement of a lever. Within this phase, the problems were made increasingly difficult. Later, the therapist asked the subjects to verbalize or otherwise describe their next moves, and he tried in this and other ways to interact verbally with the patients.

In Phase III, the therapist and the patient worked as a team on the levers, starting with the simpler lever problems and moving up to the more complex. Then two subjects worked as a team. Finally other subjects were brought into the room to observe before they themselves worked as members of a team. Every subject had to team up with every other.

The experimental subjects were compared with control groups of patients who received either psychotherapy, group therapy, or occupational therapy. The experimental subjects were found in the ward itself to have a higher level of verbalization, decreased nervousness, and greater likelihood of transfer to better wards.

Thus, in both studies, three factors appeared to be important in influencing patient behavior on the ward: (1) the patients were successful in a variety of tasks; (2) the patients were successful in increasingly difficult tasks; and (3) the patients received persistent support and encouragement from the therapists. The question remains as to how much each of these factors contributed separately to the patients' improvement. On the other hand, it is most likely that in the face of the hopelessness of schizophrenics, a combination of all three is necessary. In both the studies, the experimenters appear to have had to use encouragement mostly in the early sessions, while later the effectiveness appears to have stemmed from the success on the tasks.

Both studies can be interpreted as demonstrating that the experimental treatments had at least four effects. First, the subjects developed a higher level of hopefulness on the particular tasks on which they succeeded in the experimental situation and on similar ones. Second, the treatment led to a higher general level of hopefulness, a greater sense of personal effectiveness among the patients. Since the subjects were increasingly effective on more and more difficult and varied tasks, they could not but acquire a schema that they themselves were increasingly competent with regard to tasks and problems in general. This higher order schema of general competence then influenced lower order schemas relevant to it and to particular problem situations. Their higher levels of expectations led to more effort and, probably, to more success. This outcome, the translation into expressions of greater effort and success, was what was noticed by ward personnel.

This is not to argue that the patients perceived themselves to be completely incompetent beforehand or that an entirely new schema had to be developed. Certainly, they had expectations greater than zero of solving problems; but their expectations were, as we have indicated, not much greater. Therefore it cannot be argued that a previously acquired, rather than a new, schema of hopefulness was being invoked. The extent and the intensity of the experience necessary to establish hopefulness argue for the establishment of relatively new schemas. At the same time, some patients already have some hopeful schemas; these schemas merely need to be invoked. These patients would be those whose lives have been more successful generally until the point of illness.

A third effect of the experimental treatments in these studies stems from the very intense and persistent efforts by important people to help the patient. The patient could not help but change his negative schemas about other people at least a little as a result of this experience. The change was probably enhanced by the positive experience that the patient had with other patients in the final phases of both studies.

A fourth probable effect was that the patients not only developed a greater sense of competence but also felt more competent to cope with their own difficulties, anxieties, and symptoms. They could, therefore, invoke a particular schema about their own illness —presumably hopeful—and begin to attack and overcome their anxieties. The need for this "attack" may be the reason why the establishment of hope is a requisite antecedent to cure.

CHAPTER 12

The Therapy of Hope

As the previous chapter has shown, schizophrenic patients can become hopeful through a "total push" in which all aspects of the patient's life are directed to communicating hopefulness. First, the hopeful communications come from the staff, in the form of direct verbalizations and communications through policies and actions. These actions signify respect for the patient, a hopeful catering to his strengths rather than his pathology. Second, the patient acquires hopefulness as he succeeds at his tasks, either as an individual or, more typically, as a member of a group. This hopefulness applies not only to the specific tasks and situations used in treatment, but also to more general tasks and situations, because of the great variety involved in these total push types of treatment.

The most convincing data about this type of effort come from studies in which an experimental paradigm has been applied as much as possible—patients assigned either randomly or by some matching procedure to an experimental or control group. Sanders, Weinman, Smith, Smith, Kinney, and Fitzgerald (1962) assigned patients to one of four groups. The first group was placed in a therapeutic community, which consisted of the following treatment: the patients were moved from their old wards to a small building in which each of them had a private room and key (a rather effective way of communicating respect and hopefulness); both the staff and patients were taught, at meetings, that the patients could recover by assuming responsibility; the patients were told that the goal was discharge in six to twelve months, that all activities prior to that time were preparatory, and that they would be given a series of jobs with increasing responsibilities; the patients participated in regular social gatherings; and the patients formed an "alumni" club to help in the transition to the outside world. In addition, this group received "core and interaction treatment," which consisted of having small group sessions in which the patients were trained by social therapists to handle four difficult interpersonal situations that they would have to face in life. These patients also received group therapy and had an active patient government.

The second group received the core and interaction treatment only; the third had the therapeutic community only; and the fourth, a control, received none of these treatments. All of the experimental groups had a higher discharge rate than the control. Furthermore, the first and second groups stayed out of the hospital longer than the third or the control. Thus, when the patients had their hopefulness increased by the treatment in which they were treated as increasingly responsible persons, they were more ready for discharge and were better able to cope with the problems they would face outside the hospital.

Fairweather, Simon, Gebhard, Weingarten, Holland, Sanders, Steve, and Reahl (1960) divided patients into four groups. The first group lived apart from other patients, ran a newspaper, participated in group work and group living, and received group psychotherapy. The second received individual work assignments and individual psychotherapy and planned for departures. The third received the same treatment as the second, except that group psychotherapy was used as well. The fourth group was the control; they received only individual work assignments. The first group was rated by ward personnel as improving the most in ward behavior. Further, the first three groups had a higher percentage of discharged patients who were employed than did the control group.

In another study, Fairweather (1964) divided patients into a "traditional" and "small-group" treatment program. He describes the different routines of the two groups in the following table, with his comments cited below.

DAILY WARD SCHEDULE

	Small-Group Ward	Traditional Ward
A.M.		
6:00– 6:30	Lights on in dormitory	Lights on in dormitory
6:30– 7:30	Bedmaking, shaving, bathing	Bedmaking, shaving, bathing
7:30– 7:55	Breakfast	Breakfast
7:55– 8:00	Medication	Medication
8:00– 9:00	Task group ward housekeeping	Individual work assignments
9:00–10:00	Ward meeting hour	Individual work assignments
10:00–11:00	Recreation hour	Ward meeting hour
11:00–12:00	Autonomous meetings of task groups	Recreation hour
P.M.		
12:00–12:05	Medication	Medication
12:05–12:30	Free time	Free time

12:30– 1:00	Lunch	Lunch
1:00– 4:00	Individual work assignments	Individual work assignments
4:00– 5:30	Ward activity—patients' choice (recreation, shower, socialize, *etc.*)	Ward activity—patients' choice (recreation, shower, socialize, *etc.*)
5:30– 6:10	Dinner	Dinner
6:10– 9:00	Off-ward recreation, *i.e.,* library, dance, *etc.*	Off-ward recreation, *i.e.,* library, dance, *etc.*
9:00– 9:05	Medication	Medication
9:05–10:00	Free time	Free time
10:00	Bedtime	Bedtime

This table shows that the only differences between each day in the treatment programs, with regard to patient assignments are the hours from 8:00 to 9:00 and from 11:00 to 12:00 on the small-group ward. During those two hours, the task groups met on the ward. From 8:00 to 9:00 they engaged in a ward housekeeping task, and from 11:00 to 12:00 they held task group meetings during which decisions and recommendations about group members were discussed. To provide a control for these two hours, patients participating in the traditional program had work assignments. The differential use of these two hours in the treatment programs provided the time and the social atmosphere for the development of problem-solving task groups, which is the major experimental variable in the study.

As shown in Table 3.1, the patients participating in both programs spent two hours of their day in a large-group meeting directly followed by a recreation hour. The first of these two hours spent in a ward meeting . . . was attended by all patients, the nurse, nursing assistants, and a group leader. A psychologist, the group leader, served in this role for the daily meetings on both experimental wards. The recreation hour on both wards was similar and allowed patients to engage in any activity of their choosing within the confines of the ward. . . . The remainder of the patients' day on both wards was spent in regularly scheduled work assignments which were made on an individual basis.

For further contrast, it is necessary to trace the course of events in a patient's life for the first few days on the small-group ward as compared with the traditional ward. When a patient arrived on the traditional ward, which usually occurred in the afternoon, he was interviewed by the ward psychologist. Historical information was gained from the patient during this interview, and an attempt at rapport was made. His clinical file was studied. After he was informed of the treatment program including job assignment, ward regulations governing money and passes, and other policies, he was seen by the nurse and a bed assignment was made. He soon was sent to be interviewed about and to receive his job assignment. After the first day, he followed his assigned schedule and was informed that he could request an appointment with the appropriate staff members for discussion of money, passes, problems, and the like. To obtain money and a pass for the weekend, he signed a roster on the bulletin board indicating the days he wished passes and the weekly money request. The roster was then given to the ward psychiatrist for approval or rejection. The patient daily attended his large-group meeting where he was free to discuss anything he wished. He remained on the ward following this meeting for the recreation hour, where he could engage in a chosen activity. On this traditional ward, a list of regulations governing passes, money, medication, among other things, was posted on the bulletin board.

By contrast, a patient arriving on the small-group ward was briefly seen by the psychologist and informed that he was now a member of a particular patient task group. It was pointed out to him that the task group was responsible for orienting him to the ward and explaining the program to him. He was shown the bulletin board which displayed only the list of requirements for each step level that he must fulfill to complete successfully the program, and the rewards associated with them, as well as a list of patients who were members of his newly assigned task group. A note was placed in the group's box informing them of their new member, and it now became their responsibility to orient him to the program. On the first day, he met with his task group where he was introduced to the ward procedures. These included an explanation of the treatment program, the handling of passes and money, what he should do about personal, and other problems. At this point he became a group member.

But the arrival of a new patient in the small-group program was his only introduction into a new social system. This system required that each patient remain in his assigned task group from the day he arrived until he left the ward. To complete successfully the program, the patient had to progress through four steps. The group was responsible, as a unit, for each of its individual member's progress through these steps. The first step level was personal care, punctuality on assignments, and orientation of new members. When in this step, the member received

$10.00 and a one-day pass per week. Each patient ordinarily had some money in his personal funds to be used for expenditures, and the approved funds were taken from these accounts. Step 2 required adequate performance in Step 1 as well as qualitatively acceptable work on the job assignment. After successful completion of step 1, patients were advanced to step 2. In step 2 the member received $15.00 per week and overnight pass every other week. In step 3, members were responsible for steps 1 and 2 and, in addition, recommended their own money and passes commensurate with individual step level. Members were eligible for $20.00 per week and three overnight passes for the four weekends per month. In step 4, the patient had unlimited withdrawal of money and passes and was responsible for departure plans. While in step 4, the patient was responsible for all preceding steps.

The task groups operated in the following manner: Four out of every five days they met in their own room without staff members present. Here they evaluated each other and prepared recommendations for the staff when they met with them on the fifth day. During the autonomous task group meetings, the patients had recourse to request any staff member to appear before the group and to ask him for factual information, which was needed to enable them to make a decision. The staff member could not recommend a course of action, but did reveal facts that were needed by the group to arrive at reasonable decisions.

On the fifth day, the staff met with the task group. The group presented specific recommendations about how their problems should be solved. This involved not only recommendations about more adequate group performance but also about how each member's money, privileges, job assignment, and problems should be handled. The staff then adjourned and made decisions regarding the merit of the task group recommendations.

It is important here to point out the role requirements of the patients and the staffs in the two different treatment programs. First, the patients' roles in the programs will be described. In the traditional program, all problems regarding the patient are taken up with him as an individual matter. His role is very clearly a subordinate one in which he relies upon the staff for their final decisions without any voice about possible courses of action. On the other hand, the social system of the small-group treatment program clearly delineates the patient's role as that of participant in group discussion and recommendations. Although the final decision regarding such recommendations rests with the staff, each patient's task group has the responsibility and is re-

> warded for recommending realistic and meaningful courses of action for each of its members, with particular emphasis on daily living and future plans (pp. 29–31).

The results of this differential treatment were various. During the recreation hour the small-group patients were more active physically and interpersonally. In the large-group meetings, the small-group patients spoke out more often, directed their speeches more toward other patients, interfered less with the topic under discussion and were more prompt. They spent less time in silence; and, more frequently, two or more of them spoke at the same time. On a sociometric measure, the small-group patients made more choices of other patients as friends. Over a period of time, the small-group patients had increased their expectations of advancement on their jobs after discharge, but the traditional patients tended to become more pessimistic. The small-group patients also expected to spend more leisure time in interaction with others, and did not lose whatever positive attitudes they had toward marriage, as did the traditional patients. The small-group patients were discharged sooner from the hospital. Six months after discharge, 54 per cent of the small-group patients were employed, as compared to 38 per cent of the traditional. Furthermore, the small-group patients were more sociable after discharge. No comment is really necessary after this list of consequences. The patients' success in forming groups that were functionally successful obviously had profound effects.

The experimental work cited above shows clearly that mental patients can be greatly influenced by their social and physical environment. We can now turn with more confidence to reports from nonexperimental observations in hospitals of changes in the social and physical experience of the patients and of how these changes influence patients, in the direction sometimes of hopefulness, sometimes of hopelessness. In these reports, the various actions of the staff communicate hopefulness or hopelessness to the patients. The patients can, of course, also acquire hope or hopelessness through their own successes or failures and through their interactions with and perceptions of other patients.

The first group of reports concerns the effects of administrative changes on the patients. Rashkis and Swan (1957) describe a change in the treatment of a group of female chronic schizophrenics who had been hospitalized from four to twenty-five years. This change has a family resemblance to the types of changes found to be effective in more experimental studies. These patients were transferred to a new, quite attractive, "research" building, where the staff-to-patient ratio was very high. Special medical treatment was given to some of the longer-term patients. Nurses encouraged the patients to take care of themselves better, for example, to feed themselves, if they hadn't previously. After twenty-eight weeks, the nurses and doctors involved report that thirty-nine of the forty-eight patients improved in motor activity levels, in taking personal care of themselves, and in interpersonal relationships. Obviously, the atmosphere of hopefulness among the staff both about the program and about the patients' capabilities must have been communicated to the patients, with the expected effects.

Sometimes the communication of hopeful expectations can be accomplished with good effects by placing demands on the patient, the implication of these demands being that the patient is capable of fulfilling them. Of course, the demands cannot be too far beyond the patient's functional level at that particular time. If the demands are not realistic, the patients are unlikely either to accept them or to meet them. Nevertheless, the demands could be raised as each higher level of performance is attained. In this way, a benign circle of expectation and accomplishment is established. Scher (1957) insisted that a group of rather chronic schizophrenic patients work, take care of their personal needs themselves, stop "acting out," stop secluding themselves. Participation in the program was mandatory. As a consequence, there was general improvement of behavior on the ward, less hopelessness among patients, more sense of responsibility. The general tone of Scher's communication to the patients is suggested by his statement: ". . . respect is communicated by the insistence on function, rather than the disrespect of directly or indirectly communicating to him that he is capable only of performing in an aberrant fashion or of doing nothing at all (p. 537)."

Clark, Hooper, and Oram (1962) report about a ward of chronic, "disturbed" schizophrenic women who had been segregated from the rest of the hospital. Despite considerable resistance from the staff, they instituted a program of giving the patients more responsibility for running the domestic routine of the ward. This program led to much more informal social interaction among patients and to a higher rate of discharge.

Although they interpret the effect of what they did in much more behavioristic terms, Ayllon and Haughton (1962) also improved the behavior of schizophrenic patients by demanding (expecting) that they behave in a more mature manner. Their patients were schizophrenics who had received many of the traditional forms of treatment for problems in eating, such as spoon feeding, tube feeding, intravenous feeding, electric shock, coaxing, and eating with the patient. They report that only some of the patients responded to this treatment and even then required constant attention. Ayllon and Haughton had these procedures stopped. At first, the patients engaged in a wide range of behaviors directed at seeking help from the nurses. When this help was refused, they started coming to the dining room on their own without coaxing. Later, the patients learned to get a penny from the nurse, which was to be turned in at the dining room to gain admittance. Finally, the patients learned that two patients together had to press buttons in order to get the tokens. Each level of achievement provided a basis for hope to achieve at a higher level.

In a therapeutic *tour de force,* Wilmer (1958) explicitly and deliberately employed communication of his high expectations of patients as a therapeutic procedure. He describes a remarkable change that he instituted as the new director of an admission ward in a naval neuropsychiatric hospital. Before he took over the ward, it had been managed by conventional hospital practices, employing restraints, large amounts of sedation, and seclusion as methods of control. The corpsmen (aides) were at first quite skeptical of the new approach because it differed so radically from the methods they had been accustomed to using.

> Gradually, however, through their experience on the ward, the corpsmen were largely relieved, at least consciously, of their fears that the patients would do violence. And, with the patients relieved of their fears of harsh treatment, a spirit of mutual cooperativeness developed. In commenting on the difference between the old way and the new, one corpsman said to me, "You should have been here before. It didn't matter how good the corpsmen were; it was how much meat they had on their bones." He was referring to the physical struggles, which he rather vividly described, that had frequently taken place in putting patients in the seclusion room (p. 84).

Changes were introduced when a therapeutic community was established on the ward:

> The basic departure of the therapeutic community from traditional plans of mental hospital management stems from its different view of staff-patient roles and relationships. On the traditionally managed ward the role of the patient is to be sick. Staff attitudes are consequently based on the expectation of sick behavior. It is even possible that certain clinical syndromes or characteristic ways of behaving in a hospital environment are actually a response to this expectation.
>
> In the therapeutic community, in contrast, the role assigned to the patient is that of a responsible member of a social group, and the expectation is that his behavior will conform as nearly as possible to the norms of society. It is assumed that even the patient, who, on initial contact, might appear dangerous will often become actively uncontrolled only if the staff reinforce his dangerous potentialities by acting as if something terrible might happen. Therefore, in the community, staff fears are not projected into staff-patient relationships. The expectation is, rather, that each member can and will exercise self-control, and staff attitudes toward patients are based on this expectation. As a result, procedures are designed to foster self-control, rather than to impose controls from without. The use of locks, mechanical restraints, seclusion, punishment, and suppression of ideas and feel-

> ings is abandoned whenever possible. Such methods defeat the therapeutic purpose of fostering the self-control on which acceptable modes of social behavior are based (p. 10).

Wilmer reports that it was quite easy to integrate the administrative and therapeutic roles, and that he continually assumed the role of being an officer in charge of his men. He did not allow the patients to withdraw from reality—in their case, the necessity of maintaining the role of Navy men, bound to all the routine demands made of the enlisted man—although he obviously recognized that they were ill. "I found my identification with the Navy in a role clearly defined by military custom—my authority, not only as a doctor but as an officer—gave force to my expectation that others would remain in their roles, however sick they were; that this was their task (pp. 68–69)." There were definite limits to the freedom of the patients, and these limits were explicitly communicated. Also, cleanliness and courtesy were expected in the regular meetings of the ward staff and patients, as much as they would be with any group. The director apparently always treated the patients with great courtesy and respect. Profanity when nurses were present was taboo. Wilmer emphasizes the necessity for setting very strict limits on certain kinds of behavior and for issuing direct commands in instances of flagrant violations. He reports that he got the support of the patients for this policy, and it was not just a matter of threat. "But when they were met only with the insistent expectation of good behavior, and when they see other people responding to this expectation, and social pressure to conform will have more force than a threat (p. 261)." The net effects of the changes Wilmer introduced were: a decline in the use of medication; discontinuance of the use of the seclusion room, a drop in interpersonal violence on the ward; and a general improvement of patient behavior.

Sometimes the higher level of expectations of patients is communicated by establishing the "open door" policy. This policy also reduces anxiety due to confinement itself. Wisebord, Herman, Dember, Charater, and Travis (1958) interviewed female patients who were in the first ward in a hospital to have their doors opened. They asked the patients about the meaning of the change to them. They report:

> Many of the patients referred to the opening of the doors as a symbol of trust, and this in turn increased their self-esteem, level of aspiration, and sense of reliability. Common responses included: "It makes you feel trusted . . . It makes you feel you are more responsible." One lady made this syllogism as she described the honor card system: "Before we had honor cards which meant that you were honorable. No honor card meant that you were dishonorable. If you were honorable, you had to live up to it and now this is changed." One answered with pride, "It shows that patients are trustworthy and no one is dangerous and we are not prisoners;" or again, "It shows the doctors have faith in the patients" and with added hope, "There is less wrong with me." The statement, "It makes me feel more confident in myself" was often repeated (p. 519).

Sometimes administrative changes can communicate hopelessness, however inadvertently. Caudill (1958) has described a case in which an administrative change in a hospital led to dramatic deterioration of patient behavior. A breakdown in communication among staff members had led to moving the three patients who were in a closed ward into an open ward.

> This had the effect of turning the open ward into a locked ward owing to the increased security precautions that were necessary, and served the implicit function of bringing the activities of the open ward under the direct control of the nurses. This move came about because of a misunderstanding between the Director of Nurses and the head of the hospital. The head of the hospital, in giving permission, believed that the more disturbed male patients would be moved to the open ward only during the afternoon while the locked ward was being cleaned and painted, and that these patients would return to the locked ward each night. What happened was that these more disturbed male patients lived in the open ward for a week. Without prior notification, the situation simply broke upon the open ward patients and the nurse on duty late one afternoon.
>
> One of the things that happened was that the aides who had been only on the locked ward now were working on the

> open ward and this apparently disturbed some of the patients quite a bit. To quote one patient, "It does make it nice to have the joy-boys (aides) staring at us." Two of the open ward patients who had been patients at the same time in the locked ward some months ago, continued conversation about the old days in the hospital. They reverted to their old pattern of behavior on the locked ward of riding the joy-boys.
>
> One of the interesting things that accompanied the movement of the locked ward patients was the "mass regression" of the open ward patients. All the patients on the open ward had previously come to breakfast shaven and dressed, but, in the days that followed, they came out unshaven in their pajamas. The level of conversation became more primitive and indicative of anxiety on the part of all the patients; the ward became littered with cigarette butts on the floor; and there were more demands made of ward personnel for service (pp. 163–165).

Here we see the patients' misunderstanding of intent of an administrative change, a change that was never explained to them (or to the charge nurse), in any case. The administrative change occurred for reasons having nothing to do directly with the progress of the open ward patients. The meaning communicated to the patients, however, was that the staff saw them as having regressed to the same level as the three more disturbed patients from the closed ward. And it appears that the consequent loss of hopefulness led to a rise in anxiety and general deterioration of behavior.

Our review of case studies of the communication of expectations from staff to patients has thus far concentrated on changes in administrative procedures as a way of communicating. We now turn to reports of more direct, face-to-face communications of expectations.

As Scheff (1963) has pointed out, the staff's explicitly held expectations of a patient can have decided influence over his behavior. Stanton and Schwartz (1954) tell of the power of a patient's reputation for maintaining her pathology and how "experimental alteration" of her reputation led to great changes in her integrative ability. In their description, the concept of a patient's reputation can be understood as the staff's expectations of the patient, combined with the diagnostic rationale that normally accompanies these expectations:

> The reputation of one particular patient, a seriously disturbed schizophrenic patient whose condition had been static for some months, was systematically explored. To find out what her reputation was, the psychiatrist asked everyone in direct contact with her what he thought was the "really fundamental problem." . . . Then two actions were taken at the same time. First, the reputation was presented to the staff-nurses, aides, physicians, and occupational and recreational therapists—in various meetings, and was criticized as devastatingly as possible. This was easy since the reputation, like all such oversimplified statements, was logically indefensible, internally contradictory, and so vague as to be seen as meaningless when held to such criticism. Secondly, the patient was moved into another room at her own request, against the unanimous mild protest of others in contact with her, in a blunderbuss attempt to change what could be changed. Such an action in the face of general disagreement was very unusual for the psychiatrist, but in this case was perhaps justified by the failure of previous measures. The questioning itself served to renew interest in the patient and furnished a rather dramatic background for the presentations at conferences (p. 223).

The rationale for the patients' reputation was found to consist of a series of propositions:

> Proposition 1: Miss Willard's music is an expression of her illness and she can never get well as long as she continues with it.
>
> Proposition 2: Miss Willard can never succeed in her music because she is too competitive.
>
> Proposition 3: Miss Willard should not be permitted to make a superficial recovery, but must go through psychosis in order to work out the "basic" problem.
>
> The changes following these maneuvers were dramatic. . . . She changed from a person wildly confused, frequently assaultive, engaging in no activities of a generally accepted sort such as her music, regularly incontinent of feces and urine, into a patient who was generally clear in her speech, with occasional fifteen-to-thirty minute episodes of confusion, who was not assaultive, was entirely continent, and had arranged realistically for her dental work. Her therapist thought she was again moving in treatment, better than she had since he had known her (pp. 113–114).

Clearly, the staff's expectations were vital for the progress of this patient.

The same sort of emphasis on hopefulness in individual therapy in hospitals has also been shown to have a strong positive effect. Kennedy (1964) reports three cases of treatment of schizophrenics by what she calls *behavior therapy,* but which can just as readily be termed *communicating hopefulness.* The first case was of a man who had married and had had children prior to his illness. The treatment emphasized talk about jobs and about practical problems of family living, and involved arguing with the patient's paranoid statements. She reports that this patient did very well on leaving the hospital. The second case was a paranoid woman who demanded explicit definitions of the hospital rules. She was given a set of "do's and don'ts." Her social relationships improved greatly and she did very well after discharge. The third case was a very paranoid and withdrawn woman on whom all sorts of therapy had failed. Kennedy discouraged her from talking about her delusions or she ignored them. Kennedy saw her as much as possible outside the hospital, in the surrounding area. In local shops, making purchases, she was found to act responsibly. She was able to get and hold a job. Unfortunately, her pathological relationship with her father, with whom she lived, led to her return to the hospital.

Whitehorn and Betz (1954) developed a measure of improvement based on the hospital records of patients. The measure involved discharge, social interaction with other patients on the ward, "increased clinical activity," and less odd behavior. Based on these measures, they found several therapists whose patients typically had high rates of improvement and several who had low rates, although both treated the same clinical types of patients. Whitehorn and Betz found that the more successful therapists appeared to place more emphasis on growth and problem-solving by the patient than on insight into symptoms. They were more active in the psychotherapy situation, taking the initiative more, making sympathetic inquiries, expressing more honest disagreement, challenging more the patients' self-deprecation, setting realistic limits as to what they would accept in patient behavior. Whitehorn and Betz (1957) found essentially the same results in a subsequent study. And, three years later, Whitehorn and Betz (1960) report that 70 per cent of the improved patients in the previous studies were still improved.

Whitehorn and Betz (1957) also gave the good and poor therapists the Strong Vocational Interest Blank. The good therapists' interests were similar to those of lawyers and accountants while they were unlike those of printers and high school mathematics or physics teachers. Whitehorn and Betz were also able to use the Strong to predict the therapeutic ability of other doctors, both in the original hospital they studied and in other hospitals. They interpret these results by pointing out that law and accounting are both problem solving professions, professions that face and solve the ambiguously defined problems of practical living. Printers and mathematics teachers are more likely to deal with problems which are more clearly defined and whose solutions are either right or wrong. Whitehorn and Betz point out that poor therapists were more likely to "play by the rules." Thus, the therapists who had greater success were those who took an active, problem solving orientation to their patients, who had confidence that the patients as well as they themselves could overcome difficulties.

McNair, Callahan, and Lorr (1962) report a failure to replicate the results obtained by Whitehorn and Betz, but their measures of outcome were based either on the subjects' test scores, which are highly suspect, or the therapist's ratings of his own patients' progress, which are even more suspect. Whitehorn and Betz measured many more variables without including test scores or the subjective ratings of the therapists' own patients' progress.

Not only are the effects of directly communicated expectations manifest in hospitals; they also influence the course of a patient's behavior after he leaves the hospital. If the expectations are high, the patient is more likely to do well after discharge. Carstairs (1959) found that ex-patients were more likely to stay out of the hospital if the key person in their households had more positive expectations of them, or expected them not to be dangerous. Furthermore, if the patient went back to full responsibility as head of a household he was more likely to stay out of the hospital than if he returned home as a "son" or had been displaced as head of the household. Simmons and Freeman (1959) summarize the results of the follow-up study of a large number of ex-patients as follows:

> Our findings suggest that the family milieux characterized by expectations that are high at the time the patient was released and remain so, and in which there are no other actors available to occupy or share the occupancy of roles normatively prescribed for the adult male, are the most likely to encourage movement toward higher performance (p. 241).

It was pointed out in Chapter Seven that an individual's hopefulness would be influenced not only by other people's expectations but also by the behavior of other people whose goals were to be achieved jointly or cooperatively. The ability and dependability of these other people could also influence a person's hopefulness.

The patient enters a hospital with at least a minimum of expectation that one of the goals of the hospital as an institution is to help patients. Moreover, since the patient has not been able to achieve the goal of mental health unaided, he must depend on the hospital staff to assist him. Thus, both his needs and the ostensible goals of the hospital make the patient a junior partner to the staff in their joint enterprise, the achievement of his mental health. As pointed out above, the patient would then come to be hopeful or hopeless, in part, depending upon his confidence in the hospital staff. If the hospital staff, however, does not have confidence in itself, or is not motivated strongly toward their joint goal, it would be delusional for the patient to assume that the staff could help him. On the other hand, the patient is faced with a situation about which he has few guideposts. Furthermore, he lacks the confidence to evaluate the guideposts that he does find. He must depend on the staff for an evaluation of the prospects for their joint enterprise. The staff, then, is in the very peculiar position of being both the source of the patient's hopefulness and the judge of its own ability in this enterprise. The patient must rely on the staff in both these ways—as actual helper and as evaluator of the help.

The discussion can be summarized by pointing out that the patient asks two related questions of the hospital staff. First, is your goal the same as mine? That is, helping me to get better? Second, are you confident you will be able to achieve this joint goal? If he gets positive answers to these questions, his behavior will become better integrated. The first question is often implied in the patient's quest for understanding from the staff. If he feels that the staff understands him, he infers a mutuality of interest in his ultimate welfare; and he can then go on to hope. This process is described by Stanton and Schwartz (1954):

> When a seriously disturbed patient feels or says for the first time that a staff member understands him, it marks an emotional landmark; staff member and patient both begin to hope, and to feel that solid realistic grounds for hope exist. Conversely, when a patient is not understood, it often means bleak despair. To protest that one's psychiatrist does not understand one is to invite almost certain rebuff, or even outright ridicule, and patients usually avoid it, either by retiring at least temporarily into bitter isolation and hopelessness, concealing the misunderstanding from themselves and from everyone else, or by protecting themselves in some other way from the emotional implications. No single word used at the hospital is more charged with emotional meaning, or more slippery in cognitive implications, than the word "understanding." With such patients the psychiatrist may rely upon the fact that whenever he correctly understands what a patient is saying, he will contribute to the patient's security by the very fact alone. He may also awaken hope in the patient, often with the conscious tension or misery accompanying it, or fear, or other effects, but he will nevertheless usually contribute to the patient's confidence. At least momentary improvement is the rule (p. 195).

The patient may also learn whether the staff shares his goals, through the way the staff responds to his progress. Of course, on the face of it, it would appear that the staff of any therapeutically-oriented hospital would be pleased, its morale lifted, if patients progress. But as pointed out above, the staff's perception of a situation may greatly differ from the patient's, so that staff morale in many situations may be unrelated to patient progress. It will be recalled that Caudill (1958) reports that patients considered their interactions with nurses not very therapeutic. Part of the reason may be found in the nurses' preference for working on the closed, rather than on the open wards. Their higher morale on the closed wards appears to have stemmed from quite different sources than the matter of patient progress; one nurse said:

> The nurses who work on the locked wards usually don't like the open wards. . . . I would absolutely refuse to work on the open ward under the setup as it now is. From my view, I have a feeling that the open ward is going in all directions. There is no order or plan from the top down about what should and should not be going on. . . . Another thing is the continuous view, it's an interesting place, a very warm place. The staff on the locked ward have a really genuine interest in the patient, and are interested in their work. . . . The locked ward is an easier place to be, the behavior is so different. You can put your finger on it and say: "Here is the symptom." It's not this everlasting delving into details. . . . I think the open ward mirrors more than any place else the conflicts and lack of coordination in the whole hospital. . . . Also, the locked ward is easier, as it is much more what the psychiatric nurse knows as a mental hospital. You couldn't find a psychiatric nursing textbook anywhere that could tell you about the care of the neurotic patient unless you went to a child growth and development book. I don't think the nurse has any security. No definite body of knowledge to hang her hat on with neurotics (p. 183).

The patient's other question of the staff may be formulated, as we have already, as "If you do share my goals, are you confident of your ability to achieve them?" An affirmative answer to this question has the intrinsic power to integrate patient behavior.

A review of the history of the vast variety of forms of psychotherapy illustrates that even the most outlandish forms of psychotherapy have succeeded for at least one practitioner (Appel, 1944). Generally, such a practitioner perceived himself as a pioneer, and had supreme confidence in his new methods. It is not surprising, then, that other therapists, who are more open-minded and more objective about the efficacy of a new therapy, as well as somewhat less certain, had had less success with each new method of therapy.

The effectiveness of Wilmer's (1958) ward, again, may have resulted in part from his own high level of confidence and the confidence he was able to instill in his corpsmen. He met with them apart from the nurses, thirty to forty-five minutes each week. He reports: "These meetings clearly increased their confidence and sense of personal participation in the care of the patients (p. 59)." His night crew was particularly effective, because it was given responsibility for running the ward at night without any direct supervision from him. He says: "Indeed they prided themselves on their patience and its rewards, that of seeing improvements result and of having my explicit and implicit faith and support and reassurance. Unlike the day corpsmen with their frequent change in peer group, they stood together constant and united (p. 91)."

In one hospital (Hamberg, 1957), the introduction of a new therapeutic and administrative regime produced higher morale among the staff and benefited the patients. The improvement in personnel attitudes and turnover was indicated by a marked decrease in resignation among nurses and nurses' assistants. There was also a change in attitude over time.

> A feeling of significant participation in treatment of patients and in administration of the hospital; a sense of development and progress; a sense of pride in being a part of the hospital community; and at times a feeling of optimistic enthusiasm about the therapeutic work and its probable results. There is considerable evidence that such attitudes are often transmitted to patients and it is difficult to conceive that they would not sometime facilitate the recovery process (p. 10).

This improvement in attitude occurred among all staff members in all disciplines. There is some evidence that there was also more effectiveness in the hospital over time, in terms of the rate of the patients' improvement.

The most elaborate description of an example of the process of communication of confidence comes from Stanton and Schwartz (1954). Their interpretation of the incident described below is that the outbreak of disturbance among patients was the result of a breakdown in communication among members of the staff, as a result of which the patients were subjected to conflicting pressures. Our interpretation of the incident is not inconsistent with theirs. We assume that the breakdown was closely associated and causally intertwined with a breakdown in staff self-confidence, which was at least as important as the breakdown in communication in causing the disturbance. (Etzioni [1960] points out that restoring communications in organizations does not always solve the problem.)

The incident began with an administrative change in the hospital, forced by a decrease in hospital income. One of the changes was to dismiss the 25 per cent of patients unable to pay their fees. This change caused much resentment among the staff; some even refused to help in its effectuation. A second change was to reduce the number of administrative doctors from five to two. The medical staff was quite distressed by this, and the concentration of administration led to considerable disorganization. A week or two later, disturbances occurred on the wards. Some patients escaped; others had to be returned to the disturbed ward.

It is interesting to note that the psychiatrist on the ward where much of the disturbance was centered had been extremely and openly critical of the administrative changes.

The nurses could not, of course, remain apart from all this administrative disorganization. Since they functioned as part of a total organization, their confidence in their own adequacy could be expected to be greatly reduced by disagreements, disorganizations, and breakdowns in communication. Thus, during the disturbances on the wards,

> [the nurses] said they were very much under pressure and spoke of their inability to cope with the patient or to stop this disorganization on the ward. They referred to their own inadequacies as nurses and aides and occasionally they were reduced to tears.

> Some asked for personal psychiatric help, several complained bitterly, and others asked for a transfer to another ward or threatened to quit (p. 389).
>
> Key staff members all suffered from feelings of helplessness and dealt with them by partial withdrawal from the ward (p. 395).

The effect on the patients of a breakdown of staff functioning and self-confidence is clear in the following description:

> At the height of the disturbance several patients, never all of them, simultaneously made violent protests about the inadequacy of their treatment—each for a different reason, but each with a significant undertone of not receiving enough care, attention or love, in some form. But even though many patients protested simultaneously, their protests were not at all concerted. Nearly always each patient asked for something for herself, which if granted would have been at the immediate expense of other patients. Each patient reacted in her own stereotyped way—the ordinary way in which she expressed her autistic needs. Nothing approaching a strike or a riot occurred at these times (p. 399).

It was the reassertion of leadership that brought an end to the collective disturbance.

> Generally, perhaps always, reintegration was achieved by the collective reassertion of the previous formal organization with little or no change in it. Such reaffirmation of the official structure followed the leadership of a particular person, frequently the charge nurse or the administrator (p. 398).

Much of the effectiveness of some of the studies cited throughout this volume could very well be the result of the enthusiasm and determination of the experimenter-therapists. This was probably the case in the studies by Peters and Jenkins (1954), King, Armitage, and Tilton (1960), Fairweather, *et al.* (1960), Rashkis and Swan (1957), and Scher (1957).

We have presented evidence showing that hopefulness and higher performances can be established in patients in a variety of ways, but we have treated all patients as being alike in their susceptibility to these influences. However, we pointed out earlier that differences in the degree of hopefulness that schizophrenics have upon entering a hospital can be indexed by the Phillips Scale, which distinguishes the good from poor premorbids. Since good premorbids appear to display more hopefulness than do the poor, they would also be expected to have better prognoses. Their higher potential for recovery would be based on several factors. The first is simply that with more hopefulness, the good premorbids would be motivated to a greater extent to "face life" again, to take a chance on doing well on the outside, or even in a "better" ward in the same hospital. The second factor is that their perception of the possibility of succeeding on the outside is, in part, based on reality. They generally have had better jobs, more security, more friends, a family. They have greater resources to call upon to aid them in reestablishing themselves after their illness. This realization increases their actual chances of recovery and supports the hopefulness of their outlook on leaving the hospital.

The third factor is motivation. To the extent that recovery is dependent upon the patient's coping with his own psychological problems, of dealing with his own symptoms, of facing the causes of his anxieties, his recovery will be a result in part of his motivation for dealing with his illness. If he is hopeless, his motivation for dealing with his problem will be low. We have already shown that good premorbids are more likely to attempt to overcome problems than are poor premorbids. This reasoning appears to be somewhat similar to that of Zigler and Phillips (1961) in describing the meaning of the Phillips Scale. They generally assume that persons who are high in social competence have achieved a higher level of development than persons who are not. Zigler and Phillips write:

> Central to the developmental approach is the view that the individual progresses through successive stages or levels of maturity and that individuals differ in the final level of maturity attained. At each level of maturation, society presents a complex of tasks with which the individual may cope successfully or deal with inappropriately. That is, for every maturity level there is a nor-

> mal pattern of adaptation as well as a pathological deviation from this pattern. Psychopathology then represents various forms of inappropriate resolution. . . . The various pathologies (syndromes) may be completely ordered and viewed as representing inadequate resolutions at successive stages of social maturation. . . .
>
> This position negates the view that normality is the absence of pathology and suggests instead that pathology can best be understood within the context of normal maturation. Then, it places major emphasis on the adaptive potential of the individual. The major implication of this position is that remission from the various pathologies is represented by the establishment of successful resolution of the individual's adaptive difficulties at a level appropriate to him rather than at some ideal end state. . . . Increasing maturity . . . should allow the individual to bring greater resources to bear on the mastery of the tasks set by society. Thus in pathological individuals a higher degree of maturity should imply a greater potential for undoing inappropriate solutions to their tasks. Therefore maturity level should bear a definite relation to prognosis (p. 265).

For all these reasons, the good acute schizophrenic would be expected to have a better chance than the poor. Zigler and Phillips (1961) found that good ones had a better chance of being discharged from the hospital, stayed in the hospital for shorter periods of time, and if discharged, were more likely to remain out of the hospital. Farina, Garmezy, and Barry (1963) traced schizophrenics for five and a half years following admission and classified them as recovered if they were hospitalized for no more than six months and as non-recovered if hospitalized for at least five years. The recovered group showed inferior social and sexual adjustment prior to illness. Farina, Garmezy, Zalinsky, and Becker (1961) found that recovered patients were more likely than non-recovered to have had good social relationships before entering the hospital. Farina and Webb (1956) found that good premorbids have a better chance of doing well on trial visits home and of staying out of the hospital after discharge. Pascal, Swenson, Feldman, Cole, and Bayard (1953) found that married patients, more than single patients, were more likely to return to their previous levels of adjustment.

In sum, then, there are a number of studies that indicate that good premorbid schizophrenics have a greater tendency to try to overcome failures and difficulties, and this tendency, in part, leads to a higher rate of improvement. These tendencies can readily be interpreted as indicating that, regardless of the factors originally leading to a good *versus* a poor premorbid life, the good premorbid has more basis for hopefulness.

CHAPTER 13

Hope and Other Patients

In the previous chapter, we considered the ways in which the therapist-experimenter-authority influenced the hopefulness and performances of patients. Because of the schizophrenic's low self-esteem, such influence can be quite powerful. On the other hand, the schizophrenic's tendency to withdraw from difficulties tends to thwart peer relationships. Nevertheless, in the confines of a mental hospital, complete withdrawal is impossible, so that the patient must interact with his peers at least minimally. In this chapter, we will point out how much relationships can affect the patient's level of hopefulness and anxiety. In general, there are two modes relevant to hope through which patients can relate to one another. The first is based on the patients' simply observing their similarity to and difference from the other patients. The second is based on the formation of interacting social groups. We will examine these two modes in turn.

The hopefulness of patients may be affected by their perception of the fate of others similar to themselves (other patients). Wilmer (1958) describes the influence on other patients of putting one patient in the seclusion room—in itself a genuine indication of staff hopelessness about the patient so confined. "However, the effects of isolating patients from the group reach out to the ward as a whole. When a patient is locked in the quiet room, particularly if he is removed from the ward by force, the other patients become extremely apprehensive. It intensifies in some way their anxiety over their own sanity . . . (p. 122)." If one of the patients on a hopeful ward becomes upset, other patients on the same ward tend to become upset. From a hospital other than the one cited above, we have the following report (Dunham and Weinberg, 1960):

> A frequent type of ward deviant persistently complains about his personal condition and arouses the anxieties of other patients. Although many patients complain about their difficulties, this deviant complains indiscriminately and continually so that other patients either avoid him or try to change him.
>
> Patients compete for discharge. The discharge of one accentuates the desire of others to leave. The apprehensions of some patients, particularly those who are uncertain about their discharge, multiply as time passes (p. 88).
>
> The following comment by another patient reflects clearly the attitude which makes "going home" a competitive value. When a patient is ready to go home, some other patients may gossip. "Oh, she's not as well as I. How come she's going home so soon? I'm at least as well as she is." And the other may nod and say the same thing about herself (p. 104).

Identification with other patients may become so intense under certain circumstances as to lead to an imitation of other patients' symptoms. This was seen in the case of a schizophrenic patient, Mr. Esposito, who acquired certain manic-depressive symptoms because of his contacts with a manic-depressive patient (Caudill, 1958). Gruenberg (1957) has reviewed studies of "socially shared psychopathology" and points out that one of the more frequently cited explanations for the many instances in history of "contagion" of mental illness is the individual's identifying with another. This identification leads to manifesting the same form of psychopathology.

Conversely, if patients perceive that others are getting better, this may very well renew hopefulness in themselves.

> . . . . [T]hey saw desperately psychotic patients improve and even relinquish or change their symptoms, just as the others saw the "bad men" become tractable. It was this quick tempo of change, occurring often enough to be in the memory of at least some members of the community at all times, which gave a special tone of hopefulness and interest to the meetings and to life on the ward. A situation existed where the "outsider" was the person who himself closed the door (Wilmer, 1958, p. 26).

Schooler and Spohn (1960) asked patients why they preferred to associate with healthier patients. Some replied that being close to a healthier patient would enable them to "borrow" some of his status. This is very like Kelley's (1951) finding that low status normals like to communicate about nonrelevancies with those of higher status, especially if they have little possibility of achieving higher status themselves. Although such achievement is possible for patients, it is not easily accomplished.

On the other hand, patients sometimes merely contrast themselves with others, feeling healthier and more hopeful because someone else is sicker and more hopeless, or perhaps feeling more sick and more hopeless because someone else is feeling better. Stanton and Schwartz (1954) describe some of this process among a group of patients:

> In their competitiveness with each other, the concern which was uppermost was with the fact that another patient was achieving a value which they were not, rather than with the desirability of the object itself. Such dissatisfaction was part of the general pattern of noting, comparing, and equating the care, privileges, and

> values accorded each group member. This was prompted by a fear of losing out in the distribution of values. "Mental illness" and "health" were items in such balancing and measuring: for example, Mrs. Stillman refused to room with Miss Hixon and expressed her attitude eloquently: "She is much sicker than I am" (p. 185).

Sometimes the process of contrasting himself with others on a sort of health dimensional scale leads the patient to increase the distance between himself and other, sicker patients; in other words, increases his hopefulness. But when will patients contrast themselves with other patients, and when will they identify with one another? It appears that the social structure of the patient groups is a prime determinant. Patients appear to identify with patients in the same social category as themselves, and contrast themselves with those in a different category. The different categories of patients depend in part upon the formal social structure of the hospital—the categorization of wards and the designation of the wards as being hopeful, hopeless, or acute. Patients in the hopeful wards will contrast themselves with patients in the agitated and chronic wards. A clear, formal boundary between the hopeful and the hopeless patients permits the latter to contrast themselves. However, even within the same ward, an informal social structure may develop in which patients are grouped separately by their levels of hopefulness. The hopeful patients take great pains to distinguish themselves from the other, hopeless patients. Dunham & Weinberg (1960) report from one hospital:

> Short-term and long-term patients have different routines and do not mingle as a rule. The hospital patients regard long-timers in various ways. Confident of release, some feel sorry for the "old timers." "I hate to see people spend the remainder of life in this place," said one patient. "It must be terrible." Others, apprehensive about getting out, desire not to be identified with the long-time group and are anxious to acquire the attitudes of this group.
>
> Many hopeful patients feel that the long-timers must really be ill or they would have been released. In contrast, they consider their own condition as transient and their stay as a recuperative period. Short-time patients often cannot agree that

> anybody can become reconciled to the institution. They regard long-time patients as either devoid of ambition or without the necessary drive to recover. "Some old fellows look happier here," remarked a patient. "How can anyone be happy in this kind of place?"
>
> Hopeful patients tend to feel different from agitated patients. Though expressing sympathy for them, because of their defensive position they avert identification. They regard anyone as slightly disturbed who is so "sensible." They feel that disturbed patients should be transferred to other wards because they are unable to conform to ward standards and they upset other patients (pp. 112–113).

From another hospital, we have the following report (Belknap, 1956).

> As Ward 30 was organized, the fourth-level patients [hopeful] were grouped in a fashion which excluded all the fifth level [hopeless] from personal association, except for an occasional probationer. The fourth-level patients regarded themselves literally as mentally sound and the patients below them as "crazy people." Such phrases were used continually by the fourth-level patients, and by the attendants as well, in speaking of the two or three incidents in which members of the fourth-level repulsed members of the lower groups who attempted to converse or play dominoes or cards with them. The attendants, who understood this situation if they remained on the ward, never assigned any patient from the fifth level to work with the various groups of fourth-level patients unless this patient was acceptable to these latter. In this sense, the fourth-level patients, rather than the attendant or the doctor, ultimately determined upward mobility in the ward for the majority of patients and thus the actual discharge potentiality of the average patient in the hospital (p. 196).

Sometimes the social situation is so structured that patients compare themselves with non-patients. If they do, these comparisons obviously lead to a lower level of hopefulness, manifest in a lower level of self-esteem. This assumption was confirmed in a study by Manasse (1965). He measured the self-esteem of a group of day center patients who had been discharged from the hospitals to their families but were unable to hold remunerative employment or to manage their own daytime activities independently. The day center provided a sheltered setting in which these patients engaged in various activities of a recreational, educational and pre-vocational nature. Manasse compared their self-esteem with that of a group of patients in the best of the chronic wards of the hospital associated with the day care center. The only reason that the hospitalized patients were not discharged was that no families could be found for them. This group then had the highest status among hospitalized patients. The day center patients, on the other hand, were confronted every evening and every morning with relatives who were competent and responsible. They therefore had much lower self-esteem than the hospitalized group. Clearly, Manasse points out, if the steps from the hospital to discharge were more gradual with each increment not too far above the patients' previous level of performance, then patients would have been better off.

In addition to contrasting and identifying themselves with other patients, patients may develop small, face-to-face groups with their own social roles and ideology. The strength of such groups is suggested by the difficulty some patients face in leaving the hospital and their circle of friends. One patient said,

> I have established a circle of friends that I am comfortable with. I guess that is security. The problem of insecurity for me will be making a new circle of friends and not having the bond of mental illness in common. Instead of being an integral part of a group I will be isolated while still knowing I'm not yet well (Caudill, 1958, p. 176).

Most of the studies suggesting the power and significance of face-to-face social groups among patients appear to come from hospitals in which there is a more hopeful atmosphere generated by the staff, providing a basis for the patient's overcoming his well-established fear of others. Murray and Cohen (1959) studied the social interaction among patients in wards of different types, including wards in which milieu therapy was practiced. Milieu therapy is therapy in which the staff makes a concerted effort to use all aspects of the patient's life in what they term a therapeutic fashion.

Murray and Cohen found that there was a higher level of positive social interaction in milieu therapy wards than in other wards, including those receiving milieu treatment previously. Without staff-engendered hopefulness, the patients avoid one another.

The patients' social groupings can serve a variety of functions pertinent to their hopefulness and progress. First, the patients may simply help one another. Caudill (1958) reports that patients perceive their contacts with one another to be quite helpful and therapeutic. Second, the patients' entry into a social group may give them a chance, desperately needed, to interact with other persons. Third, the groups may develop ideologies or social norms concerning illness that will influence the hopefulness of the group. These efforts at interaction and group formation are illustrated in the following cases.

Stanton and Schwartz (1954) present the following description of a "sewing circle" of women patients on the ward:

> Out of the gossip and continuous discussion there arose a number of shared attitudes and expectations. Most of these concerned personnel reactions to patients and relations with them and the sewing circle's own attempt to maintain a set of "therapeutic" norms. Their expectations in regard to the personnel represented the kind of treatment they would like to receive from them. They expected the hospital as a whole to be run for the benefit of the patients and the activities of all its employees to be "therapeutically" oriented. The administrator of the ward ought to accede to their requests, indulge their wishes, and meet their needs. The therapist should be completely accepting and understanding. The nursing personnel on the ward should all be analyzed, should be mature, sensitive, and anxiety-free in their handling of patients, should always be concerned about their recovery, should not put too much pressure on them and should accept their unorthodox behavior without resentment or retaliation. A quite different set of standards was applied to patients. Because they were mentally ill, they could not help acting as they did; they had no control over their symptoms and therefore were not responsible for their behavior. The very role of staff member implied better mental health, greater self-control, and therapeutic responses; therefore, what was permissible for patients was unacceptable from the personnel (p. 182).

Caudill (1958) describes the ideology and norms established among patients. He describes the patients on the ward as developing an implicit set of values, which they impose upon new arrivals.

> The content and organization of the values held by patients would vary with the type of hospital and the nature of the patients, but in the small psychodynamically oriented hospital in this study, such a set of values might partially be stated as follows: (1) In his attitude toward himself: a patient should not deny the reality of being in the hospital for therapeutic purposes, should try to give up what the other patients consider his defenses, and should try to bring himself to a middle ground where he neither engages in extreme regressive behavior nor attempts to carry on life as if the hospital did not exist. (2) In his actions toward other patients: a patient should suspend judgment, and make an effort to see all sides of a person, should support others, and if requested, should try actively to help other patients by providing a sympathetic sounding board for their problems. (3) Toward psychotherapy and the therapist: a patient should believe in the ability of his doctor, cooperate in working with him, and feel that, for the time being, it is better to receive treatment in the hospital than in the outside world. (4) Toward nurses and other personnel: a patient should try to be thoughtful and pleasant, and abide by the rules of the hospital up to the point where either the demands of the nurses become unreasonable or the rules conflict with more important values toward other patients.
>
> The value system of the patients as sketched above tended to be put into action by ascribing to each new arrival what might be called the *role of a patient*. This role required that the patient act in accordance with the foregoing expectations concerning behavior. In addition, it was anticipated by the patients that each individual would take a personal role which was rooted in his background outside the hospital. A new patient, then, had the task of integrating his personal role with the role of a patient; or, at least, seeing to it that the values and behavior characteristic of his personal role did not conflict directly with those of the patient role (p. 327).

Caudill says the pressure on a new patient to conform to these expectations is often impressive, and usually results in the patient's conforming.

> If a patient would accept the ascribed role of a patient, then the group would, in turn, support the patient in his personal role. Particularly this was true if the personal role of the patient served some positive function in the group (p. 328).
>
> The patient group . . . consists largely of a clustering of patients into a number of friendship or clique groups. In the hospital reported on here, one function of the clique was to increase the opportunities among its members for social interaction. A second function was to act as a sort of "mutual therapy" group within which patients could talk over their problems and test out new ways of relating to others that they may have arrived at as a result of psychotherapy. On the other hand, of course, the clique provided a convenient setting for acting out personal conflicts, but the combined effect of the other members of the clique on an individual who was obviously acting out was to dampen and restrict such behavior instead of increasing it. . . . A third function of the clique was to provide an opportunity for letting off steam, and thus act as a safety valve, since it was not always easy for a patient to maintain a constant attitude of toleration and support toward all other patients (pp. 326–327).

One area in which the consensus reached by the patient group appears to be especially potent is that of the definition, and consequence, of mental illness. The significance of this consensus is in its implications for the degree of hopelessness and hopefulness of the patients. The patients appear to attempt to arrive at a definition that, on the one hand, recognizes that they are "ill," but, on the other hand, does not imply that they are incapable of action in at least some aspects of life. The difficulty of arriving at a realistic yet hopeful definition of their illness leads them to be particularly sensitive to the ideas of their fellow patients in their social group.

Wilmer (1958) gives a vivid description of his patients' attempt to develop a consensus about the meaning of mental illness. This attempt to resolve the dilemma of being sick, while maintaining the belief that the illness did not destroy all hope, revolved around the use of the term "crazy." Wilmer points out that this was an extremely frightening word, and all of them had to deal with it in some way or another—sometimes by joking about it, sometimes by denying it, sometimes by attributing craziness to others—

but it was always a problem. Many times, apparently, the patients tried to find out exactly what "crazy" meant.

> The first patient repeated, "People think NP patients are out of their heads." There was another long silence. I finally said, "I wonder what this means—out of your head?" A patient replied, "It means a break; you don't know your name, you don't know who you are, and you can't make sense; a total break, you're gone, you're insane. But I'm not really qualified to say." (An insane person does not go out of his head, or out of his mind, but wholly "in his mind" as Santayana said.)
>
> Several other patients also gave tentative explanations, always stating, however, that they were not really qualified to answer this question. In effect, they wanted me to answer it. I did so, and at the end of my discussion the patient who had first tried to define the term asked, "Is it true that people who fear they are going insane never do; that everybody at some time feels this way?" Through the rest of the hour the group discussed the question of what insanity means, in an attempt to arrive at rational conclusions about themselves and their current condition. One comment which was widely accepted was that sometimes people "act crazy" to reassure themselves that they are in control of themselves and that the NP status sometimes gives them the license to do so. In support of this view, examples were cited of a patient who had "behaved like a nut" on the day when a certain captain had made inspection and a patient who had urinated under the quiet room door on one of the wards as the Admiral passed by on inspection (p. 256).

Dunham and Weinberg (1960) give a graphic description of patients' attitudes toward their illness.

> Most patients do not refer to their condition as "insanity," but describe it in socially acceptable terms, such as "nervousness" or "nervous breakdown." This denial, which begins as an individual defense, is reinforced by other patients who also hesitate to discuss the stigma of the hospitalization. Striving to eliminate this stigma, as well as the hospital discomfort, the patients aspire toward discharge and renewed relationships with the "outside world." Some patients may from impulsive anger call other patients "crazy" or "not responsible" but this reference is infrequent. They hesitate to use these terms in the presence of outsiders or hospital staff. Many patients also do not label their

condition "insanity," even among themselves, unless one patient becomes disturbed. "I've been here a long time," stated one patient, "but I've seldom heard a patient volunteer or admit that she was insane, although some must realize it." Some patients try to narrow the concept of mental disorder to faulty memory, unclear thinking, or to agitated impulsiveness. Many do not consider their profound conflicts as long as they retain personal awareness. Paranoids who have marked delusions become genuinely puzzled that they are considered mentally ill. Some paranoids consider their ideas of reference as accurate interpretations of reality; they regard the people who hospitalized them as having "ganged up" on them.

However, the more nearly oriented patients must reconcile themselves to the self-definition of "mentally ill" as long as they are confined to the hospital. Some try to resolve this notion by claiming they do not belong in the mental hospital. Others "hope against hope that the diagnosis is wrong." But in becoming a part of the patient group, they often revise their ideas and become more sympathetic to the mentally disordered (pp. 68–70).

The power and significance attained by the relationship among patients is strongly suggested by Caudill's (1958) report that a period of disturbance among patients on a ward was precipitated in part by the transfer of certain patients who were important to the social groups.

Certain events on the ward grossly upset the equilibrium among the patients, and they were unable to communicate adequately their anxiety about these events to the staff. The main upsetting events seemed to be the following: (1) Two new patients were admitted to the open ward whose behavior was very disruptive for the other patients. (2) Two old patients were discharged from the open ward who were key persons in the structure of the ward. (3) The discharge of these two key patients greatly lessened the ability of the remaining patients to plan their activities and they immediately requested first Miss Wright, the group activities worker, and secondly, the anthropologist, who was on the ward at the time, to organize activity for them. Miss Wright refused to do so on the grounds that she would first have to obtain approval at the administrative conference, and the anthropologist refused because he felt it was outside his research role. Various patients then attempted to contact their individual therapists, and those patients who did receive individual approval

> then left the hospital for the evening. (4) As indicated earlier, the patients, who had previously gone out in groups of four or five, left the hospital on this particular evening in pairs or as isolated individuals, and all returned in an upset state which, in succeeding ways, spread through the ward (pp. 107–108).

In this chapter we have seen that a patient's hopefulness can be influenced by his fellow patients in a variety of ways: by generalizing from the others to themselves, by contrasting themselves to others, and by forming groups that are directly helpful to the members by giving them experience in relating to others and through the development of group norms relevant to the members' hopefulness. The data indicate, however, that patients react to one another even when such groups are not formed, even when no ordinary communication appears to take place. The patients' observations of one another appear to have direct consequences.

Epilogue

A Framework for Hope

In the opening chapters, the nature of hope, hopefulness, and hopelessness were analyzed within a systematic framework consisting of seven rather simple propositions. These propositions not only have considerable face validity but they have been put forth, directly or indirectly, by other theorists and by "common-sense" psychology. Some additional definitional assumptions concerning mostly the not-very-startling-notion that an individual can perceive his own behavior and develop concepts and schemas about it provided the basis for interpreting data and problems from many varied chapters in the textbooks of psychology. In short, a rather simple theory has been used to find a common thread running through many types of problems.

This analysis has shown that an everyman's psychological concept like hope can be treated within a more formal theoretical framework, which, in turn, can find a comfortable place in scientific psychology. Using this framework, the psychologist does not have to wince even slightly as he encounters the term in print and in conversation. He does not have to ignore it as something he does not deal with as a scientific psychologist, while as a human being he recognizes hope and awareness as part of the universe. Admittedly, treating hope within this framework is not enough. The usefulness of the framework in inspection and integration of psychological data is the ultimate criterion. The breadth of range of data to which the framework has been applied is especially significant since the framework relies so heavily on cognitive explanatory notions, such as the schema. The justification for using terms like *schema* is that data of diverse types can fit neatly into the system. When such a fit is made, it violates the principle of parsimony not to use a cognitive framework.

The present approach has been amply vindicated by the kaleidoscope of different problems it has dealt with. To sample some salient ones to remind the reader: positive and negative goal gradients; the effects of success and failure on motivation and performance; the distinction between apathy and anxiety; the effects of partial schedules of reinforcement on reaction to extinction (persistence); persistent reactions in the face of painful stimuli; anxiety as a result of inability to respond adequately; reaction to psychological conflict; the effects on an individual's performance and anxiety of other people's expectations and performance; the function of behavior and of other people in anxiety-reduction; interpersonal aggression; the application of this theory to persons with emotional disturbance; the development of these disturbances, the resultant behavior and individual processes. Relevant data have come from both human and animal studies. It would appear that the scope of these data meet the stipulation that the theory have a broad range of applicability.

Furthermore, the schema approach makes it possible to examine social influences on actions and emotions in the same context as "non-social" influences. These social influences can be of two varieties that can be described as communicational and observational, both varieties influencing hope, action, and anxiety. These social influences become especially obvious in the examination of the social world of the emotionally disturbed person, both before and after he enters a mental hospital. Other approaches to motivation often ignore social influences or treat them needlessly as a kind of distinct phenomenon.

As more is learned through research about the nature of cognitive processes, of the process of the individual's developing complex higher order schemas, of the relationships between orders of schemas, the additional knowledge can be applied directly to schemas concerning goal attainment, anxiety, action, and so on. The present approach provides an avenue of linkage between these "different" areas of concern. Furthermore, as more is learned about the determinants of the acceptance or rejection of communication from other people, this additional knowledge can also be integrated with propositions about motivational and emotional spheres by means of the present approach.

The data cited in the present volume are not the only types to which the approach might be applied fruitfully. For instance, the only individual differences that have been a major concern in this volume are those between the good and poor premorbid schizophrenics. One reason for this limitation is that, unlike most individual differences, this distinction among schizophrenics was based not on a test score but on the patient's pre-hospitalization history. There are few problems of response sets, reliability, and so on, to confuse the interpretation, such as are encountered on the usual questionnaire or personality measure of individual differences. Furthermore, there has been relatively little research attention given to the antecedent conditions of given scores on a personality test, and these conditions would be important for a proper application of the present theory.

Nonetheless, the theory does suggest a way of approaching

some types of personality test scores. For example, instead of viewing scores on a test anxiety scale solely as diagnostic of response tendencies in the individual, the scores can also be seen as describing the individual's response to his subjective knowledge of his own previous performances on tests. An individual who, in fact, does poorly on tests would, in fact, be expected to feel anxious, prone to withdraw from the test. Since it has been found that persons with a high level of anxiety during tests do more poorly than persons with low anxiety on complex tasks described to them as psychological tests, it would be surprising if these people did not perform poorly in real-life test situations. The highly anxious people may be so because they do do poorly on tests. Furthermore, poor past performances of these highly anxious people lead them to expect to do more poorly on future tests, and part of the reason they do poorly is that they expect to do so. Their poor performance then enhances the anxiety, and the vicious circle continues.

Another area to which the present approach could be quite cogently and usefully applied is that of processes of social change, such as the rise of black America. Leaders in this social movement frequently refer to hope as being a key determinant of the reactions of black Americans. The poetry of the movement concerns hope. The occasional violence that has characterized the movement is, of course, motivated by many purposes, such as that of communicating effectively with white Americans. Nevertheless, some of the aggression is no doubt a result of a high state of anxiety resulting from the frustration of progress toward goals that are both very important and impossible to give up except at great psychological, social, and moral cost.

It is my hope that this volume has achieved the multiple goals of showing that a subjective term like *hope* can be treated meaningfully in scientific psychology, of leading to an integration of a number of areas of psychological research and concern, and of contributing to a solution to the problems humans face.

References

AMSEL, A. "The Role of Frustrative Nonreward in Noncontinuous Reward Situations," *Psychological Bulletin,* 1958, *55,* 102–119.

AMSEL, A., and HANCOCK, W. "Motivational Properties of Frustration: III. Relation of Frustration Effect to Antedating Goal Factors," *Journal of Experimental Psychology,* 1957, *53,* 126–131.

AMSEL, A., and PENICK, E. "The Influence of Early Experience on the Frustration Effect," *Journal of Experimental Psychology,* 1962, *63,* 167–176.

AMSEL, A., and ROUSSEL, J. "Motivational Properties of Frustration: I. Effect on a Running Response of the Addition of Frustration to the Motivational Complex," *Journal of Experimental Psychology,* 1952, *43,* 363–368.

ANDERSON, O. D., and LIDDELL, H. S. "Observations on Experimental Neurosis in Sheep," *Archives of Neurology and Psychiatry,* 1936, *34,* 330–354.

ANDERSON, O. D., and PARMENTER, R. "A Long-term Study of the Experimental Neurosis in the Sheep and Dog," *Psychosomatic Medicine Monographs,* 1941, *2* (3 & 4).

APPEL, K. "Psychiatric Therapy." In J. McV. Hunt (Ed.), *Personality and Behavior Disorders.* New York: Ronald Press, 1944, *2.*

ARIETI, S. "Schizophrenia: The Manifest Symptomatology, the Psychodynamic and Formal Mechanisms." In S. Arieti (Ed.), *American Handbook of Psychiatry, Vol. 1.* New York: Basic Books, 1959a.

ARIETI, S. "Manic-depressive Psychosis." In S. Arieti (Ed.), *American Handbook of Psychiatry, Vol. 1.* New York: Basic Books, 1959b.

ARIETI, S. "The Family of the Psychiatric Patient." In S. Arieti (Ed.), *American Handbook of Psychiatry, Vol. 1.* New York: Basic Books, 1959c.

ARSENIAN, J. M. "Young Children in an Insecure Situation," *Journal of Abnormal and Social Psychology,* 1943, *38,* 225–249.

ATKINSON, J. W. *An Introduction to Motivation.* New York: Van Nostrand, 1964.

AUER, E. T., and SMITH, K. U. "Characteristics of Epileptical Convulsive Reactions Produced in Rats by Auditory Stimulants," *Journal of Consulting Psychology,* 1940, *36,* 255–259.

AYLLON, T., and HAUGHTON, E. "Control of the Behavior of Schizophrenic Patients by Food," *Journal of the Experimental Analysis of Behavior,* 1962, *5,* 343–352.

BANDURA, A. "Self Insight and Psychotherapeutic Competence," *Journal of Abnormal and Social Psychology,* 1956, *52,* 333–337.

BARTEMEIR, L. H., KUBIC, L. S., MENNINGER, K. A., RAMANO, J., and WHITEHORN, J. C. "Combat Exhaustion," *Journal of Nervous and Mental Diseases,* 1946, *104,* 358–389.

BATESON, G., JACKSON, D., HALEY, J., and WEAKLAND, J. H. "Toward a Theory of Schizophrenia," *Behavioral Science,* 1956, *1,* 251–264.

BATTLE, E. S. "Motivational Determinants of Academic Task Persistence," *Fels Research Institute Mimeo,* 1965.

BATTLE, E. S. "Motivational Determinants of Academic Competence," *Journal of Personality and Social Psychology,* 1966, *4,* 634–642.

BAXTER, J. C., and BECKER, J. "Anxiety and Avoidance Behavior in Schizophrenics in Response to Parental Figures," *Journal of Abnormal and Social Psychology,* 1962, *64,* 432–437.

BAYTON, J. A., and CONLEY, H. W. "Duration of Success Background on the Effect of Failure upon Performance," *Journal of General Psychology,* 1957, *56,* 179–185.

BEBRING, E. "The Mechanism of Depression." In P. Greenacre (Ed.), *Affective Disorders.* New York: International Universities Press, 1953.

BECKER, E. "Toward a Comprehensive Theory of Depression: A Cross Disciplinary Appraisal of Objects, Games, and Meaning," *Journal of Nervous and Mental Disorders,* 1962, *135,* 26–35.

References

BELKNAP, I. *Human Problems in a State Mental Hospital.* New York: McGraw-Hill, 1956.

BENTON, A. L., JENTSCH, R. C., and WAHLER, H. J. "Simple and Choice Reaction Times in Schizophrenia," *AMA Archives of Neurology and Psychiatry,* 1959, *81,* 373–376.

BERKOWITZ, H. "Effects of Prior Experimenter-subject Relationships on Reinforced Reaction Time of Schizophrenics and Normals," *Journal of Abnormal and Social Psychology,* 1964, *69,* 522–530.

BERKOWITZ, L. *Aggression: A Social Psychological Analysis.* New York: McGraw-Hill, 1962.

BERKUN, M. M. "Factors in the Recovery from Approach-avoidance Conflict," *Journal of Experimental Psychology,* 1957, *54,* 65–73.

BERNSTEIN, B. "Extinction as a Function of Frustration Drive and Frustration-drive Stimulus," *Journal of Experimental Psychology,* 1957, *54,* 89–95.

BERSH, P. J., MATTERMAN, J. M., and SCHOENFELD, W. M. "Extinction of a Human Cardiac-response During Avoidance Conditioning," *American Journal of Psychology,* 1956, *69,* 244–251.

BETTELHEIM, B. *The Informed Heart.* Glencoe, Ill.: Free Press, 1960.

BEVAN, J. R. "Learning Theory Applied to the Treatment of a Patient with Obsessional Convictions." In H. Eysenck (Ed.), *Behavior Therapy and the Neuroses.* New York: Macmillan, 1960.

BIJOU, S. W. "A Study of 'Experimental Neurosis' in the Rat by the Conditioned Response Technique," *Journal of Comparative and Physiological Psychology,* 1943, *36,* 1–20.

BIRCH, D. "Incentive Value of Success and Instrumental Approach Behavior," *Journal of Experimental Psychology,* 1964, *68,* 131–139.

BITTERMAN, M. E., and WARDEN, C. J. "The Inhibition of Convulsive Seizure in the White Rat by the Use of Electric Shock," *Journal of Consulting Psychology,* 1943, *35,* 133–137.

BOURNE, L., GOLDSTEIN, S., and LINK, W. E. "Concept Learning as a Function of Availability of Previously Presented Information," *Journal of Experimental Psychology,* 1964, *67,* 439–448.

BRADY, J. V. "Ulcers in 'Executive' Monkeys," *Scientific American,* 1948, *199,* 95–100.

BRIDGER, W., and MANDEL, F. J. "Abolition of the PRE by Instructions in GSR Conditioning," *Journal of Experimental Psychology,* 1965, *69,* 476–482.

BRODSKY, M. J. "Interpersonal Stimuli as Interference in a Sorting Task," *Journal of Personality,* 1963, *31,* 519–533.

BROWN, J. S., and FARBER, I. E. "Emotions Conceptualized as Intervening Variables—With Suggestions Toward a Theory of Frustration," *Psychological Bulletin,* 1951, *48,* 465–495.

BROWN, R. T., and WAGNER, A. R. "Resistance to Punishment and Extinction Following Training with Shock or Non-reinforcement," *Journal of Experimental Psychology,* 1964, *68,* 503–507.

BUSS, A. H., and LANG, P. J. "Psychological Deficit in Schizophrenia: I. Affect, Reinforcement, and Concept Attainment," *Journal of Abnormal Psychology,* 1965, *70,* 2–24.

CAHILL, H. E., and HOVLAND, C. I. "The Role of Memory in the Acquisition of Concepts," *Journal of Experimental Psychology,* 1960, *59,* 137–144.

CANNON, W. B. "Voodoo Death," *Psychosomatic Medicine,* 1957, *19,* 182–190.

CARLSON, N. J., and BLACK, A. H. "Traumatic Avoidance Learning: The Effect of Preventing Escape Responses," *Canadian Journal of Psychology,* 1960, *14,* 21–28.

CARSTAIRS, G. M. "The Social Limits of Eccentricity: An English Study." In M. K. Opler (Ed.), *Culture and Mental Health.* New York: Macmillan, 1959.

CARTWRIGHT, D. "The Effect of Interruption, Completion and Failure upon the Attractiveness of Tasks," *Journal of Experimental Psychology,* 1942, *31,* 1–16.

CARTWRIGHT, D. "Emotional Dimensions of Group Life." In M. Reymart (Ed.), *Feelings and Emotions.* New York: McGraw-Hill, 1950.

CAUDILL, W. *The Psychiatric Hospital as a Small Society.* Cambridge, Mass.: Harvard University Press, 1958.

CAVANAUGH, D. K. "Improvement in the Performance of Schizophrenics on Concept Formation Tasks as a Function of Motivational Change," *Journal of Abnormal and Social Psychology,* 1958, *17,* 8–12.

CAVANAUGH, D. K., COHEN, W., and LANG, P. J. "The Effect of 'Social Censure' and 'Social Approval' on Psychomotor Performance of Schizophrenics," *Journal of Abnormal and Social Psychology,* 1960, *60,* 213–218.

CHAMPION, R. A. "Studies in Experimentally Induced Disturbance," *Australian Journal of Psychology,* 1950, *2,* 90–99.

CHAPMAN, D. W., and VOLKMANN, J. A. "A Social Determinant of the Level of Aspiration," *Journal of Abnormal and Social Psychology,* 1939, *34,* 225–238.

CHAPMAN, L. J. "Distractibility in the Conceptual Performance of Schizophrenics," *Journal of Abnormal and Social Psychology,* 1956, *53,* 286–291.

CLARK, D. F. "Fetishism Treated by Negative Conditioning," *British Journal of Psychiatry,* 1963a, *109,* 404–407.

CLARK, D. F. "The Treatment of Spasm and Agoraphobia by Behavior Therapy," *Behavior Research and Therapy,* 1963b, *1,* 245–250.

References

CLARK, D. F. "The Treatment of Monosymptomatic Phobia by Systematic Desensitization," *Behavior Research and Therapy,* 1963c, *1,* 63–68.

CLARK, D. H., HOOPER, D. F., and ORAM, E. G. "Creating a Therapeutic Community in a Psychiatric Ward," *Human Relations,* 1962, *15,* 123–146.

CLARKE, A. R. "Conformity Behavior of Schizophrenic Subjects with Maternal Figures," *Journal of Abnormal and Social Psychology,* 1964, *68,* 45–53.

COFER, C. M., and APPLEY, M. H. *Motivation: Theory and Research.* New York: Wiley, 1964.

COHEN, A. R. "Situational Structure, Self-esteem, and Threat-oriented Reactions to Power." In D. Cartwright (Ed.), *Studies in Social Power.* Ann Arbor: Institute for Social Research, 1959.

COHEN, B. D. "Motivation and Performance in Schizophrenia," *Journal of Abnormal and Social Psychology,* 1956, *52,* 186–190.

COHEN, M. B. "The Therapeutic Community and Therapy," *Psychiatry,* 1957, *20,* 173–175.

COHEN, R. A. "Some Relations Between Staff Tensions and the Psychotherapeutic Process." In M. Greenblatt, D. J. Levinson, and R. H. Williams (Eds.), *The Patient and the Mental Hospital.* Glencoe, Ill.: Free Press, 1957.

COOK, S. W. "Production of 'Experimental Neurosis' in the White Rat," *Psychosomatic Medicine,* 1939, *1,* 293–308.

COOK, S. W., and HARRIS, R. E. "The Verbal Conditioning of the Galvanic Skin Response," *Journal of Experimental Psychology,* 1937, *21,* 202–210.

CRANDALL, V., KATKOVSKY, W., and PRESTON, A. L. "Motivation and Ability Determinants of Young Children's Intellectual Achievement Behavior," *Child Development,* 1962, *33,* 643–661.

CROMWELL, R. L., ROSENTHAL, D., SHAKOW, D., and ZOHN, T. P. "Reaction Time, Locus of Control, Choice Behavior, and Descriptions of Parental Behavior in Schizophrenic and Normal Subjects," *Journal of Personality,* 1961, *29,* 363–380.

CRUMPTON, E. "Persistence of Maladaptive Responses in Schizophrenia," *Journal of Abnormal and Social Psychology,* 1963, *66,* 615–618.

D'ALESSIO, G. R., and SPENCE, J. T. "Schizophrenic Deficit and Its Relation to Social Motivation," *Journal of Abnormal and Social Psychology,* 1963, *66,* 390–393.

DAVIS, R. H., and HARRINGTON, R. W. "The Effect of Stimulus Dose on the Problem Solving Behavior of Schizophrenics and Normals," *Journal of Abnormal and Social Psychology,* 1957, *54,* 126–128.

DESOTO, C., COLEMAN, E. B., and PUTNAM, P. L. "Predictions of Sequences of

Successes and Failures," *Journal of Experimental Psychology,* 1960, *59,* 41–46.

DIBNER, R. "Ambiguity and Anxiety," *Journal of Abnormal and Social Psychology,* 1958, *56,* 165–173.

DIGGORY, J. C. *Self-Evaluation: Concepts and Studies.* New York: Wiley, 1966.

DIGGORY, J. C., KLEIN, S. J., and COHEN, M. "Muscle Action Potentials and Estimated Probability of Success," *Journal of Experimental Psychology,* 1964, *68,* 449–455.

DIGGORY, J. C., and LOEB, A. "Motivation of Chronic Schizophrenics by Information about their Abilities in a Group Situation," *Journal of Abnormal and Social Psychology,* 1962, *65,* 48–52.

DIMMICK, F. L., LUDLOW, H., and WHITEMAN, A. "A Study of 'Experimental Neurosis' in Cats," *Journal of Comparative Psychology,* 1939, *28,* 39–43.

DINSMOORE, J. A., and CAMPBELL, S. L. "Escape-from-shock Training Following Exposure to Inescapable Shock," *Psychological Reports,* 1956, *2,* 43–49.

DITTES, J. E. "Effect of Changes in Self-esteem upon Impulsiveness and Deliberation in Making Judgments," *Journal of Abnormal and Social Psychology,* 1959, *58,* 348–356.

DITTES, J. E. "Impulsive Closure as Reaction to Failure-induced Threat," *Journal of Abnormal and Social Psychology,* 1961, *63,* 562–569.

DOLLARD, J., MILLER, N. E., DOOB, L. W., MOWRER, O. H., and SEARS, R. R. *Frustration and Aggression.* New Haven: Institute of Human Relations, Yale University Press, 1939.

DUNHAM, H. W., and WEINBERG, S. K. *The Culture of the State Mental Hospital.* Detroit: Wayne State University Press, 1960.

DUNN, R. E. "Schizophrenia, Socio-sexual Adjustment, Evaluation, and Involvement with People." Unpublished doctoral dissertation, University of Washington, 1964.

DURKHEIM, E. *Suicide.* Glencoe, Ill.: Free Press, 1951.

DWORKIN, S., BAXT, J. O., and DWORKIN, E. "Behavioral Disturbances of Vomiting and Micturition in Conditioned Cats," *Psychosomatic Medicine,* 1942, *4,* 75–81.

EASTERBROOK, J. A. "The Effect of Emotion on Cue Utilization and the Organization of Behavior," *Psychological Review,* 1959, *66,* 183–201.

EDWARDS, A. L. *The Social Desirability Variable in Personality and Research.* New York: Holt, 1957.

ERWIN, W. J. "Confinement in the Production of Human Neuroses: The Barber's Chair Syndrome," *Journal of Behavior Research and Therapy,* 1963, *1,* 175–183.

ETZIONI, A. "Interpersonal and Structural Factors in the Study of Mental Hospitals," *Psychiatry,* 1960, *23,* 13–23.

References

FAIRWEATHER, G. W. (Ed.). *Social Psychology in Treating Mental Illness: An Experimental Approach.* New York: Wiley, 1964.

FAIRWEATHER, G. W., SIMON, R., GEBHARD, M. E., WEINGARTEN, E., HOLLAND, J. L., SANDERS, R., STEVE, G. B., and REAHL, J. E. "Relative Effectiveness of Psychotherapeutic Programs: A Multicriterion Comparison of Four Programs for Three Different Patient Groups," *Psychological Monographs,* 1960, *74* (5, Whole no. 492).

FARBER, I. E., HARLOW, H. F., and WEST, L. J. "Brainwashing, Conditioning, and DDD (Debility, Despondency, and Dread)," *Sociometry,* 1957, *60,* 277–285.

FARINA, A., GARMEZY, L., and BARRY, H. "Relationship of Marital Status to Incidence and Prognosis of Schizophrenia," *Journal of Abnormal and Social Psychology,* 1963, *67,* 624–630.

FARINA, A., GARMEZY, N., ZALINSKY, M., and BECKER, J. "Premorbid Behavior and Prognosis in Female Schizophrenic Patients," *Journal of Consulting Psychology,* 1961, *26,* 56–60.

FARINA, A., and WEBB, W. W. "Premorbid Adjustment and Subsequent Discharge," *Journal of Nervous and Mental Disease,* 1956, *124,* 612–613.

FEATHER, N. T. "The Study of Persistence," *Psychological Bulletin,* 1962, *69,* 94–115.

FEATHER, N. T. "Effects of Prior Success and Failure on Expectations of Success and Subsequent Performance," *Journal of Personality and Social Psychology,* 1966, *3,* 287–298.

FEFFER, M., and PHILLIPS, L. "Social Attainment and Performance Under Stress," *Journal of Personality,* 1954, *22,* 284–297.

FEIGL, H. "The 'Mental' and the 'Physical.'" In H. Feigl, M. Scriven, and G. Maxwell (Eds.), *Minnesota Studies in the Philosophy of Sciences* (*II*). Minneapolis: University of Minnesota Press, 1958.

FESHBACH, S. "The Function of Aggression and the Regulation of Aggressive Drive," *Psychological Review,* 1964, *71,* 257–272.

FESTINGER, L. "Wish, Expectation, and Group Standards as Factors Influencing Level of Aspiration," *Journal of Abnormal and Social Psychology,* 1942, *37,* 184–200.

FISHER, E. H. "Task Performance of Chronic Schizophrenics as a Function of Verbal Evaluation and Social Proximity," *Journal of Clinical Psychology,* 1963, *19,* 176–178.

FRANK, J. D. "The Influence of the Level of Performance on One Task and the Level of Aspiration in Another," *Journal of Experimental Psychology,* 1935, *18,* 159–171.

FRANK, J. D. *Persuasion and Healing.* Baltimore: Johns Hopkins, 1961.

FREEMAN, G. L., and PATHMAN, J. H. "The Relation of Overt Muscular Discharge to Physiological Recovery from Experimentally Induced Displacement," *Journal of Experimental Psychology,* 1942, *30,* 161–174.

FREIDMAN, S., CHODOFF, P., MASON, J. W., and HAMBERG, D. A. "Behavioral Observations on Parents Anticipating the Death of a Child," *Pediatrics,* 1963, *32,* 616–625.

FRENCH, E. A. "Some Characteristics of Achievement Motivation," *Journal of Experimental Psychology,* 1955, *50,* 232–236.

FRENCH, T. M. *The Integration of Behavior: Vol. 1, Basic Postulates.* Chicago: University of Chicago Press, 1952.

FRENCH, T. M. *The Integration of Behavior: Vol. 3, The Reintegration Process in a Psychoanalytic Treatment.* Chicago: University of Chicago Press, 1958.

FREUD, S. *The Problem of Anxiety.* New York: Norton, 1936.

FREUD, S. *Collected Papers. Vol. 1, On Psychotherapy.* London: Hogarth, 1953.

FREUND, K. "Some Problems in the Treatment of Homosexuality." In H. Eysenck (Ed.), *Behavior Therapy and the Neuroses.* New York: Macmillan, 1960.

GAGNÉ, R. M., MAYOR, J. R., GARSTENS, H. L., and PARADISE, N. E. "Factors in Acquiring Knowledge of a Mathematical Task," *Psychological Monographs,* 1962, *76* (Whole no. 526).

GANONG, W. F. Discussion of Paper by H. W. Magoun, in Kaiser Foundation, *The Physiology of Emotions.* Springfield, Ill.: Thomas, 1960.

GANTT, W. H. "The Origin and Development of Nervous Disturbances Experimentally Produced," *American Journal of Psychiatry,* 1942, *98,* 475–481.

GEBHARD, M. E. "The Effect of Success and Failure upon the Attractiveness of Activities as a Function of Experience, Expectation, and Need," *Journal of Experimental Psychology,* 1948, *38,* 371–388.

GEWIRTZ, H. B. "Generalization of Children's Performance as a Function of Reinforcement and Task Similarity," *Journal of Abnormal and Social Psychology,* 1959, *58,* 111–118.

GILL, W. S. "Interpersonal Affect and Conformity Behavior in Schizophrenics," *Journal of Abnormal and Social Psychology,* 1963, *67,* 502–505.

GLASS, A. J. "Psychotherapy in the Combat Zone," *American Journal of Psychiatry,* 1954, *110,* 725–731.

GOFFMAN, E. "Characteristics of Total Institutions." In M. R. Stein, A. J. Vidich, and D. M. White (Eds.), *Identity and Anxiety.* Glencoe, Ill.: Free Press, 1960.

GOFFMAN, E. *Asylums: Essays on the Social Situation of Mental Patients and Other Inmates.* Chicago: Aldine, 1961.

References

GOLDSTEIN, A. P. *Therapist-patient Expectancies in Psychotherapy*. New York: Pergamon Press, 1962.

GOLDSTEIN, K. *Human Nature in the Light of Psychopathology*. Cambridge, Mass.: Harvard University Press, 1940.

GOODRICH, K. P. "Performance in Different Segments of an Instrumental Response Chain as a Function of Reinforcement Schedule," *Journal of Experimental Psychology*, 1959, *57*, 57–63.

GOODSON, F. E., and MARX, M. H. "Increased Resistance to Audiogenic Seizure in Rats Trained on an Instrumental Wheel-turning Response," *Journal of Comparative and Physiological Psychology*, 1953, *46*, 225–230.

GRAYSON, N. M., and OLINGER, L. B. "Simulation of Normalcy by Psychiatric Patients on the MMPI," *Journal of Consulting Psychology*, 1957, *21*, 73–77.

GREEN, C., and ZIGLER, E. "Social Deprivation and the Performance of Retarded and Normal Children on a Satiation Type Task," *Child Development*, 1962, *33*, 499–508.

GREENBLATT, M., and LIDZ, T. "Some Dimensions of the Problem." In M. Greenblatt, D. J. Levinson, and R. H. Williams (Eds.), *The Patient and the Mental Hospital*. Glencoe, Ill.: Free Press, 1957.

GRIFFITHS, W. J. "The Production of Convulsions in the White Rat," *Comparative Psychology Monographs*, 1942, *17* (8).

GRINKER, R. R., and SPEIGEL, J. P. *War Neuroses*. Philadelphia: Blakiston, 1945a.

GRINKER, R. R., and SPEIGEL, J. P. *Men Under Stress*. Philadelphia: Blakiston, 1945b.

GRINKER, R. R., *et al. The Phenomena of Depressions*. New York: Hoeber, 1961.

GROSSLIGHT, J. H., and CHILD, I. L. "Persistence as a Function of Previous Experience of Failure Followed by Success," *American Journal of Psychology*, 1947, *60*, 378–387.

GRUENBERG, E. M. "Socially Shared Psychopathology." In A. H. Leighton, J. A. Clausen, and R. N. Wilson (Eds.), *Explorations in Social Psychiatry*. New York: Basic Books, 1957.

HAAS, H. I., and MAEHR, M. L. "Two Experiments on the Concept of Self and the Reaction of Others," *Journal of Personality and Social Psychology*, 1965, *1*, 100–105.

HAGGARD, E. A. "Some Conditions Determining Adjustment During and Readjustment Following Experimentally Induced Stress." In S. S. Tompkins (Ed.), *Contemporary Psychopathology*. Cambridge, Mass.: Harvard University Press, 1946.

HAGGARD, E. A. "Psychological Causes and Results of Stress." In *Human Fac-*

tors in Undersea Warfare. Washington: National Research Council, 1949.

HAGGARD, E. A., and FREEMAN, G. L. "Reactions of Children to Experimentally Induced Frustration," *Psychological Bulletin,* 1945, *38,* 581.

HALL, C. S., and WHITEMAN, P. H. "The Effects of Infantile Stimulation upon Later Emotional Stability in the Mouse," *Journal of Comparative and Physiological Psychology,* 1951, *44,* 61–66.

HAMBERG, D. A. "Therapeutic Aspects of Communication and Administrative Policy in the Psychiatric Section of a General Hospital." In M. Greenblatt, D. J. Levinson, and R. H. Williams (Eds.), *The Patient and the Mental Hospital.* Glencoe, Ill.: Free Press, 1957.

HAMBERG, D. A., HAMBERG, B., and DEGOZA, S. "Adaptive Problems and Mechanisms in Severely Burned Patients," *Psychiatry,* 1953, *16,* 1–20.

HARLOW, H. F. "The Formation of Learning Sets," *Psychological Review,* 1949, *56,* 51–65.

HARLOW, H. F. "Primary Affectional Patterns in Primates," *American Journal of Orthopsychiatry,* 1960, *30,* 676–684.

HARLOW, H. F., and ZIMMERMAN, R. R. "Affectional Responses in the Infant Monkey," *Science,* 1959, *130,* 421–432.

HAYGOOD, R. C., and BOURNE, L. E., JR. "Attribute- and Role-learning Aspects of Conceptual Behavior," *Psychological Review,* 1965, *72,* 175–195.

HEIDER, F. *The Psychology of Interpersonal Relations.* New York: Wiley, 1958.

HERON, W. "The Process-reactive Classification of Schizophrenia," *Psychological Bulletin,* 1962, *59,* 329–343.

HERTZMAN, M., and FESTINGER, L. "Shifts in Explicit Goals in a Level of Aspiration Experiment," *Journal of Experimental Psychology,* 1940, *27,* 439–452.

HESLIN, R., and DUNPHY, D. "Three Dimensions of Member Satisfaction in Small Groups," *Human Relations,* 1964, *17,* 99–112.

HILL, K., and STEVENSON, H. "The Effects of Social Reinforcement vs. Nonreinforcement and Sex of E on the Performance of Adolescent Girls," *Journal of Personality,* 1965, *33,* 30–36.

HOKANSON, J. E., and BURGESS, M. "The Effects of Three Types of Aggression on Vascular Processes," *Journal of Abnormal and Social Psychology,* 1962a, *64,* 446–449.

HOKANSON, J. E., and BURGESS, M. "The Effects of Status, Types of Frustration and Aggression on Vascular Processes," *Journal of Abnormal and Social Psychology,* 1962b, *65,* 232–237.

HOKANSON, J. E., and EDELMAN, R. "Effects of Three Social Responses on

Vascular Processes," *Journal of Personality and Social Psychology*, 1966, *3*, 445–447.

HOKANSON, J. E., and SHETLER, S. "Effect of Overt Aggression on Physiological Arousal Level," *Journal of Abnormal and Social Psychology*, 1961, *63*, 446–448.

HOLDER, W. B., MARX, M. H., HOLDER, E. E., and COLLIER, G. "Response Strength as a Factor of Delay of Reward in a Runway," *Journal of Experimental Psychology*, 1957, *53*, 316–323.

HOLLINGSHEAD, A. B., and REDLICH, F. C. *Social Class and Mental Illness*. New York: Wiley, 1958.

HONIGFELD, G. "Relationships among Physicians' Attitudes and Response to Drugs," *Psychological Reports*, 1962, *11*, 683–690.

HONIGFELD, G. "Physician and Patient Attitudes as Factors Influencing the Placebo Response in Depression," *Diseases of the Nervous System*, 1963, *24*, 1–4.

HORNEY, K. *The Neurotic Personality of Our Time*. New York: Norton, 1937.

HORWITZ, M. "The Veridicality of Liking and Disliking." In R. Tagiuri and L. Petrullo (Eds.), *Person Perception and Interpersonal Behavior*. Stanford, California: Stanford University Press, 1958.

HUNT, J. MCV. "Psychological Government and the High Variability of Schizophrenic Patients," *American Journal of Psychology*, 1936, *48*, 64–81.

HUNT, J. MCV., and COFER, C. "Psychological Deficit." In J. McV. Hunt (Ed.), *Personality and the Behavior Disorders, Vol. II*. New York: Ronald Press, 1944.

HUNT, J. MCV., and SCHLOSBERG, H. "Behavior of Rats in Continuous Conflict," *Journal of Comparative and Physiological Psychology*, 1950, *43*, 351–357.

HURLOCK, E. B. "The Value of Praise and Reproof as Incentives for Children," *Archives of Psychology*, 1924, *71*.

HURLOCK, E. B. "An Investigation of Certain Incentives used in School Work," *Journal of Educational Psychology*, 1925, *16*, 145–159.

HUSTON, P. E., SHAKOW, P., and RIGGS, L. A. "Studies of Motor Function in Schizophrenia: II. Reaction Time," *Journal of General Psychology*, 1937, *16*, 39–82.

HUTCHINSON, A. L., and AZRIN, H. H. "Conditioning of Mental Hospital Patients to Fixed-ratio schedules of Reinforcement," *Journal of the Experimental Analysis of Behavior*, 1961, *4*, 87–95.

HUTT, M. L. "A Clinical Study of Consecutive and Adaptive Testing with the Revised Stanford Binet," *Journal of Consulting Psychology*, 1947, *2*, 93–103.

JACOBSON, E. *Progressive Relaxation.* Chicago: University of Illinois Press, 1929.

JAMES, W. *The Principles of Psychology.* New York: Holt, 1890.

JAMES, W. T. "The Formation of Neurosis in Dogs by Increasing the Energy Requirement of a Conditioned Avoiding Response," *Journal of Comparative Psychology,* 1943, *36,* 109–124.

JANIS, I. L. *Psychological Stress: Psychoanalytic and Behavioral Studies of Surgical Patients.* New York: Wiley, 1958.

JANIS, I. L., and RIFE, D. "Persuasibility and Emotional Disorder." In C. I. Hovland and I. L. Janis (Eds.), *Personality and Persuasibility.* New Haven: Yale University Press, 1959.

JESSOR, R. "The Generalization of Expectancies," *Journal of Abnormal and Social Psychology,* 1954, *49,* 196–200.

JOHANNSEN, W. J. "Responsiveness of Chronic Schizophrenics and Normals to Social and Non-social Feedback," *Journal of Abnormal and Social Psychology,* 1961, *62,* 109–113.

JOHANNSEN, W. J. "Effect of Reward and Punishment on Motor Learning by Chronic Schizophrenics and Normals," *Journal of Clinical Psychology,* 1962, *18,* 204–207.

JOHANNSEN, W. J., FREIDMAN, S. H., LEITSCHUK, R., and AMMONS, H. "A Study of Certain Schizophrenic Dimensions and Their Relationship to Double Alternation Learning," *Journal of Consulting Psychology,* 1963, *27,* 375–382.

JOHNSON, H. J. "Decision Making, Conflict, and Physiological Arousal," *Journal of Abnormal and Social Psychology,* 1963, *67,* 114–124.

JOHNSON, R. C., and ZARA, R. C. "Relational Learning in Young Children," *Journal of Comparative and Physiological Psychology,* 1960, *53,* 594–597.

JONES, E. E., and GERARD, H. B. *Foundations of Social Psychology.* New York: Wiley, 1967.

JONES, M. C. "The Elimination of Children's Fears," *Journal of Experimental Psychology,* 1924, *7,* 383–390.

JONES, M. C. "A Laboratory Study of Fear: The Case of Peter." In H. Eysenck (Ed.), *Behavior Therapy and the Neuroses.* New York: Macmillan, 1960.

JOST, K. C. "The Level of Aspiration of Schizophrenic and Normal Subjects," *Journal of Abnormal and Social Psychology,* 1965, *50,* 315–320.

KAMIN, L. J. "Traumatic Avoidance Learning: The Effects of the GS-US Interval with a Trace-conditioning Procedure," *Journal of Comparative and Physiological Psychology,* 1954, *47,* 65–72.

References

KARDINER, A. "The Neuroses of War." In S. Tompkins (Ed.), *Contemporary Psychopathology.* Cambridge, Mass.: Harvard University Press, 1946.

KASH, S., and FRENCH, J. R. P. "The Effects of Occupational Status on Physical and Mental Health," *Journal of Social Issues,* 1962, *18* (3), 65–89.

KATZ, D., and KAHN, R. L. "Some Recent Findings in Human Relations Research in Industry." In G. E. Swanson, T. M. Newcomb and E. L. Hartley (Eds.), *Readings in Social Psychology.* New York: Holt, 1952.

KEISTER, M. E. "The Behavior of Young Children in Failure." In R. G. Barker, J. S. Kounin, and H. E. Wright (Eds.), *Child Behavior and Development.* New York: McGraw-Hill, 1943.

KELLEY, H. H. "Communication in Experimentally Created Hierarchies," *Human Relations,* 1951, *4,* 39–56.

KENDLER, H. H., and KENDLER, T. S. "Vertical and Horizontal Processes in Problem Solving," *Psychological Review,* 1962, *69,* 1–16.

KENNARD, E. A. "Psychiatry, Administrative Psychiatry, Administration; A Study of a Veterans Hospital." In M. Greenblatt, D. J. Levinson, and R. H. Williams (Eds.), *The Patient and the Mental Hospital.* Glencoe, Ill.: Free Press, 1957.

KENNEDY, T. "Treatment of Chronic Schizophrenics by Behavior Therapy: Case Reports," *Behavior Research and Therapy,* 1964, *2,* 1–6.

KIEV, A. (Ed.) *Magic, Faith, and Healing: Studies in Primitive Psychiatry Today.* New York: Free Press, 1964.

KING, G. F., ARMITAGE, S. G., and TILTON, J. R. "A Therapeutic Approach to Schizophrenics of Extreme Pathology: An Operant-Interpersonal Method," *Journal of Abnormal and Social Psychology,* 1960, *61,* 276–286.

KISSEL, S. "Stress-reducing Properties of Social Stimuli," *Journal of Personality and Social Psychology,* 1965, *2,* 378–384.

KOBLER, A. L., and STOTLAND, E. *The End of Hope: A Social-clinical Study of Suicide.* New York: Free Press, 1964.

KOGAN, W., and KOGAN, K. Cited in A. L. Edwards, *Social Desirability Variable in Personality Assessment and Research.* New York: Holt, 1957.

KOHLER, W. "Relational Determination in Perception." In L. A. Jeffress (Ed.), *Cerebral Mechanisms in Behavior.* New York: Wiley, 1951.

KRASNOGORSKI, M. I. "The Conditional Reflexes and Children's Neuroses," *American Journal of Diseases of Children,* 1925, *30,* 753–768.

KUENNE, M. R. "Experimental Investigation of the Relation of Language to Transposition Behavior in Young Children," *Journal of Experimental Psychology,* 1946, *36,* 471–490.

LANE, E. A., and ALBEE, W. "Early Childhood Intellectual Differences between

Schizophrenic Adults and Their Siblings," *Journal of Abnormal and Social Psychology,* 1964, *68,* 193–195.

LANG, P. J. "The Effect of Aversive Stimuli on Reaction Time in Schizophrenia," *Journal of Abnormal and Social Psychology,* 1959, *59,* 263–268.

LANG, P. J., and LAZOWIK, D. A. "Experimental Desensitization of a Phobia," *Journal of Abnormal and Social Psychology,* 1963, *66,* 519–525.

LANGNER, T. S., and MICHAEL, S. T. *Life Stress and Mental Health.* New York: Collier-Macmillan, 1963.

LANTZ, B. "Some Dynamic Aspects of Success and Failure," *Psychological Monographs,* 1945, *59* (1, Whole no. 271).

LANZETTA, J. T. "Group Behavior under Stress," *Human Relations,* 1955, *8,* 29–52.

LAWRENCE, D. H. "The Nature of a Stimulus: Some Relations between Learning and Perception." In S. Koch (Ed.), *Psychology: Study of a Science, Vol. 5.* New York: McGraw-Hill, 1963.

LAWRENCE, D. H., and DE RIVERA, J. "Evidence for Relational Transposition," *Journal of Comparative and Physiological Psychology,* 1954, *47,* 465–471.

LAWRENCE, D. H., and FESTINGER, L. *Deterrents and Reinforcements: The Psychology of Insufficient Reward.* Stanford, Calif.: Stanford University Press, 1962.

LAZARUS, A. A. "Group Therapy of Phobia Disorders by Systematic Desensitization," *Journal of Abnormal and Social Psychology,* 1961, *63,* 504–510.

LAZARUS, R. S. *Psychological Stress and the Coping Process.* New York: McGraw-Hill, 1966.

LAZARUS, R. S., and ERICSON, C. W. "Effects of Failure Stress upon Skilled Performance," *Journal of Experimental Psychology,* 1952, *43,* 100–105.

LEFCOURT, H. M. "Internal Versus External Control of Reinforcement: A Review," *Psychological Bulletin,* 1966, *65,* 206–220.

LEFCOURT, H. M., and LADWIG, G. W. "The Effect of Reference Group upon Negroes' Task Persistence in a Biracial Competitive Game," *Journal of Personality and Social Psychology,* 1965, *1,* 668–671.

LEIGHTON, A. H., and LEIGHTON, D. C. "Elements of Psychotherapy in Navaho Religion," *Psychiatry,* 1941, *4,* 515–523.

LEIGHTON, D. C., HARDING, S., MACKLIN, B., MACMILLAN, M., and LEIGHTON, A. H. *The Character of Danger.* New York: Basic Books, 1963.

LERNER, M. J. "Responsiveness of Chronic Schizophrenics to the Social Behavior of Others in a Meaningful Task Situation," *Journal of Abnormal and Social Psychology,* 1963, *67,* 295–299.

LERNER, M. J., and FAIRWEATHER, G. W. "Social Behavior of Chronic Schizophrenics in Supervised and Unsupervised Work Groups," *Journal of Abnormal and Social Psychology,* 1963, *67,* 219–225.

LEWIN, K. *Field Theory in Social Science.* New York: Harper, 1951.

LEWIN, K., DEMBO, T., FESTINGER, L., and SEARS, P. "Level of Aspiration." In J. McV. Hunt (Ed.), *Personality and the Behavior Disorders.* New York: The Ronald Press, 1944.

LICHTENBERG, P. "A Definition and Analysis of Depression," *Archives of Neurology and Psychiatry,* 1957, *77,* 519–527.

LICHTENSTEIN, P. E. "Studies of Anxiety: I. The Production of a Feeding Inhibition in Dogs," *Journal of Comparative and Physiological Psychology,* 1950, *43,* 16–29.

LIDDELL, H. "The Role of Vigilance in the Development of Animal Neurosis." In P. M. Hoch and J. Zubin (Eds.), *Anxiety.* New York: Grune and Stratton, 1950.

LIDDELL, H. S., JAMES, W. T., and ANDERSON, O. D. "The Comparative Physiology of the Conditioned Motor Reflex," *Comparative Psychological Monographs,* 1936, *11* (51).

LIDZ, T., and FLECK, S. "Schizophrenia, Human Integration, and the Role of the Family." In D. D. Jackson (Ed.), *The Etiology of Schizophrenia.* New York: Basic Books, 1960.

LIDZ, T., CORNELISON, A., FLECK, S., and TERRY, D. "Intrafamilial Environment of Schizophrenic Patients: VI. The Transmission of Irrationality," *Archives of Neurology and Psychiatry,* 1958, *79,* 305–316.

LIKERT, R. *New Patterns of Management.* New York: McGraw-Hill, 1961.

LINDLEY, A. H., and MAYER, K. E. "Effects of Instruction on the Extinction of a Conditioned Finger-withdrawal Response," *Journal of Experimental Psychology,* 1961, *61,* 82–88.

LINDZEY, G., LYKKEN, D. T., and WINSTON, H. D. "Infantile Trauma, Genetic Factors, and Adult Temperament," *Journal of Abnormal and Social Psychology,* 1960, *61,* 7–14.

LOEB, A., FESHBACH, S., BECK, A. T., and WOLF, A. "Some Effects of Reward upon the Social Perception and Motivation of Psychiatric Patients Varying in Depression," *Journal of Abnormal and Social Psychology,* 1964, *68,* 609–616.

LONG, R. C. "Praise and Censure as Motivating Variables in the Motor Behavior and Learning of Schizophrenics," *Journal of Abnormal and Social Psychology,* 1961, *63,* 283–288.

LOSEN, S. "The Differential Effects of Censure on the Problem Solving Behavior of Schizophrenics," *Journal of Personality,* 1961, *29,* 258–272.

LOTT, A. L., and LOTT, B. E. "Group Cohesiveness as Interpersonal Attraction:

A Review of Relationships between Antecedent and Consequent Variables," *Psychological Bulletin,* 1965, *64,* 259–309.

LOVAAS, O. I., SCHAEFFER, B., and SIMMONS, J. Q. "Building Social Behavior in Autistic Children by use of Electric Shock," *Journal of Experimental Research in Personality,* 1965, *1,* 99–109.

LU, Y. C. "Contradictory Parental Expectations in Schizophrenia: Dependence and Responsibility," *Archives of General Psychiatry,* 1962, *6,* 219–234.

MCCLELLAND, D. C., and APICELLA, F. S. "Reminiscence Following Experimentally Induced Failure," *Journal of Experimental Psychology,* 1947, *37,* 159–177.

MCCULLOCH, T. L. "The Role of Clasping Activity in Adaptive Behavior of the Infant Chimpanzee: III. The Mechanism of Reinforcement," *Journal of Psychology,* 1939, *7,* 305–316.

MCNAIR, D. M., CALLAHAN, D. M., and LORR, M. "Therapist 'Type' and Patient Response to Psychotherapy," *Journal of Consulting Psychology,* 1962, *26,* 425–429.

MAEHR, M. L., MENSING, J., and NAFZGER, S. "Concept of Self and the Reactions of Others," *Sociometry,* 1962, *25,* 353–357.

MAIER, N. R. F. "Studies of Abnormal Behavior in the Rat: IV. Abortive Behavior and its Relation to the Neurotic Attack," *Journal of Experimental Psychology,* 1940, *23,* 369–393.

MAIER, N. R. F., and GLASER, M. "Studies of Abnormal Behavior in the Rat: A Comparison of Some Convulsion-producing Situations," *Comparative Psychological Monographs,* 1940, *16* (1).

MAIER, N. R. F., and KLEE, J. B. "Studies of Abnormal Behavior in the Rat: VII. The Permanent Nature of Abnormal Fixations and Their Relation to Convulsive Tendencies," *Journal of Experimental Psychology,* 1941, *29,* 380–389.

MALAMUD, W., and PALMER, E. "Intellectual Deterioration in the Psychoses," *Archives of Neurology and Psychiatry,* 1938, *39,* 68–81.

MANASSE, G. "Self-regard as a Function of Environmental Demands in Chronic Schizophrenics," *Journal of Abnormal Psychology,* 1965, *70,* 210–213.

MANDLER, G., MANDLER, J., KREMEN, I., and SHOLITON, R. D. "The Response to Threat: Relations among Verbal and Physiological Indices," *Psychological Monographs,* 1961, *75* (Whole no. 513).

MANDLER, G. "From Association to Structure," *Psychological Review,* 1962, *69,* 415–426.

MANDLER, G., and WATSON, D. L. "Anxiety and the Interruption of Behavior." In C. D. Spielberger (Ed.), *Anxiety and Behavior.* New York: Academic Press, 1966.

MANN, J. H., and MANN, C. H. "The Importance of Group Task in Producing Group-member Personality and Behavior Changes," *Human Relations,* 1959, *12,* 75–88.

MARX, M. H. "Some Relations between Frustration and Drive." In M. Jones (Ed.), *Nebraska Symposium on Motivation.* Lincoln, Nebraska: University of Nebraska Press, 1956.

MASLOW, A. H. "Deprivation, Threat, and Frustration," *Psychological Review,* 1941, *48,* 364–366.

MASLOW, A. H. "Conflict, Frustration, and the Theory of Threat," *Journal of Abnormal and Social Psychology,* 1943, *38,* 81–86.

MASON, W. A. "Sociability and Social Organization in Monkeys and Apes." In L. Berkowitz (Ed.), *Advances in Experimental Social Psychology, Vol. 1.* New York: Academic Press, 1964.

MASON, W. A., and BERKSON, G. "Conditions Influencing Social Responsiveness in Infant Chimpanzees," *Science,* 1962, *137,* 127–128.

MASSERMAN, J. H. *Behavior and Neurosis.* Chicago: University of Chicago Press, 1943.

MAZER, M. "The Therapeutic Function of the Belief in Will," *Psychiatry,* 1960, *23,* 45–53.

MEAD, G. H. *Mind, Self, and Society from the Standpoint of a Social Behaviorist.* Chicago: The University of Chicago Press, 1934.

MENNINGER, K. A. *The Vital Balance.* New York: Viking Press, 1963.

MILLER, G. A., GALANTER, E., and PRIBRAM, K. H. *Plans and the Structure of Behavior.* New York: Holt, 1960.

MILLER, N. E. "Experimental Studies of Conflict." In J. McV. Hunt (Ed.), *Personality and the Behavior Disorders, Vol. 1.* New York: Ronald Press, 1944.

MILLER, N. E. "Liberalization of Basic S-R Concepts: Extensions to Conflict Behavior, Motivation, and Social Learning." In S. Koch (Ed.), *Psychology: a Study of a Science, Vol. 2.* New York: McGraw-Hill, 1959.

MILLER, N. E. "Learning Resistance to Pain and Fear: Effects of Overlearning, Exposure and Rewarded Exposure in Context," *Journal of Experimental Psychology,* 1960, *60,* 137–145.

MISCHEL, W., and STAUB, E. "Effects of Expectancy on Working and Waiting for Larger Rewards," *Journal of Personality and Social Psychology,* 1965, *2,* 625–633.

MORIARTY, D., and KATES, L. "Concept Attainment of Schizophrenics on Materials Involving Social Approval and Disapproval," *Journal of Abnormal and Social Psychology,* 1962, *65,* 355–364.

MOSHIN, S. M. "Effects of Frustration on Problem-solving Behavior," *Journal of Abnormal and Social Psychology,* 1954, *49,* 152–155.

MOWRER, O. H. *Learning Theory and Behavior.* New York: Wiley, 1960.

MOWRER, O. H., and VIEK, P. "An Experimental Analogue of Fear from a Sense of Helplessness." In D. McClelland (Ed.), *Studies in Motivation.* New York: Appleton-Century-Crofts, 1955.

MUENZINGER, K. F., BROWN, W. O., CROW, W. J., and POWLOSKI, R. F. "An Analysis of Electric Shock for Correct Responses into Its Avoidance and Accelerating Components," *Journal of Experimental Psychology,* 1952, *43,* 115–119.

MULDER, M., and STEMERDING, A. "Threat, Attraction to Group, and Need for Strong Leadership: A Laboratory Experiment in a Natural Setting," *Human Relations,* 1963, *16,* 317–334.

MURPHY, J. M. "Psychotherapeutic Aspects of Shamanism on St. Lawrence Indians." In A. Kiev (Ed.), *Magic, Faith, and Healing: Studies in Primitive Psychiatry Today.* New York: Free Press, 1964.

MURPHY, L. *The Widening World of Childhood: Paths Toward Mastery.* New York: Basic Books, 1962.

MURRAY, E. J., and COHEN, M. "Mental Illness, Milieu Therapy, and Social Organization in Ward Groups," *Journal of Abnormal and Social Psychology,* 1959, *58,* 48–54.

MYERS, J. K., and ROBERTS, B. H. *Family and Class Dynamics in Mental Illness.* New York: Wiley, 1959.

NARDINI, J. E. "Survival Factors in American Prisoners of War of the Japanese," *American Journal of Psychiatry,* 1952, *109,* 242–248.

NEISSER, U., and WEENE, P. "Hierarchies in Concept Attainment," *Journal of Experimental Psychology,* 1962, *64,* 640–645.

NEWCOMB, T. M. "Attitude Development as a Function of Reference Groups." In E. E. Maccoby, T. M. Newcomb, and E. L. Hartley (Eds.), *Readings in Social Psychology.* New York: Holt, 1958.

NOWLIS, H. M. "The Influence of Success and Failure on the Resumption of an Interrupted Task," *Journal of Experimental Psychology,* 1941, *28,* 304–325.

OLSON, G. W. "Failure and the Subsequent Performance of Schizophrenics," *Journal of Abnormal and Social Psychology,* 1958, *57,* 310–313.

OPLER, M. E. "Some Points of Comparison and Contrast between the Treatment of Functional Disorders by Apache Shamans and Modern Psychiatric Practice," *American Journal of Psychiatry,* 1936, *92,* 1371–1387.

OSLER, S. F. "Intellectual Performance as a Function of Two Types of Psychological Stress," *Journal of Experimental Psychology,* 1954, *47,* 115–121.

OVERMIER, J. B., and SELIGMAN, M. E. "Effects of Inescapable Shock upon

Subsequent Escape and Avoidance Responding," *Journal of Comparative and Physiological Psychology,* 1967, *63,* 28–33.

PARSONS, T. "The Mental Hospital as a Type of Organization." In M. Greenblatt, D. J. Levinson, and R. H. Williams (Eds.), *The Patient and the Mental Hospital.* Glencoe, Ill.: Free Press, 1957.

PARTON, D., and ROSS, A. O. "Social Reinforcement of Children's Motor Behavior," *Psychological Review,* 1965, *64,* 65–73.

PASCAL, G. R., and SWENSON, C. H. "Learning in Mentally Ill Patients under Conditions of Unusual Motivation," *Journal of Personality,* 1952, *21,* 240–249.

PASCAL, G. R., SWENSON, C. H., FELDMAN, D. A., COLE, M. E., and BAYARD, J. "Prognostic Criteria in the Case Histories of Hospitalized Mental Patients," *Journal of Consulting Psychology,* 1953, *17,* 163–171.

PAVLOV, I. P. *Lectures on Conditioned Reflexes.* New York: International, 1928.

PERRY, H. S., and PERRY, S. E. *The Schoolhouse Disasters: Family and Community as Determinants of the Child's Response to Disaster. Disaster Study No. II.* Washington: National Academy of Sciences–National Research Council, 1959.

PERRY, S. E., SILBER, E., and BLOCH, D. A. *The Child and His Family in Disaster: A Study of the 1953 Vicksburg Tornado. Disaster Study No. V.* Washington: National Academy of Sciences–National Research Council, 1956.

PETERS, H. N., and JENKINS, R. L. "Improvement of Chronic Schizophrenic Patients with Guided Problem-solving Motivated by Hunger," *Psychiatric Quarterly Supplements,* 1954, *28,* 84–101.

PRINCE, R. "Indigenous Yoruba Psychiatry." In A. Kiev (Ed.), *Magic, Faith, and Healing: Studies in Primitive Psychiatry Today.* New York: Free Press, 1964.

QUARANTELLI, E. L. "The Nature and Conditions of Panic," *American Journal of Sociology,* 1954, *60,* 267–275.

RABBIE, J. M. "Differential Preference for Companionship under Threat," *Journal of Abnormal and Social Psychology,* 1963, *67,* 643–648.

RAPAPORT, G. M. " 'Ideal Self' Instructions, MMPI Profile Changes, and the Prediction of Clinical Improvement," *Journal of Consulting Psychology,* 1958, *22,* 459–463.

RASHKIS, H. A., and SWAN, E. R. "Psychopharmacotherapeutic Research," *Archives of Neurology and Psychiatry,* 1957, *77,* 202–209.

RHINE, R. J. "The Effect on Problem Solving of Success or Failure as a Function of Cue Specificity," *Journal of Experimental Psychology,* 1957, *53,* 121–125.

RICHTER, C. P. "On the Phenomenon of Sudden Death in Animals and Man," *Psychosomatic Medicine,* 1957, *19,* 191–198.

RICKERS-OVSIANKINA, M. "Studies of the Personality Structure of Schizophrenic Individuals: I. The Accessibility of Schizophrenics to Environmental Influence," *Journal of General Psychology,* 1937a, *16,* 153–178.

RICKERS-OVSIANKINA, M. "Studies on the Personality Structure of Schizophrenic Individuals: II. Reactions to Individual Tasks," *Journal of General Psychology,* 1937b, *16,* 179–196.

RODNICK, E., and GARMEZY, H. "An Experimental Approach to the Study of Motivation in Schizophrenia." In M. R. Jones (Ed.), *Nebraska Symposium on Motivation.* Lincoln: University of Nebraska Press, 1957.

RODNICK, E. M., and SHAKOW, D. "Set in the Schizophrenic as Measured by a Composite Time Study," *American Journal of Psychiatry,* 1940, *97,* 214–225.

ROSENBAUM, G., MACAVEY, W. R., and GRISELL, J. L. "Effects of Biological and Social Motivation on Schizophrenic Reaction Time," *Journal of Abnormal and Social Psychology,* 1957, *54,* 364–368.

ROSENTHAL, D., and FRANK, J. D. "Psychotherapy and the Placebo Effect," *Psychological Bulletin,* 1956, *53,* 294–302.

ROSENTHAL, R. *Experimenter Effects in Behavioral Research.* New York: Appleton-Century-Crofts, 1966.

ROSENZWEIG, S. "Further Comparative Data on Repetition-choice after Success and Failure as Related to Frustration Tolerance," *Journal of Genetic Psychology,* 1945, *66,* 71–81.

ROTHAUS, P., and WORCHEL, P. "Ego-support, Communication, Catharsis, and Hostility," *Journal of Personality,* 1964, *32,* 296–312.

ROTTER, J. B. *Social Learning and Clinical Psychology.* New York: Prentice-Hall, 1954.

RUBIN, A. J. "Test-score Patterns in Schizophrenic and Non-psychotic States," *Journal of Psychology,* 1941, *12,* 91–100.

RYCHLAK, J. F. "Task Influence and the Stability of Generalized Expectancies," *Journal of Experimental Psychology,* 1958, *55,* 459–462.

RYCHLAK, J. F., and EACKER, J. N. "The Effects of Anxiety, Delay and Reinforcement on Generalized Expectancies," *Journal of Personality,* 1962, *30,* 123–134.

SANDERS, R., SMITH, R. S., and WEINMAN, B. *Chronic Psychoses and Recovery.* San Francisco: Jossey-Bass, 1967.

SANDERS, R., WEINMAN, B., SMITH, R. S., SMITH, A., KINNEY, J., and FITZGERALD, B. J. "Social Treatment of the Male Chronic Schizophrenic," *Journal of Nervous and Mental Diseases,* 1962, *134,* 244–255.

SARASON, I. G., and SARASON, B. R. "Effects of Motivating Instructions and Reports of Failure on Verbal Learning," *American Journal of Psychology,* 1957, *70,* 92–96.

SCHACHTER, S. *The Psychology of Affiliation.* Stanford, Calif.: Stanford University Press, 1957.

SCHEERER, M. "Cognitive Theory." In G. Lindzey (Ed.), *Handbook of Social Psychology, Vol. 1.* Cambridge, Mass.: Addison-Wesley, 1954.

SCHEFF, T. J. "The Role of the Mentally Ill and the Dynamics of Mental Disorder: A Research Framework," *Sociometry,* 1963, *26,* 436–453.

SCHER, J. M. "Schizophrenia and Task Orientation," *Archives of Neurology and Psychiatry,* 1957, *78,* 531–538.

SCHOOLER, C. "Affiliation among Schizophrenics: Preferred Characteristics of the Other," *Journal of Nervous and Mental Diseases,* 1963, *137,* 438–446.

SCHOOLER, C., and SPOHN, H. E. "The Susceptibility of Chronic Schizophrenics to Social Influence in the Formation of Perceptual Judgments," *Journal of Abnormal and Social Psychology,* 1960, *61,* 348–354.

SEARS, R. R. "Initiation of the Repression Sequence by Experienced Failure," *Journal of Experimental Psychology,* 1937, *20,* 570–580.

SELIGMAN, M. E., and MAIER, S. F. "Failure to Escape Traumatic Shock," *Journal of Experimental Psychology,* 1967, *74,* 1–9.

SHAFFER, L. F. "Fear and Courage in Aerial Combat," *Journal of Consulting Psychology,* 1947, *11,* 137–143.

SHAKOW, D. "Segmental Set: A Theory of the Formal Psychological Deficit in Schizophrenia," *Archives of General Psychiatry,* 1962, *6,* 1–17.

SHERMAN, M., and JOST, H. "Frustration Reaction of Normal and Neurotic Persons," *Journal of Psychology,* 1942, *13,* 3–19.

SILBER, E., HAMBERG, D. A., COELHO, G. V., MURPHY, E. B., ROSENBERG, M., and PEARLIN, L. I. "Adaptive Behavior in Competent Adolescents: Coping with the Anticipation of College," *Archives of General Psychiatry,* 1961, *5,* 354–365.

SIMMONS, O. G., and FREEMAN, H. E. "Familial Expectations and Post-hospital Performance of Mental Patients," *Human Relations,* 1959, *12,* 233–242.

SINGER, R., and FESHBACH, S. "Effects of Anxiety Arousal in Psychotics and Normals upon the Perception of Anxiety in Others," *Journal of Personality,* 1962, *30,* 574–587.

SOBELL, R., and INGALLS, A. "Resistance to Treatment: Explorations of the Patients' Sick Role," Unpublished manuscript, University of Washington.

SOLOMON, R. L. "Punishment," *American Psychologist,* 1964, *19,* 239–253.

SOLOMON, R. L., and BRUSH, E. S. "Experimentally Derived Conceptions of Anxiety and Aversion." In M. Jones (Ed.), *Nebraska Symposium on Motivation.* Lincoln: University of Nebraska Press, 1956.

SOLOMON, R. L., and WYNNE, L. C. "Traumatic Avoidance Learning: Acquisition in Normal Dogs," *Psychological Monographs,* 1953, *67* (Whole no. 354).

SOLOMON, R. L., and WYNNE, L. C. "Traumatic Avoidance Learning: The Principle of Anxiety Conservation and Partial Irreversibility," *Psychological Review,* 1954, *61,* 353–385.

SPENCE, K. W. "The Differential Response in Animals to Stimuli Varying within the Same Dimension," *Psychological Review,* 1937, *44,* 430–444.

SPERBER, Z., and SPANNER, M. "Social Desirability, Psychopathology, and Item Endorsement," *Journal of General Psychiatry,* 1962, *67,* 105–112.

SPOHN, H. E., and WOLK, W. "Effect of Group Problem Solving Experience upon Social Withdrawal in Chronic Schizophrenics," *Journal of Abnormal and Social Psychology,* 1963, *66,* 187–190.

STANLEY, W. C., and MONKMAN, J. A. "A Test for Specific and General Behavioral Effects of Infantile Stimulation with Shock in the Mouse," *Journal of Abnormal and Social Psychology,* 1956, *53,* 19–22.

STANTON, A. H., and SCHWARTZ, M. S. *The Mental Hospital.* New York: Basic Books, 1954.

STEVENSON, H. W., and CRUSE, D. B. "The Effectiveness of Social Reinforcement with Normal and Feebleminded Children," *Journal of Personality,* 1961, *24,* 124–135.

STEVENSON, I., and FISHER, T. M. "Techniques in the Vocational Rehabilitation of Chronically Unemployed Psychiatric Patients," *American Journal of Psychiatry,* 1954, *3,* 289–300.

STOTLAND, E., and BLUMENTHAL, A. L. "The Reduction of Anxiety as a Result of the Expectation of Making a Choice," *Canadian Journal of Psychology,* 1964, *18,* 139–145.

STOTLAND, E., and DUNN, R. "Identification, 'Oppositeness,' Authoritarianism, Self-esteem, and Birth Order," *Psychological Monographs,* 1962, *76* (9, Whole no. 528).

STOTLAND, E., and HILLMER, M. J. "Identification, Authoritarian Defensiveness, and Self-esteem," *Journal of Abnormal and Social Psychology,* 1962, *64,* 334–342.

STOTLAND, E., and KOBLER, A. L. *Life and Death of a Mental Hospital.* Seattle: University of Washington Press, 1965.

STOTSKY, B. A. "Motivation and Task Complexity as Factors in Psychomotor Responses of Schizophrenics," *Journal of Personality,* 1957, *25,* 327–343.

References

STRESSMAN, H. D., THALER, M. B., and SCHEIN, E. H. "A Prisoner of War Syndrome: Apathy as a Reaction to Severe Stress," *American Journal of Psychiatry,* 1955, *112,* 998–1003.

SULLIVAN, H. S. *The Interpersonal Theory of Psychiatry.* New York: Norton, 1953.

SZASZ, T. S. *The Myth of Mental Illness.* New York: Hoeber-Harper, 1961.

TALBOT, E., MILLER, S., and WHITE, R. "Some Aspects of Self-conception and Role Demand in a Therapeutic Community," *Journal of Abnormal and Social Psychology,* 1961, *63,* 338–345.

TAYLOR, J. B. "Social Desirability and MMPI Performance: The Individual Case," *Journal of Consulting Psychology,* 1959, *23,* 514–517.

TAYLOR, J. G. "A Behavioral Interpretation of Obsessive-compulsive Neurosis," *Behavior Research and Therapy,* 1963, *1,* 237–244.

TIGHE, L. S. "Effects of Perceptual Pre-training on Reversal and Non-reversal Shifts," *Journal of Experimental Psychology,* 1965, *70,* 379–385.

TINKLEPAUGH, O. L., and HARTMAN, C. G. "Behavior and Maternal Care of the Newborn Monkey," *Journal of Genetic Psychology,* 1932, *40,* 257–286.

TODD, F. J., TERRELL, G., and FRANK, C. E. "Differences between Normal and Underachievers of Superior Ability," *Journal of Applied Psychology,* 1962, *46,* 183–190.

TOLMAN, E. C. "Cognitive Maps in Rats and Men," *Psychological Review,* 1948, *55,* 189–208.

TURNER, L. H., and SOLOMON, R. L. "Human Traumatic Avoidance Learning: Theory and Experiments on the Operant-respondent Distinction and Failure to Learn," *Psychological Monographs,* 1962, *76* (40, Whole no. 559).

ULLMAN, A. D. "The Experimental Production and Analysis of a 'Compulsive' Eating Symptom in Rats," *Journal of Comparative and Physiological Psychology,* 1951, *44,* 575–581.

ULLMAN, A. D. "Three Factors Involved in Producing 'Compulsive Eating' in Rats," *Journal of Comparative and Physiological Psychology,* 1952, *45,* 490–496.

ULLMAN, L. P., KRASNER, L., and COLLINS, B. J. "Modification of Behavior through Verbal Conditioning: Effects on Group Therapy," *Journal of Abnormal and Social Psychology,* 1961, *62,* 128–132.

VERNON, D. T., FOLEY, J. M., and SCHULMAN, J. L. "Effect of Mother-child Separation and Birth Order on Young Children's Responses to Two Potentially Stressful Experiences," *Journal of Personality and Social Psychology,* 1967, *5,* 162–174.

VIDEBECK, R. "Self-conception and the Reactions of Other," *Sociometry,* 1960, *23,* 351–359.

VISOTSKY, H., HAMBERG, D., GOSS, M. E., and LEIBOWITZ, B. Z. "Coping Behavior under Extreme Stress," *Archives of General Psychiatry,* 1961, *5,* 423–448.

WAGNER, A. P. "The Role of Reinforcement and Nonreinforcement in an Apparent Frustration Effect," *Journal of Experimental Psychology,* 1959, *57,* 130–136.

WALTON, D., and MATHER, M. D. "The Application of Learning Principles to the Treatment of Obsessive-compulsive States in the Acute and Chronic Phases of Illness," *Behavior Research and Therapy,* 1963, *1,* 163–174.

WEAKLAND, J. H. "The 'Double-bind' Hypothesis of Schizophrenia and Three-party Interaction." In D. D. Jackson (Ed.), *Etiology of Schizophrenia.* New York: Basic Books, 1960.

WEBB, W. N. "Conceptual Ability of Schizophrenics as a Function of Threat of Failure," *Journal of Abnormal and Social Psychology,* 1955, *50,* 221–226.

WEGROCKI, M. J. "Generalizing Ability in Schizophrenia," *Psychological Monographs,* 1940, *50* (No. 254).

WEINSTOCK, S. "Acquisition and Extinction of a Partially Reinforced Running Response at a 24-hour Inter-Trial Interval," *Journal of Experimental Psychology,* 1958, *56,* 151–158.

WELLS, H. H. "Effects of Transfer and Problem Structure in Disjunctive Concept Formation," *Journal of Experimental Psychology,* 1963, *65,* 63–69.

WHITE, R. W. "Motivation Reconsidered: The Concept of Competence," *Psychological Review,* 1959, *66,* 297–333.

WHITE, R. K., and LIPPITT, R. *Autocracy and Democracy.* New York: Harper, 1960.

WHITEHORN, J. C., and BETZ, B. J. "A Study of Psychotherapeutic Relationships between Physician and Schizophrenic Patients," *American Journal of Psychiatry,* 1954, *3,* 321–331.

WHITEHORN, J. C., and BETZ, B. J. "A Comparison of Psychotherapeutic Relationships between Physicians and Schizophrenic Patients under Insulin," *American Journal of Psychiatry,* 1957, *113,* 901–910.

WHITEHORN, J. C., and BETZ, B. J. "Further Studies of the Doctor as a Crucial Variable in the Outcome of Treatment with Schizophrenic Patients," *American Journal of Psychiatry,* 1960, *117,* 215.

WHITEMAN, M. "The Performance of Schizophrenics on Social Concepts," *Journal of Abnormal and Social Psychology,* 1954, *49,* 266–271.

WHITEMAN, M. "Anticipated Frustration as a Determinant of Anxiety," *Journal of General Psychology,* 1957, *57,* 183–195.

WHITING, J. W. M., and CHILD, I. "Effects of Goal Attainment: Relaxation

Versus Renewed Striving," *Journal of Abnormal and Social Psychology,* 1949, *45,* 667–681.

WHITING, J. W. M., and CHILD, I. *Child Training and Personality: A Cross-Cultural Study.* New Haven: Yale University Press, 1953.

WILENSKY, H. "The Performance of Schizophrenic and Normal Individuals Following Frustration," *Psychological Monographs,* 1952, *66* (12, Whole no. 344).

WILMER, H. A. *Social Psychiatry in Action.* Springfield, Ill.: Thomas, 1958.

WING, J. K., and FREUNDENBERG, R. K. "The Response of Severely Ill Chronic Schizophrenic Patients to Social Stimulation," *American Journal of Psychiatry,* 1961, *118,* 311–322.

WISEBORD, M., HERMAN, C. B., DEMBER, R., CHARATER, F. B., and TRAVIS, J. H. "Patient Reactions to the 'Open Door,'" *American Journal of Psychiatry,* 1958, *115,* 518–521.

WOLF, M., RISLEY, T., and MEES, H. "Application of Operant Conditioning Procedures to the Behavior Problems of an Autistic Child," *Behavior Research and Therapy,* 1964, *1,* 305–312.

WOLPE, J. *Psychotherapy by Reciprocal Inhibition.* Stanford, Calif.: Stanford University Press, 1958.

WORCHEL, P. "Status Restoration and the Reduction of Hostility," *Journal of Abnormal and Social Psychology,* 1961, *63,* 443–445.

WRIGHTSMAN, L. S., JR. "Effects of Waiting with Others on Changes in Level of Felt Anxiety," *Journal of Abnormal and Social Psychology,* 1960, *61,* 216–222.

ZAHN, T. P., SHAKOW, D., and ROSENTHAL, D. "Reaction Time in Schizophrenics and Normal Subjects as a Function of Preparatory and Inter-Trial Intervals," *Journal of Nervous and Mental Diseases,* 1961, *133,* 283–287.

ZANDER, A. "A Study of Experimental Frustration," *Psychological Monographs,* 1944, *56* (3, Whole no. 256).

ZANDER, A., STOTLAND, E., and WOLFE, D. M. "Unity of Group, Identification with Group, and Self-esteem," *Journal of Personality,* 1960, *28,* 463–478.

ZANDER, A., and QUINN, R. "The Social Environment and Mental Health: A Review of Past Research at the Institute for Social Research," *Journal of Social Issues,* 1962, *18,* 48–66.

ZEILER, M. D. "Transposition in Adults with Simultaneous and Successive Stimulus Presentation," *Journal of Experimental Psychology,* 1964, *68,* 103–107.

ZELLER, A. F. "An Experimental Analogue of Repression," *Journal of Experimental Psychology,* 1950, *40,* 411–422.

ZIGLER, E. F., HODGDEN, F., and STEVENSON, H. W. "The Effect of Support and Non-support on the Performance of Normal and Feebleminded Children," *Journal of Personality,* 1958, *26,* 106–122.

ZIGLER, E. F., and PHILLIPS, L. "Psychiatric Diagnosis and Symptomatology," *Journal of Abnormal and Social Psychology,* 1961a, *63,* 69–75.

ZIGLER, E. F., and PHILLIPS, L. "Social Competence and Outcome in Psychiatric Disorder," *Journal of Abnormal and Social Psychology,* 1961b, *63,* 264–271.

ZIGLER, E. F., and PHILLIPS, L. "Social Competence and the Process Reactive Distinction in Psychopathology," *Journal of Abnormal and Social Psychology,* 1962, *65,* 215–222.

ZIMMERMAN, D. W. "Durable Secondary Reinforcement: Method and Theory," *Psychological Review,* 1957, *64,* 373–383.

ZIPF, S. "Effects of Probability of Reward and Speed Requirement on Human Performance," *Journal of Experimental Psychology,* 1963, *65,* 106–107.

Name Index

C

D

E

Name Index

Name Index

R

S

T

Name Index

Subject Index

A

Subject Index

Subject Index

T

W